Florída

Florida

Edited by Jeff Rice

Parlor Press
Anderson, South Carolina
www.parlorpress.com

Parlor Press LLC, Anderson, South Carolina, USA

© 2015 by Parlor Press.
All rights reserved.
Printed in the United States of America

SAN: 254-8879

Library of Congress Cataloging-in-Publication Data

Florida / edited by Jeff Rice. -- First edition.
   pages cm
  Summary: "Florida taps into an existing conversation regarding space, and it contributes a new approach by offering up the state as a network of both objective and personal meanings"--Provided by publisher.
  Includes bibliographical references and index.
  ISBN 978-1-60235-544-6 (paperback : acid-free paper) -- ISBN 978-1-60235-545-3 (hardcover : acid-free paper)
  1. Florida--Social life and customs. 2. Florida--History, Local. 3. Florida--Description and travel. 4. Florida--Social conditions. 5. Space--Social aspects--Florida. I. Rice, Jeff (Jeff R.)
  F311.5.F59 2015
  975.9--dc23
                           2015007498

Cover design by Amber Day
Copyediting by Jared Jameson
Printed on acid-free paper.

               1 2 3 4 5
               First Edition

Parlor Press, LLC is an independent publisher of scholarly and trade titles in print and multimedia formats. This book is available in paper, hardcover, and digital formats from Parlor Press on the World Wide Web at http://www.parlorpress.com or through online and brick-and-mortar bookstores. For submission information or to find out about Parlor Press publications, write to Parlor Press, 3015 Brackenberry Drive, Anderson, SC 29621, or e-mail editor@parlorpress.com.

Contents

Acknowledgments *vii*

1 Introduction *3*

Florida Patterns

2 A Network of Bones: Key West as Underworld *17*
  Sean Morey

3 Miami Spatial Stories *34*
  Jeff Rice

4 Florida Trouse *51*
  Charlie Hailey

Florida Narratives

5 Tampa at the Sunset of Western Civilization *73*
  Todd Taylor

6 Assembling New Port Richey, Florida *86*
  Cassandra Branham and Megan McIntyre

7 Ferris Wheels, Concertos, Sidewalks and Sassy Tongues: Negotiating Racial Performances in the Capital City *108*
  Lillie Anne Brown

8 Sort of on the Grid: An Eccentric Map of Growing Up Jewish in the Miami Suburbs, c.1975–85   *128*
Steve Newman

Florida Studies

9 West Palm   *151*
Bradley Dilger

10 The Spectator, the Spectacle, and the Spectral at the Stadium Course at the Tournament Players Club, Ponte Vedra Beach   *174*
James P. Beasley

11 Shell Games: A Eulogy Against Suburbia   *195*
David M. Grant

12 An American Beach   *212*
Sidney I. Dobrin

Florida Theory

13 EPCOT: Florida's Disney-Psychosis Dreams Foreclosed   *233*
Craig Saper with Channel Two (Adam Trowbridge & Jessica Westbrook)

14 Orlando, Florida's Ubiquitous Libidinal Boxes   *248*
Lauren Mitchell

15 "Murphy's Well-Being": The Konsult   *271*
Gregory L. Ulmer

Index   *297*

Contributors   *301*

Acknowledgments

I thank all of the contributors to *Florida* for wanting to be a part of this project. I imagined this project as a mix of personal and scholarly thoughts on a state that many of us have conflicting attachments to, whether we grew up there, studied there, or still live there. The contributors helped me realize my vision with very generous chapters. I also thank the original College Composition and Communication panel on Florida, held March 2011 in Atlanta, Georgia: Bradley Dilger, Craig Saper, and Blake Scott. Their papers inspired this collection. I thank David Blakesley and Parlor Press for eagerly working with me on this project (the second of my Florida oriented projects Parlor has published). I thank the crazy state of Florida and the slightly more bizarre city of Miami for my upbringing and college education. Go Gators.

And, as always, I thank my wife Jenny and my two kids, Vered and Judah, for being in my life. I still haven't taken any of you to Florida, and I probably never will. This book, though, is for you.

Florída

1 Introduction

Billy: We did it, man. We did it, we did it. We're rich, man. We're retirin' in Florida now, mister.

Captain America: You know Billy, we blew it."

—*Easy Rider*

I am bad at remembering. Very little from my past sticks with me. Homes. Neighborhoods. People I went to school with. Family vacations. High school friends. Places we ate at. I cannot recall anything significant. In that way, I am a bad nostalgic storyteller. I cannot draw upon the details of my life. I lack, therefore, an ability to embrace and share narratives of my life. It would be nice if I could begin this collection of Florida-based chapters, in which each author ties a space in Florida with his/her own life, with my own vivid memories of growing up in Miami. It would be nice if this collection began with a traditional and powerful anecdote to set the tone of the collection as a whole. It would be nice, but I cannot do that.

Even though I lived in Miami from 1971 to 1987 (with a couple of returns after that), I have no such memories. I am bad at recollection. No grand stories stick with me. If I am a product of a Florida upbringing, it might not be immediately apparent to those who know me or who have read my work. Nothing about me says "Florida." My wife, in fact, calls me a "New Yorker" because of how I talk; my tendency to yell, "I'm walking here," if a car turns into the crosswalk; and because of my supposedly intense attitude. If I am a product of a Florida upbringing, it might not be evident what part of Florida has shaped me or helped formulate my outlook on my professional or personal life. If Florida has interpellated me, it is not clear how.

Florida, thus, begins without clarity. Still, my memories are not incomplete; nor do I lack a narrative overall. Such a point is often the case when associations, place, and history collide. Those items that refuse to stand out as complete, remembered experiences are overshadowed by fragments and disconnected details. Whatever imaginary map I use to locate myself in the space called Florida, I find fragments of experience. This collection, too, is about fragments as much as it is about narratives. *Florida* assembles diverse positions on place, personal narrative, the state's politics and culture, and theoretical speculation not to deliver a comprehensive vision of Florida as a state or even as a site of contention or difference. Instead, this collection delivers fragments and details. While such a delivery may feel uncommon among other volumes devoted to discussions of place, rhetoric, writing, or related material, *Florida* is meant to stand apart from common discussions. Florida is not a common state, and the ways we write about the state are not required to be common either. Florida's disconnect, however, should not distract or disorient but instead tap into the disconnect that often accompanies not just my own incomplete memories or narrative, but the majority of incomplete memories and narratives that accompany discussions of place. Contributors to *Florida* were not asked to tell a complete story of Florida. Instead, they were encouraged to foreground experiences around their connections to the state, even if those connections do not offer a thorough worldview.

Place, therefore, is personal even as it may be fragmented. I begin this collection, then, with my own incomplete story of Florida fragments: Sitting in Pumpernick's with my grandparents and learning about the space shuttle explosion, a parrot biting my father's thumb after he stuck it in a cage at Parrot Jungle, bowling in Kendall Lakes, calzones from The Big Cheese off of Dixie Highway, buying double album cassettes by ZZ Top and Fleetwood Mac (an album on each side) from Peaches Record and Tapes, arriving at the Tropicare Drive-In for the Sunday morning flea market before it was even open ("We have to beat the heat," my dad would say), stuffing horseshoe crabs from Matheson Hammock in jars for a highschool marine biology project, sitting on the long communal benches at Shorty's Bar-B-Que, the hour long drive to the Hollywood Sportatorium to see concerts twice a month, the motor on my dad's boat typically not running once we were ready to fish, buying beer from the Farm Stores drive-in on Dixie (clerks didn't ask for id), appearing on the *Sunday Funnies* morning TV show after winning a *Miami Herald* comic contest.

Unfortunately, these memories lack a cohesion or anchor that could transform them into the narrative I want tell, one that is total and complete.

I have the fragments; but I lack the details that make up a story. Thus, I feel I have little to share as introduction. My anecdotes are limited to fragmented markers (eating at Shorty's, for instance) rather than the larger memory that one would expect to translate into a more substantial narrative (how Miami barbecue, for instance, relates to larger, cultural trends or national barbecue standards). If anything, I wish I could reclaim that narrative via saved material artifacts that would help return my memory to me. For instance, out of all of the saved video stored on YouTube (video recovered from private home collections, we might assume), I cannot find my *Sunday Funnies* appearance. And if, by chance, we had taped the episode I appeared on, those tapes are lost forever to a trash pickup somewhere in Florida. All I have left from that moment is not the substantial narrative (appearing on the show, winning a newspaper contest, beginning a life-long interaction with media and writing), but, instead, the minor story of using the winning money I received to buy the J. Geils Band's *Love Stinks* at Spec's Records on the way home. I am left with a fragmented private memory, not the possible public memory that could be displayed if the show were saved somewhere for viewing.

Does every story need a totalizing set of details for the story to have meaning? Scholarship, of course, gravitates toward the totalizing gesture because totalizing gestures promise substance. A more substantial Florida narrative than buying a record and one that sits in the public memory rather than the private memory might focus on Florida's role in the chad controversy during the 2000 presidential election. A more substantial narrative might focus on Florida as the site of the infamous 1980 Mariel boatlift crisis. A more substantial narrative might focus on Disney World as the center of American tourism. A more substantial narrative might focus on the oddball moments often associated with the Sunshine State. "Dwarf Season Opens in Florida," a December 2012 *Weekly World News* headline declares. "Naked Florida Man Jumps Off Of Roof Onto Homeowner, Knocks Television Over, Empties Vacuum Cleaner, Masturbates," a January 2013 *Gawker* headline proclaims. Such narratives might recall Florida's role as a primary figure in Hollywood movies such as *Goldfinger* (though Sean Connery was not filmed in the Miami scenes), *There is Something About Mary* (Mary's office is in Brickell Park, downtown), and *Scarface* (at 728 Ocean Drive, Tony Montana watches a man be chainsawed to death). These are narratives of substance, whether they seem trivial or monumental. They frame a state as overall experience. These narratives, indeed, mark more substantial approaches toward discussing Florida. They provide recognizable markers from which we can identify the state: politics, immigration, tourism, craziness, film. We could easily add other markers in order to construct more substantial narratives. We could do so, but the authors represented in this collection have opted not to.

New Media Storytelling

The rationale for choosing another approach to discussions of space is tied to the logic of new media. While my inability to offer a substantial narrative regarding my upbringing should be a point of self-reflective critique (I am unable to construct a narrative; I am a terrible storyteller), instead, I find it to be a focal point of new media storytelling and the overall influence of network culture on how we respond to a number of activities or moments, as well as places. I also find this inability acts as a platform from which to introduce a book about Florida. Often, in lieu of grand narrative gestures, cultural or spatial memories are traced in digital spaces as fragmented moments, such as my own memories. The fragment provides authors and readers a type of "digital" marker for spatial identification. Facebook, in particular, showcases this effect (the kind of effect Marshall McLuhan might have "inventoried" in *Medium is the Massage* as a human extension). Facebook is a site of fragmented moments: updates, posts, embedded videos, commentary, personal photographs. With or without a Timeline, Facebook aggregates these fragmented moments, and individual stories are told (one's politics, one's family situation, one's running habits, one's professional views). We might call the kinds of narratives told in many online spaces, such as Facebook, fragmented narratives. The fragmented narrative is familiar to what is offered by Twitter users or Storify users as well as to what we find in communities built around Google + circles. Fragmented narratives are not concerned with overall cohesion or extended meaning. Instead, they offer selected moments one can draw upon, pass over, focus on, or merely enjoy. As Roland Barthes writes, "a text on pleasure cannot be anything but short" (*Pleasure of the Text* 18). Florida can be one such pleasure text, one defined by the fragmented (short) logic new media evokes. The logic is not problematic for generating short attention spans, as critics such as Nicholas Carr attest. The logic, in contrast, allows for another form of expression not dependent on totalizing gestures, as popularized in typical scholarship on place, or even on Florida. The status update, as one such fragment, comes and goes; it glosses over, it showcases brevity, it provides a piece of a larger narrative. It appears to not be substantial. It only needs to capture a piece of the story. And it has become a dominant form of networked expression. *Florida* contributions are meant to capture pieces of various stories.

Florida, too, has been caught within this system of fragmented narratives. Take two Facebook pages as examples: "I Grew Up in South Florida in the '60s, '70s, and '80s"[1] and "Old Florida"[2]. On these pages, page owners and fans share postcards, old photographs, newspaper clippings, and other material artifacts that often stand for memories of Florida and its many spaces.

None of these isolated posts offer a complete narrative on their own, but one could read through the posts and construct a variety of stories out of the fragments. The fragments, it seems, intend to provoke further reflection or storytelling. Many of those who post ask: "Anyone remember?" or "Who remembers?" alongside the posted material. Some of the material is public (newspaper clippings, Miami Dolphins promotional material); some of it is personal (a snapshot of a person in her waitress uniform at an unknown oyster restaurant). On a random day, I encounter a photograph from Miami circa 1978 (black and white, it showcases cars parked downtown), a reward poster for the whereabouts of Adam Walsh (who was abducted in Hollywood in 1981 and later found murdered), and ads for the original Pizza Palace on Eighth Street in Miami. The banner image for "I Grew Up in South Florida" is a photograph of Zayre, a discount department store chain that had stores in Miami. Embedded in the banner is a photo of the iconic record crate from the Peaches Records and Tapes logo. Growing up initially in Perrine (south of Miami), I have vague, fragmented memories of shopping at Zayre near the Cutler Ridge Mall. My fragmented memories of Peaches are stronger. By then, I was a teenager with an endless appetite for buying records. Behaviors, as some of the contributors to this collection demonstrate, often shape perceptions of places, past and present.

Figure 1 Facebook Screen shot. The old Zayre.

If not posted to a network space such as Facebook, and if not posted in a space with tens of thousands of fans (indicated by the "likes" noted on every Facebook page), these memories likely would be lost. They would be lost because without the networked fragmented narrative I can engage with in a space such as Facebook, I would never consider bringing back those memories. Neither Zayre nor Peaches occupy my thoughts in any regular manner. Indeed, since leaving Florida, the one space I have devoted considerable effort to writing about is Detroit, a city I lived and worked in for only five years, yet it produced more scholarship for me than Florida has to date.[3] In that sense, the narrative device I've found that I need regarding the state I grew up in is something akin to an internal Facebook Florida page (internal to me), a virtual, digital space where all of my fragments can be collected and shared as aggregated moments (one would just read the aggregation, not the overall story). An internal Facebook page, read as a whole, offers Florida and its many locales a narrative space, a spatial story that is told across users and images. An internal Facebook page networks Florida's fragments together. I need stronger networks to tie me to the state I will always have some type of relationship with, superficial or otherwise. I need a stronger connection between my internal Facebook and other metaphorical, external sites of spatial meaning. I need to connect to other writers, other objects, other memories, other "status updates." I don't need to worry, as singer Patty Griffin does, that someone might let me die in Florida.[4] My fragments will sustain me if they connect.

Networked Florida

This collection, too, attempts to network some of Florida's spaces as internal meanings (what the author holds onto) are shifted to the external site of the page (the contributed chapter). The contributors to this collection maintain and are sustained by various network positions within the spaces they write about. Contributors grew up in, studied in, or lived in these spaces, and they thus offer narratives of their experiences as a part of the network of study they wish to engage with. While traditional approaches to place often distance the writer from the object of study, *Florida's* contributors embrace their relationship to the state as a space to study. Some of the contributors problematize these spaces they have studied or worked in by reading the space's current status against past history. Some of the contributors trace the benefits and problems of these spaces as such spaces continue to function for the authors as heuristics and sites of invention. Some of the contributors explore narratives of their lives in these spaces. Some of the contributors blend their lives with the spaces under questions. Each contribution functions as a virtual fragment, a moment aligned with other networked moments. The move from self-contained memories (the memory belongs to me) to networked spaces of shared memories (such as a Facebook page) marks a move from narrative to fragment. As the contributions to this collection show, that move is not only found online, but in the ways academics work to make sense of their shared spatial memories. I find these chapters to be status updates of a sort; moments of observance, reflection, theory, appreciation, and memory. I find these chapters, networked together, to offer an alternative approach to academic writing regarding space.

Within a more traditional academic approach, studies of space often gravitate toward the familiar approach of critique. For the most part, academic writing has treated spatial memory regarding Florida as the site of critique. Andrew Ross's treatment of Disney's Celebration City in *The Celebration Chronicles* or Henry Giroux and Grace Pollock's *The Mouse that Roared: Disney and the End of Innocence* are prime examples of such work. In the typical Florida critique, one finds fault for how the space represents or is represented, or one warns the reader to be weary of the space's hegemonic impulse. Ross's *The Celebration Chronicles* unravels the façade of Celebration so that the Disneyfication of Main Street, America is revealed. Ross's narrative of his year-long residence in Celebration City is the overall narrative of critique, one that situates the local (Celebration) as representative of the global (American culture). As he writes of the initial sale of property in Celebration:

> This was a different kind of promise. It seemed to be channeling the sharp rush of baby-boomer hunger to be homeward bound to a place that lies well off the century's main drag- behind the fast curve of modernity, where their grandparents had once lived. At prices ranging from $150,000 for a townhouse all the way to a cool million for a mansion, it would not be a cheap detour. (19)

Accurate or not, Ross's narrative runs the gauntlet of the familiar, the commonplace, a topos, and as a critique, the cliché: we should know before we read Ross that inequality will be discovered (it is) and that Celebration is hardly an accurate representation of small town America (it isn't). "A different kind of promise," as Ross attests, is a broken one. One *expects* Ross to point out the contradictions and inconsistencies found in Disney's narrative (as many others have done as well). In this "revelation," the small hometown is actually an expensive simulacrum. And Disney, we can *expect* to be told, is racist (since such a declaration follows all questions of representation and corporatization). As Giroux and Pollock make clear, Celebration City reflects America's unease with people of color. "Disney's nostalgia machine is premised on an appeal to a safer past and on the assumption that any 'friendly' community is essentially middle-class and white" (68). This point, too, is a commonplace or topos of Disney and of Florida. Disney is an easy target to force this gesture upon, as are many of the expected responses that label all cultural or rhetorical phenomena as in need of decoding so that power and discrimination can be revealed. Critique may or may not have run out of steam, as Bruno Latour attests, but it can be highly predictable. And as this collection attempts to trace, critique is not always the most appropriate response to a given condition.

Instead of critique as primary response, we can consider the pattern as a principle mode of expression generated within a culture informed largely by new media practices (such as networks and fragments). Pattern formation—exemplified in network studies—reveals the ways items, people, ideas, concepts, and places (among other things) connect or disconnect in moments where meaning may be found. And while pattern formation might be typically associated with scholarship represented as "digital" or "computer based," patterns are found in the narratives we tell about place as well. That a typical critique of Florida returns, often, to Disney World reveals a pattern. The expected pattern which is often as commonplace as a Disney critique—Florida is the Sunshine State or Miami is a city of fun—are not represented in this collection. Instead, authors, and the collection as a whole, trace patterns that connect disparate narratives of Florida's spaces across very different memories and approaches to Florida. Such patterns include sludge, mounds, canals, racism, John Kennedy, school, Disney, suggestion and the imagination, disasters, storms, boxing, drugs, religion, golf, ethnicity, dividing lines, class, homes, spaceships, celebrities, and others. Readers might encounter these patterns in obvious ways (i.e., two or more chapters mentioning golf), or they might trace out the less obvious or conceptual patterns played out in the chapters' very personal, associative, historical, or theoretical discussions of Florida (such as the treatment of disaster). Network patterns are not always obvious; the tracing of a network is what reveals the items (obvious or not) that construct the network. The chapters presented in this volume do a considerable amount of tracing.

Chapter Breakdown

We might call such patterns the moving topoi of Florida, or more specifically, Florida's chora. Chora, as Gregory Ulmer, Jacques Derrida, and others have demonstrated, marks the moving places of meaning. Whereas topoi remain constant (Florida is the Sunshine State; Disney is a simulacrum) so that assumption is reflected via the commonplace (i.e., sunshine state as a topos may appear in posters, post cards, movies, books because it is an assumed meaning), chora allows meanings to move (Florida may demonstrate multiple meanings). Florida, as a pattern, is choral rather than static. When one moves through the space we identify as Florida (conceptual or physical), one moves through a variety of meanings and patterns. And as the state's patterns become the basis of a Florida many of us eventually reimagine and display, narrative becomes the primary means for discussing the state. We tell our stories by showing the patterns. In this introduction, I am doing that work as well. My own memories of Florida are reduced to fragments, isolated moments, patterns I struggle to identify and connect. Thus, I try and tell a story. I look to narrative. What follows in *Florida* are a series of narratives, each a node within a larger network of meaning, a network of choral stories, spaces, figures, and personal moments. In turn, these chapters produce a scholarship of Florida, but one not tied down to fixed expectations of scholarship. As it does in the physical space called Florida, in the volume called *Florida*, the personal blends with the object of study. We discover choral movements, patterns that move throughout the chapters.

The first three chapters exemplify the importance of pattern formation to discussions of spaces. Sean Morey discovers in patterns another Key West than the one common topoi point to, one outside of the traditional narratives associated with the country's most southern city. In this patterned Key West, Morey finds mood as it is anchored in the repetitive images of bones scattered from Florida storms. Charlie Hailey locates his Spartan trailer in Homestead as a continuing pattern of Florida mobility. The trailer is a site of dwelling, but within this site, other meanings dwell. I turn to Miami in order to trace its spatial story as one of a series of patterns of dwelling, movements among various cultural markers that begin with mobility (migration) and end in a hurricane, what Hailey identifies as his rationale for living in the Spartan in the first place. These three chapters work off of Morey's sense of mood as invention. The authors feel their way around Florida.

Following this mood, the next four chapters locate mood in their authors' personal narratives of the state. Todd Taylor remembers Tampa as a middle-class experience, a migration from the Midwest to Disney, skateboarding, and sports events. Cassandra Branham and Megan McIntyre retrace their blue-collar upbringing in New Port Richey as an assemblage of photographs and personal stories, where drug usage, subdivisions, crime, racism, and economic inequality are merged with fragmented memories. Like the chapters in the previous section, a storm is featured. Lillie Anne Brown's story of growing up in Tallahassee reminds us of the state's racist history, particularly for how race informs class divisions as well. Steve Newman, growing up Jewish in Kendall (as I did), finds race and class merge along the city's internal grid, a grid that patterns the physicality of the city.

In the next section, Bradley Dilger connects the state's physical features by tracing its canal system (a grid) in West Palm Beach as also a system of political positions and attitudes. For Dilger, muck is more than the mud embedded in the canals; it is also a rhetorical movement through West Palm. James Beasley follows the Ponte Vedra Beach golf course's mounds in order to identify an ideology of spectatorship and the gaze. David Grant identifies the Tampa suburb of Town 'n' Country as a shell game, a physical shell (the spatial features of it and key buildings) and emotional shell (his father's activities) and cultural shell (the suburbs as merely a shell of authentic existence). As Morey read the bones of Key West as a choral movement of place, Sidney Dobrin reads the Florida beach through the bodies that occupy these spaces. The beach, Dobrin shows us, tells the story of Civil Rights and racial discrimination. Dobrin reminds us of the previous sections' emphasis on the African-American bodies of Tallahassee or the Jewish bodies of Miami as they are represented in state history.

Finally, Craig Saper, Adam Trowbridge, and Jessica Westbrook make no effort to represent EPCOT as the traditional anti-Disney critique I mention here in the Introduction. Instead, EPCOT offers these authors a narrative of psychosis, in the site itself and in the visitors (such as the authors) who remember it from childhood. Lauren Mitchell's vision of Orlando (what Taylor notes as synthetic and where the previous chapter situates its discussion of EPCOT), too, is a psychotic one, where boxes mark the city's desire. Orlando boxes are the "immaterial forces" that shape relationships to space. As with the first three sections' work, desire has been present in all of *Florida's* contributions. In this way, personal impressions drive a number of positions. Gregory Ulmer concludes this type of work by returning his concept of the *popcycle*, a personalized sense of organization that ties together narrative and discourse at the metaphoric "knot" of cognitive awareness: the pattern. The *konsult* Ulmer proposes for an accident (echoing the previous chapters' interest in storms and failures), promises no clear answers to problem solving (as Mitchell suggests for her own contribution), but instead offers a series of suggestions motivated by desire, emotion, and mood so that some sense of identification develops (as opposed to critique or argument). Ulmer writes that the *konsult* "intimates (it neither reveals nor conceals) to the community what is known, what may be learned, in a way that is useful, leading perhaps to some action." The collection, then, ends without a totalizing gesture, but a suggestion for a plan, a design concept, or even the outline Ulmer leaves us with regarding this gesture. We are left with a nod towards *some action. Florida*, therefore, is a design concept. Our stories have no final conclusions. They offer fragments, moments of identification, suggestions for other thoughts and writings on space.

I identify with Florida. The contributors to this collection do as well. I ask that readers of *Florida* not consider this collection as an authoritative history or cultural critique of the state. Instead, I ask readers to approach *Florida* as an alternative method for writing about space, one that allows personal and non-personal meanings to direct narrative at the level of pattern formation so that a variety of identifications might occur. Florida, as I hope this volume demonstrates, is a choral site of meaning. Florida is a network. It is a series of patterns. And, by chance, it is the place I grew up and studied in. *Florida* helps me internalize my own sense of status updates and fragmented memories. When the chapters presented here come together into their own network, I find a Florida both new and familiar to me. I also hope that this process of writing about space allows readers to consider their own spaces in similar ways, acknowledging that an alternative methodology exists here that may be appropriated by readers for their own purposes of expression, narrative, and invention.

Because I struggle with transforming anecdotes or memories into substantial narratives, I conclude this introduction with an anecdote (I must prove to myself the ability to tell one kind of semi-complete story) so that my narrative here can settle with some overall gesture, and the other narratives in this collection can begin. I conclude with an anecdote that plays off patterns similar to those among the volume's contributions. In 1984, I was in ninth grade. Along with some friends, I purchased tickets to a Black Sabbath/Night Ranger concert at the Sunrise Musical Theater, in Sunrise, Florida, north of Kendall. While waiting outside of Arvida Junior High—located in Kendall—for one of our parents to pick us up and drive us an hour north to the show, a friend said to me: If you push the walk/don't walk button on the traffic light five times in a row, the police will show up. For whatever reason, I pushed the button on the traffic light outside of the school five times.[5] Five minutes later, two squad cars pulled up to where we stood. Two police officers began to question us and frisk us. In my flannel shirt pocket was a small bag of marijuana. I began to panic over the thought of missing the concert once busted for possession. I had waited a long time to see Black Sabbath. Even without Ozzy, Black Sabbath was a major concert goal for me. It likely did not help that my long hair and three earrings obviously made me a target of a pat down. When the police discovered nothing (by luck), they left, and the designated driver parents arrived. This incident would be worth mentioning by itself, except, in the middle of Night Ranger's opening act, already high from at least an hour of smoking, I went to light a small pipe, filled again with marijuana, and I lit my hair on fire instead. This, unfortunately, is my substantial narrative. Whatever conclusions (or lack of), I draw, I allow its disastrous or humorous ending to lead readers into the rest of this volume. I leave the reader with this supposedly important moment so that one incident—that I feel is worth mentioning—can provide the departure point for all the incidents *Florida*'s authors will consequently tell as well.

Notes

1. http://www.facebook.com/pages/I-Grew-Up-in-South-Florida-in-the-60s-70s-and-80s/203472476342271
2. http://www.facebook.com/OldFlorida1
3. *Digital Detroit: Rhetoric and Space in the Age of the Network* (Southern Illinois University Press, 2012).
4. Listen to "Don't Let Me Die in Florida" by Patty Griffin, *American Kid*.
5. My wife insists that I am making this story up each time I tell it. She believes that the traffic light pushing is merely a myth. I present the anecdote here as a story, a spatial story, as I will tell again later in this collection.

Works Cited

Barthes, Roland. *The Pleasure of the Text*. Trans. Richard Miller. New York: Hill and Wang, 1975. Print.

Giroux, Henry and Grace Pollock. *The Mouse that Roared: Disney and the End of Innocence*. New York: Rowan and Littlefield, 2010. Print.

Lane, Frank. "Dwarf-Tossing Season Opens in Florida." *Weekly World News*. 3 Dec 2012. Web.

McLuhan, Marshall and Quentin Fiore. *The Medium is the Massage: An Inventory of Effects*. Corte Madera: Gingko Press, 2001. Print.

Ross, Andrew. *The Celebration Chronicles: Life, Liberty, and the Pursuit of Property Values*. New York: The Ballantine Publishing Group, 1999. Print.

Sargent, Jordan. "Naked Florida Man Jumps Off Of Room Onto Homeowner, Knocks Television Over, Empties Vacuum Cleaner, Masturbates." *Gawker*. 22 Jan 2013. Web.

Florida Patterns

2 A Network of Bones: Key West as Underworld

Sean Morey

She was the single artificer of the world In which she sang. And when she sang, the sea, Whatever self it had, became the self That was her song, for she was the maker.

—Wallace Stevens, "The Idea of Order at Key West"

I invent Key West. Or, I invent, here, a particular networked image of Key West that has been developing for both millions of years and only a few decades. You may have read of other Key Wests, those that involve pirates, smugglers, wreck-salvagers, and unsavory characters running to or from something. You may know Key West and the Florida Keys as a far-removed place of refuge for the fringe of society, yet also a location for high-status vacationers. You may have even been to Margaritaville. All of those Key Wests are here. But unlike other tourist spots in Florida, Key West has a unique way of tapping into the visitor's unconscious, creating an attunement between the traveler and the space through which she passes. As Tim Dorsey writes, "that was Key West. It searched out and exploited the hairline crack in each person's stability and crowbarred it open" (309). I'm interested in my own unconscious connection to Key West, where I grew up before attending the University of Florida. Below, I explore this crack for myself, and use Gregory L. Ulmer's practice of choragraphy as the crowbar.

Island Choragraphy

People often speak of the mystery our island possesses, but everyone is at a loss to explain it.

—Christopher Shultz and David L. Sloan,
Quit Your Job and Move to Key West

In the *Timaeus,* Plato presents chora as a third space, not a topological place (*topos*), but a meta-space that allows for spaces and places to happen.[1] Epicurus refines the distinction between chora and topos by positing that chora is a space that bodies move through while topos "is a space when occupied by a body" (Algra 38). But even this summary is problematic. Gregory L. Ulmer notes that chora "is one of the least understood, most puzzling, most resistant to interpretation of any of Plato's works" (*Heuretics* 63). Thomas Rickert agrees that "while it is customary to translate chōra as 'space,' strictly speaking, it is untranslatable" (270). Edward Casey analogizes chora to a mirror that "is amorphous and has no quality or structure of its own" (*Getting Back into Place* 359). A mirror allows images to take form and pass through, but does not hold the image once it is gone. Thus, a Platonic understanding of chora as "receptacle" is refuted by Casey and also Derrida, who explains that, like a mirror, "*Khōra* must not receive for *her own sake,* so she must not *receive,* merely let herself be lent the properties (of that) which she receives" (98, emphasis in original). So, although chora is not a tangible thing, it provides a network, or as Casey writes, "it is a locatory matrix for things" (*The Fate of Place* 34).

I mention the difficulty of defining chora because I see similarities between chora and Key West. Although perhaps not strictly a choral space, Key West presents "a congeries of questions about identity" (Pottle 286) and functions much like Casey's mirror where identities mingle, shift, sort, and leave. As a choral space, Key West only reflects those identities that pass through it. Chora and Key West, both undefinable, share an affinity between method and object of study.

But as Derrida, Ulmer, and Rickert stress—either explicitly or implicitly—defining an essence for chora is less important than using it, for chora "is not only a matter of theoretical inquiry—it is of practical use" (Rickert 253). So how does one use chora in a practice of choragraphy? "The key to choragraphy is the recognition and formation of pattern" (Ulmer *Electronic*

Monuments 205). The chorographer gathers material into the choral space, and after sifting, notices a pattern accruing between likes and unlikes; for a spectacle-driven, new media environment, the pattern emerges from repeating images: "A chora gathers information at the level of images by means of the repetition of signifiers" (Ulmer *Electronic Monuments* 186). However, just as chora is not itself a "thing," a choragraphy does not produce a pattern that expresses an object, but a state of mind, an emotion, an atmosphere (Ulmer *Electronic Monuments* 186). Thus, as I explore Key West, mapping its relationships across identities, I explore the identity of a mood. In contrast to topos, which "collects entities into universal homogenous sets based on shared essences, necessary attributes," chora "gathers singular ephemeral sets of heterogeneous items based on associations of accidental details. Yet chora paradoxically becomes categorical (general) through the aesthetic evocation of an atmosphere by means of these details" (*Electronic Monuments* 120). Even as chora itself is unrepresentable, the image and related mood that choragraphy produces can be recognized like an image reflected in mirror.

As an experiment, choragraphy requires a variable. Composing Key West as a networked, choral space depends on me as a unique node in this network so that chora may be put to work. To learn about Key West through this method, I must learn about Key West through my personal relationships to the media that compose popular ideas of Key West. As Rickert notes, "Such self-reflexivity is further appropriate for the electronic age, where near-total mediation, feedback loops, co-adaptive systems, and ecological systems theory are culturally and epistemologically ascendant, if not dominant" (267). The image and mood that result from this choragraphic exercise is specific to me, although it has the potential (without guarantee) to be recognized and experienced by others. Therefore, this space, this method, will be my own, for as Byron Hawk writes, "doing choragraphy means inventing your own method for mapping your particular conditions of possibility" (241).

More than a geographical place, Key West is marketed as a state of mind. I offer a parallel mood created from the media-network I assemble, not an argument that Key West has a particular essence. As Rickert explains, the "hypermedia composer constructs not arguments per se but an 'information environment' through which a user will choose a path (268).[2] My path is skeletal, and following it I explore and invent Key West from its media portrayals via marketing, advertising, history, literature, and other perspectives, out of which I will create a personal, accidental account that anchors Key West as the opposite of its popular, promoted atmosphere: Key West not as paradise at the southernmost point of Florida, but Florida's metaphorical (and in some ways, literal) underworld, filled with both psychic and physical bones.

Cayo Hueso

This sanguinary battle strewed this island with bones, as it is probable the conquerors tarried not to commit the bodies of the dead to the ground, hence the name of the island, Cayo Hueso.

—William H. Whitehead[3]

"The ground is full of bones, millions of crushed, bleached-out bone fragments, mixed in with dirt and sand" (McKeen 13). These bones were most likely of a Native American tribe, and while no one is sure from which, at least some DNA appears to be Calusa. On Sugarloaf Key, I lived near Indian Mounds subdivision, with streets named after these tribes, such as the Seminole, Matecumbe, and Tequesta. These bones might have been from a burial ground, or the remains of a final battle between the Calusa and a warring tribe. Whatever the case, when the "Spaniards arrived in the early seventeenth century, not all the skeletons had been crushed to powder by human feet. Piles of bones formed prehistoric landfills and even hale and hearty explorers were taken aback" (McKeen 14).

Thus, these Spaniards named the island Cayo Hueso, "Isle of Bones," which became Anglicized to Bone Key and eventually Key West. This specter of death hides beneath the English name, chosen by John Simonton and his business partner John Whitehead, who bought the key from Juan Pablo Salas. Since "Bone Key" didn't sound business-friendly (especially with tales of pirates about), they changed the name for marketing purposes: "Visitors might be spooked by the constant reference to the decayed corpses and piles of bones, so in 1821 they took the Spanish name Cayo Hueso and morphed it into 'Key West'" (McKeen 16). Cayo Hueso, however, continues to be spoken and used to market restaurants, merchandise, and even the "Bone Island Shuttle."

These bones were not the first. Beneath the Calusa skeletons are dead coral formations. As coral grows, it excretes calcium carbonate, forming larger skeletons. The reefs become the spine for the entire ecosystem, as other plants and animals make a living in, from, and around the coral formations. Key West was alive once, about 130,000 years ago when sea levels were 25 meters higher. 30,000 years later, sea levels fell, exposing much of the peninsular shelf, changing the Keys from a reef into a boneyard. Once the sea rose again, dead vegetation acidified the water, eroded limestone, formed oolites, combined with the skeletons of dead bryozoans, and created the limestone fossils that remain. Bones upon bones.

The current sea levels have added other casualties. Both living and dead reefs remain submerged, treacherous hazards to ships navigating the Keys. Since the ancient reef and peninsular shelf extend many miles west of Key West, these hazards are plentiful. While a skilled captain with a maneuverable ship and a clear day can discern the deeper cuts, dark storms have caused many skippers to wreck throughout the area. As Simonton once remarked, "capitalists will always go where profit is to be found" (Ogle 6)—even underwater—and so wreckers and salvagers became a major part of Key West's identity and economy in the nineteenth century, vultures picking at the bones of sunken ships. While the reef formed the backbone of the Keys, it often broke the back of ships, tolls paid in treasure to the ocean floor below, more bodies and bones deposited among the calcium-rich substrate. Increased ship traffic led to more wrecks, and during the early 1800s "there was plenty for everyone" (Ogle 31). With the Florida Straits, shallow reefs, and intertidal flats mostly uncharted, plus the frequent thunderstorm or hurricane, "the experienced and inexperienced alike would founder on the reef. Key Westers studied the horizon constantly, pacing the rooftop decks of their houses, waiting for signs of a ship aground" (Ogle 32). More vulturing.

If "capitalists will always go where profit is to be found," so will those who seek to steal profit. Blackbeard, one of the more notorious pirates of the region, died over one hundred years before Cayo Hueso became Key West, but once he "set up ship in the waters around Key West, a tradition of lawlessness began that carried through well into the twentieth century" (McKeen 18). This tradition includes not only swashbuckling piracy, but gun and drug smuggling in later, more recent decades. Pirates threatened shipping and wrecking operations and the future development of the island. To counter this danger, David Porter, "The bad ass of the open sea" (McKeen 19) eliminated piracy in a year, and soon "there were shops, bars, hotels, homes . . . but piracy continued in the form of free enterprise, as wreckers rescued cargo from the ships that ran aground on the rocks and kept much of the booty as payment" (McKeen 19). Remember that most infamous image of a pirate: The Jolly Roger — skull and crossbones.[4]

In these early days, several other bones also contributed to the island's identity and economic development: cigar manufacturing (bone is slang for cigar) and sponging. The sponge's skeletal structure was a desirable commodity, and although sponging is no longer as lucrative, small fleets of spongers still make their living from the shallow flats. From time to time, piloting my skiff through the shallow waters west of Key West, travelling over other unseen wrecks—possibly unfound pieces of the Nuestra Señora de Atocha and her crew—I notice against the sunset's red, fiery sky the outline of a Cuban-American. He poles his small wooden boat across the flat, like one poles a

Venetian gondola. Finding a sponge, he stabs it with his pole, piles it in his boat, and looks for another.[5]

Mile Marker Zero

> *The Keys . . . It's a creeping rot, inoperable gangrene moving up a limb, starting at Mile Zero and crawling east along U.S. One.*
>
> —Tim Dorsey, *Torpedo Juice*

These weren't the last bones committed to the sea. Along US 1, the only road in and out of the Keys, the department of transportation posts signage reminding motorists to drive carefully, including the annual number of US 1 fatalities. I drove by the southernmost sign daily while traveling to and from Key West High School. Because of the relatively slow speed limit and lack of passing lanes, motorists can become impatient and attempt ill-advised vehicular maneuvers, causing serious accidents that stop traffic for miles. Of course, Key West has its share of drunk drivers traveling US 1 after a night at the bars, but reaching Key West from the mainland has always been deadly, and to understand Key West as an underworld also means understanding the journey, the catabasis, required to get there.

Driving US 1, the traveler will notice advertisements for different tourist destinations ahead. T-shirt shops, shells and sponges, fishing charters, dive shops, hotels and resorts, restaurants, and other ads beckon the motorist. But one also notices the mile markers, starting at MM 127 in Florida City and counting down to MM 0 at the corner of Fleming and Whitehead Streets, the end of a road that began in Fort Kent, Maine. Besides the most marketed mile marker in the Keys (sold as a bumper sticker to tourists), the other mile markers become significant, used by local businesses to help customers navigate. For the motorist driving the whole length of the Keys, they provide a constant countdown to the end.

Part of the Key West allure includes severing one's connections by isolating oneself on an island. Forty-two bridges provide links, ligaments between these islands that offer the illusion of separation but still allow easy access to Key West. However, the trip to Key West via US 1 facilitates not just an end destination, but a journey in itself, a "crucial part of the Key West experience" (Steinberg 126). This sense of journey gives the Keys a particular mood of remoteness, of being at the end of the world. "The drive to Key West thus is used to forge both distance and nearness . . . Through the drive, one constructs Key West as a safe space of adventure: a space that is beyond the normal but at the same time permanently connected, a space that is part of the mainland and yet uniquely marginal" (Steinberg 129). "Safe," however, is a construction by the tourism industry, for tourists have frequently encountered fatal and sometimes exotic ends in the Keys, either from wrecks, hurricanes, or more recently, Dengue fever (also known as "breakbone" fever).

The original Overseas Highway (another name for this stretch of US 1) was completed in 1938, a project prioritized after the 1935 Labor Day hurricane destroyed the Overseas Railway. As Hemingway described the scene: "The foliage absolutely stripped as though by fire for forty miles and the land looking like the abandoned bed of a river. Not a building of any sort standing" (421). The Keys were stripped clean to the bone. Dead bodies twisted into the mangroves and embedded into the limestone, turning the Keys into a true wasteland: "they burst when you lifted them, rotten, running, putrid, decomposed" (422). Yet, thanks to Franklin Roosevelt, "From the wreckage of the rail rose a new lifeline to the mainland . . . a two-lane road piggybacking on the remaining track" (McKeen 6). Again, bones upon bones. The modern Overseas Highway, rebuilt during the 1970s, was constructed parallel to the old highway, itself built on Henry Flagler's Florida East Coast Overseas Railway which, after seven years, $127 million, and seven hundred deaths, sent its first train to Key West with a frail and practically blind Flagler onboard. I visited with Flagler's ghost daily, as my commute took me to 2100 Flagler Avenue: Key West High School. Our school's fight song began by referencing our colors: "On with the crimson! On with the grey!" Blood and death surrounded me, and I hadn't noticed.

In Plato's *Myth of Er*, the underworld functions, for most, as a place of limbo where ghosts gather until reincarnated. In 2006, fifteen Cubans landed on a disconnected section of the old Seven Mile Bridge. The US maintains a wet-foot/dry-foot policy regarding Cuban immigration: if picked up at sea, refugees are returned to Cuba; if they reach land, they gain freedom, or the perception thereof. Was this fragment *wet* or *dry*? The US Coast Guard argued that the bridge was equivalent to a buoy at sea, and thus, *wet*. Advocates for the refugees claimed that the section—since once connected to land—was still a bridge and therefore *dry*. Moreover, the state maintains these sections for their historical significance (tourist attractions). The judge, persuaded by this latter argument, ruled that the bridge was contiguous despite its isolation. The two sides, however, agreed to drop the case if the refugees were granted entry visas, and "the meaning and implications of this bridge fragment . . . remain contested" (Steinberg 137). The bridge section becomes a fragment that is neither officially part of the Keys nor part of the sea: its identity is in limbo. The Cubans, sent home pending the verdict, were also placed in limbo between their upper-world (US) and underworld

(Cuba). The Cuban government did not grant the fifteen refugees exit visas, and so the Keys became another ending.

Twenty-three miles beyond Key West, past the Southernmost Point, I regularly fish the Marquesas Keys, named after Marquis de Cadereita, the commander in charge of the Atocha and Santa Margarita fleet that wrecked nearby. The Marquesas Keys form the only atoll in the Atlantic, created not from a volcano, but from a meteorite. I often see abandoned refugee boats that, upon high tide, drift onto the flats and become lodged. For many of these boats, the Coast Guard intercepts them at sea, removes the passengers, and paints "U.S.C.G" onto the hull. On one wreck I see no "U.S.C.G.": only the letters "FREDOM."

Margaritaville

You know Death will get you in the end, but if you are smart and have a sense of humor, you can thumb your nose at it for awhile.

—Jimmy Buffett, *A Pirate Looks at Fifty*

Driving down the Keys, Sid Dobrin has a rule: no Jimmy Buffett music in the car once upon the Overseas Highway. Not that Dobrin dislikes Buffett, only that the Keys has enough of him already. Buffett was able to capture a particular identity associated with the Keys and make it sellable: "Suddenly, the Key Westers realized that Buffett was taking their day-to-day and packaging it for mass consumption. Buffett was serving the chamber-of-commerce function for the mass audience . . . who imagined a paradise with cold drinks and pretty women in tiny swimsuits, and a life monumentally perfect and serene" (McKeen 166). More than any other song, Buffett's "Margaritaville" has come to epitomize the laid-back state of mind that many associate with the Keys and Key West. While the song doesn't reference any Key West landmarks by name, "everyone knew where Margaritaville was" (McKeen 169).

The Key's Tourist Development Council has sold this mood in a variety of packages. Over the years, ad campaigns have instructed tourists to "Go all the Way" and drive the Overseas Highway; marketed Key West and the Florida Keys as the "Smilin' Islands"; defined the Keys as "Close to Perfect, Far from Normal"; informed the LGBT community that "Your Fantasy is Our Reality"; painted Key Largo as "The Dive Capital of the World" and Islamorada as "The Sportfishing Capital of the World"; and, most recently, invited everyone to "Come as You Are." Such is the atmosphere Buffett facilitated in the 1970s, and just in time. His album *Changes in Latitude, Changes in Attitude*—which includes "Margaritaville"—helped to save the town's economy as the Navy pulled anchor, just as Hemingway's presence had helped Key West during the Great Depression. "Now, because of the song, there was a new influx of tourists" (McKeen 167). However, while "Margaritaville" allowed Buffett to make money, it also began the end of his stay in Key West, signaling another ending. "Chris Robinson, his downstairs neighbor on Waddell Street, saw the change happen just as 'Margaritaville' was all over the radio. Having a hit song about Key West was death to an artist who might want to hang out in the town that inspired the song" (McKeen 171). Buffett and his family moved to Aspen just as the tourists started flooding ashore. Buffett's success simultaneously saved and killed the very place he sang about.

But "Margaritaville's" lyrics more than "bottled up the essence of Key West in an effervescent, maddeningly memorable pop song" (McKeen 168). They told not only of an ideal setting, a tropical version of the Elysian Fields—they hinted at a darker side of Key West. Margaritaville is not where one necessarily drinks and parties, but where one "wastes away." This state of mind is not only a laziness of relaxation, but also a lethargy of decay—literally, a forgetting of a previous life and present one, as if the river Lethe flowed from the taps at Sloppy Joe's Bar. One might say that "Margaritaville" is a song about Freud's death drive, barely hanging on, trying to live without feeling.

"Margaritaville," although disguised by the lyrics and melody, has a deathly past that undergirds its creation. Like the Keys, Buffett's music remains categorically open to interpretation, resisting easy classification. His success outside of conventional genres was created by a loss that left him devastated. Jim Croce, his close friend who died in 1973, proved to ABC Records (also Buffett's label) "that there was a market out there for sensitive-singer-songwriters-who-could-also-be-up-tempo-and-who-couldn't-really-be-classified" (McKeen 162), a market that Buffett would tap into. Yet, Buffett's success is not only built on the bones of Key West and Croce, but on another icon's death, Elvis Pressley. During the television series *CMT Crossroads*, Buffett revealed that the song was originally written for Elvis, who died before he could record it. Elvis, perhaps more than any other celebrity, exists as a ghost-image, haunting us with regular "sightings" and theories about his vital state.

Once I arrived in the Keys, Buffett was himself already a ghost, perhaps because he had departed after turning the Keys into Margaritaville. While one might think he received regular radio airtime, only a daily "Jimmy Buffett Break" played on US 1 Radio, a signal that locals appreciated Buffett's ideals, but couldn't engage with Margaritaville-the-mood in the same way as tourists. Buffett has become a living ghost for Key West, ubiquitously present on the island through images and tourist bars—such as his Margaritaville restaurant chain—but also absent, self-exiled because of the commodification he helped create and continues to capitalize on. If Hemingway provides a literary aura that drew in writers, Buffett brings in not musicians, but tourists looking for their own "lost shaker of salt," whatever this fetish object represents for them.

"Margaritaville"—while referring to the drink and a state of mind—also signals an epiphany, that one sees something previously invisible. In the song, Buffett comes to realize that the woman is not to blame, but himself—he is the cause of his own problems. If he has lost Key West, "it's my own damn fault." The song also summons the ghost of the Santa Margarita and her sunken fate. While the origin of the alcoholic margarita is murky, it may have derived from the drink called the Daisy (substituting tequila for brandy). Margaritaville is not only a place where one drinks to excess, lives out fantasies, and finds paradise, but also endings. Margarita, which is Spanish for daisy, provides a *memento mori* that we will one day push up daisies. Or, if we die in Key West, add our bones to all the others.[6]

To Have and Have Not

[I]t would be difficult to find an author who has written of death as often and as consistently as has Hemingway. At one time or another he has described the death of ants, salamanders, grasshoppers, and fish; how hyenas die, how to kill kudu, the proper way to execute horses, how bulls are slain, how soldiers die, death in Italy, in Cuba, in Africa and in Spain, death in childbirth and death by suicide, death alone and death in a group; selfish death, sacrificing death, and graceful death.

—Thomas Cash Jr., "Ernest Hemingway and Death"

Go to Key West . . . It's the best place for Ole Hem to dry out his bones.

—Letter from John Dos Passos to Hemingway[7]

Hemingway didn't die in Key West, but he left his ghost there, an image that continues to haunt the island and frustrate writers. Although many authors have contended with Key West besides Hemingway, no author's image has so dominated the perception of Key West and writing, and no author's image has been so dominated by Key West. As Lawrence R. Broer writes, Key West is "the place where he can be understood best" (45).

Key West was a place of loss during Hemingway's residency (1928–1939) as the Great Depression sunk the island's economy. In contrast, Hemingway was becoming prosperous, pumping money into the island. Yet, he experienced many loses as well. Artistically, his works published during this time reflect as much: *A Farewell to Arms* (1929), *Death in the Afternoon* (1932), *Winner Take Nothing* (1933), *To Have and Have Not* (1937), and *For Whom the Bell Tolls* (1940). Despite this productive period, critics claim Hemingway experienced "lost years" in Key West, for as Kirk Curnutt writes, "of all the exotic locales with which this peripatetic author is associated, Key West is the only one deemed detrimental to his art" (1), for in Key West, Hemingway's embodiment of "hard work . . . gave way to the facile poses of the sportsman and adventurer" (2).

Hemingway also experienced personal loss during this period, what Gail D. Sinclair calls "Hemingway's Decade of Loss." Key West was the last place Hemingway saw his father before the latter killed himself, and "family frictions . . . caused another important loss: an irrevocable break between Ernest and his sister Carol" (62). Hemingway lost many of his friends during this period, straining or breaking friendships with F. Scott Fitzgerald and Archibald MacLeish; his close relationship with John Dos Passos became "ruined beyond repair" (67). He also started to lose his second marriage to Pauline Pfeiffer. While Hemingway started the 1930s with "a new hometown, a new wife, a growing family, and a rising career" (75), he would lose, or begin to lose, much of this; although he did not literally die on the island, and would not kill himself for more than two decades, "the dark seed was already deeply imbedded" (75) during his time in Key West.

In 1928, Hemingway was already "a living legend" (McKeen 39), filled the island with his presence, and became more public and "increasingly consumed with and by his own image" (Pottle 289). This image, which started to bifurcate into his literary ghost and his bodily ghost, would haunt other writers. Even though Key West changed post-Hemingway, "in the end, Key West is still Key West. Young writers still come down Highway 1, looking for the ghost of Hemingway" (McKeen 242). These writers included "Tom McGuane, Jim Harrison, Phil Caputo . . . eventually every young male writer of that generation came south, needing to deal with Hemingway's ghost" (McKeen 26). Key West was a sacred stopping ground to pay tribute (or contest) Hemingway's spirit before coming into one's own success (or failure).

Hemingway's ghost, of course, haunts my discipline of English and writing studies. While my high school English classes certainly assigned Hemingway's texts, my most vivid memory of the author comes not from his literature, but from the Hemingway Day's Festival, a carnivalesque event to attract more tourists. The festival culminates in the Ernest Hemingway Look-Alike contest, held at Sloppy Joe's Bar, where the "Winners are waistline-challenged and white-haired, unlike the film-star figure Hemingway cut in the 1930s" (Pottle 297). Instead of focusing on Hemingway's literary achievements, the festival celebrates his physical body. "Mounting the stage at Sloppy Joe's and spilling out the bar's doors, the look-alike contest interrogates . . . in the vernacular of carnival" (Pottle 296). In this carnival a séance occurs, a summoning of a Hemingway whose aura has become the image of a cartoon: the skeleton of an image, a stick-figure. In this carnival we see a liminality that makes Key West a choral space where a ghost such as Hemingway's can circulate, shift, and thrive. In this celebration, carnival's etymological roots emerge: the removal of meat, leaving just the bones, bones that can then be sorted into any formation one likes.

For the 1999 festival, my brother—only seventeen at the time—entered the competition against "contestants with big bellies and grey beards who bore little resemblance to the Hemingway of Key West" (Kerstein 185). Rather than dress in the guise of Yousuf Karsh's famous portrait of an old Hemingway, he entered the contest as a young Hemingway, just back from his stint as an Italian Ambulance driver, wearing an army uniform and standing on crutches, leg wrapped with bandages. To help his cause, he passed out flyers to show the crowd this less-known image, a Hemingway we were never taught, that we never see—an invisible Hemingway that must have haunted the author since "his formative 1918 wounding . . . initiated him in the metaphysical quandary of death" (Curnutt 2). Even though he couldn't drink yet, perhaps my brother understood the relationship between Hemingway and Key West better than anyone else in the bar.[8]

CHUMMING FOR GHOSTS: A NEKUIA

I told you I could always think good with my bones and my bones are thinking heavy right now.

—Letter from Ernest Hemingway to Archibald MacLeish, *Selected Letters*

[T]he bonefish is atomic—or, as some say . . . he is driven by 10,000 frightened devils.

—Burton J. Rowles, "The Bonefish: Ghost of the Shallows"

In the *Timaeus*, where we find Plato's most detailed treatment of chora, we also find Critias telling the legend of Atlantis, how it sank due to "the moral decay of its once virtuous population" (Ulmer, *Heuretics* 76). As Ulmer points out, a consensus once believed that Columbus had found Atlantis; another theory proposes that one of his crew, Juan Ponce de León, spotted Key West to the North but kept silent, sailing back later with his own ship. Was Key West Atlantis? Ulmer offers that the real lesson of Atlantis lies not as a parable against moral decay, but the relation between memorial and catastrophe, that we can't stop looking for the exotic, especially when buried treasure is involved. "The choral quality of 'Atlantis' concerns this power of fascination, this capacity to motivate the practice of search" (*Heuretics* 76). Key West has certainly been a location for catastrophe and fascination, a place of intrigue where people come looking for treasure and sometimes meet their end.

Geographically, Key West aligns with possible locations for Atlantis: beyond the Straits of Gibraltar. However, the Homeric underworld, as described in *The Odyssey* and in Greek mythology generally, also exists past these straits, past the setting sun. In *Book X*, Circe instructs Odysseus to "make a journey of a different kind, and find your way to the Halls of Hades . . . across the River of Ocean" (148). Although Odysseus undertakes a catabasis, a journey to the underworld, his goal is not to rescue a person or soul (as does Heracles or Orpheus), but to obtain information. Specifically, Odysseus performs a *nekuia*—he summons the ghosts of the underworld to question them. Those who travel down (south) and past the setting sun to Key West, traversing water, may also perform a *nekuia*, summoning ghosts to find answers, be they about writing, salt shakers, fishing, or loss.

I too look for ghosts. Bonefish (a fish endemic to the Keys and the Caribbean) were most likely named for their many bones, making them undesirable to eat. Thus, bonefish are almost always released upon capture: to catch one entails a loss. Bonefish live transitory lives: as larvae, they grow, shrink, morph, and then grow again; they provide a link between eels and modern fishes; they appear above and below the surface; feeding in the shallowest of water, bonefish often expose their caudal fins, called "tailing." The beginning of a fight with this fish often begins with its end. And because the bonefish is so difficult to see directly, one must look for their tails or shadows as an index of their presence; thus, Zane Grey dubbed them the "gray ghost of the flats."

Often, to attract bonefish, one makes a sacrifice by cutting shrimp into pieces, throwing them into a sandy spot, chumming the waters as Odysseus pours sheep blood for his shades. I regularly use this method to summon these ghosts, offering a sacrifice for my own nekuia. But what is the question? What am I trying to learn? What can they tell me? Perhaps I'm not seeking information, but summoning a mood. As one casts bones to perform a reading from the *I Ching*, I cast [to] bones to perform a feeling.

The only way to reach the underworld is over water, particularly by ferry; the first incarnation of US 1 required forty-one miles of ferry travel. In Greek mythology, the guide who ferried souls to the underworld was Charon, poling their shades across the River Styx. Charon provides a clue. His traditional representation depicts a skeleton clothed in a hooded garment, standing on the back of a wooden skiff, poling shades to the gates of Hades. In this image, I see a pattern: that figure is me. Like the sponger working the flats, I too pole a boat. I perform Charon as I pole my flats skiff across the shallow water, looking for grey ghosts to bring aboard.

Charon also provides another clue: his name begins with the Greek letter *Chi*, pronounced "Key" and written ☒. This X "marks the spot" for pirates, wreckers, and those who have come to Key West looking for treasure, adventure, inspiration, or whatever fetish X represents. Symbolically, X'd-out eyes signify death, and the femur bones on the Jolly Roger crisscross to make an X. Mentioned above, *Book X* informs Odysseus of his fate. To investigate Key West is to think in the key of X, the repeated signifiers that point to Charon as he points to me and to the island of X West.[9]

So what is the pay off? This chapter presents a cognitive map, which may be recognized by others, or not. Either way, this experiment relays a method for making one's own map, using chorography to chart the connections between self, place, and the media that circulate a location's identities. For me, X really does mark the spot. And what treasure do I expect to find under X? As a scholar, my treasure comes not as pieces of eight, but knowledge.[10] As an example of pattern recognition, a moment of eureka when a picture is seen from a new perspective, Ulmer offers the famous duck-rabbit image, where a gestalt switch is flipped and one can see both duck and rabbit simultaneously. I now see Key West as both paradise and underworld, not as heaven/hell, but of living/dead, happiness/melancholy, a place where ghosts haunt and may be summoned. Or, I experience Key West in both the moods of Margaritaville and loss. I now perceive Key West as a perverse chiasmus, where both states eXist simultaneously—and with this knowledge, an insight into my mood: while I am happiest in Key West, I'm also saddest; while I'm not sure why, I now have a spot to start digging.

Pattern recognition is also akin to getting a joke, requiring local knowledge to understand its language play. The joke for Key West is in its name, "Isle of Bones," not just those from ancient reefs and Native Americans, but also more recent bones that litter the island and continue to haunt visitors and residents alike. If nothing else, I've learned that the methodology of chorography can produce new knowledge, but I've also discovered that the same media network that creates the popular image of Key West can also create the unpopular—two sides of the same piece of eight. Or, another metaphor: when I fish for bones/ghosts, I fish for bones/ghosts trying to summon those spirits that haunt my Key West experience, some I'm aware of and some

I am not. Each time I visit Key West, I experience the atmosphere of loss around me, but only now, after this choragraphic experiment, does it become an image. As such, Perhaps Thomas McGuane best expresses an emblem for this perpetual mixed mood of paradise and underworld: "This spring they dug up the parking lot behind some clip joint on lower Duval and found an Indian grave, the huge skull of a Calusa seagoing Indian staring up through four inches of blacktop at the whores, junkies and Southern lawyers" (6–7).

Acknowledgments

Thanks to Scot Barnett and Jeff Rice for their insightful comments and suggestions. And thanks to bonefish.

Notes

1. While some of the authors quoted below spell "chora" and "choragraphy" differently, I rely on Ulmer's spelling in *Electronic Monuments*.
2. Rickert also explains that, geographically, chora can refer a city's surrounding territory. When mentioning Key West, I often mean this choral sense that includes the surrounding Keys, waters, and uninhabited islands.
3. Qtd. in Brown 9.
4. Blackbeard's particular flag depicted a skeleton, spearing a human heart with one hand and toasting the devil with the other.
5. As a nautical term, "bones" refers to the foam or spray which is thrown out under the bow of a ship while underway. If fast-moving, throwing much spray, the vessel is said to have "A bone in her teeth." Since my skiff is small, crossing the rough pass from the Marquesas Keys back to Key West often produced many bones.
6. Like a cigar, bone is also slang for marijuana. Buffett played on his and his followers' pot-smoking practices in his band's name, "The Coral Reefer Band."
7. While Dos Passos told Hemingway about Key West, John Bone—Managing Editor at the Toronto Star—encouraged Hemingway as a journalist (qtd in McKeen 29)..
8. Two bones in Hemingway's fiction: (1) in *A Farwell to Arms*, Ettore Moretti states "There's a dead bone in my foot that stinks right now" (106); (2) in *The Old Man and the Sea*, Santiago ponders Joe DiMaggio's bone spur.
9. Chora begins with ☒.
10. Despite this, I always scan for floating bags of money that may have been lost by drug smugglers.

Works Cited

Algra, Keimpe. *Concepts of Space in Greek Thought*. Leiden; New York; Köln: E. J. Brill, 1994. Print.

Broer, Lawrence R. "Only in Key West: Hemingway's Fortunate Isle." *Key West Hemingway: A Reassessment*. Eds. Kirk Curnutt and Gail D. Sinclair. Gainesville: U of Florida P, 2009. 44–58. Print.
Browne, Jefferson B. *Key West: The Old and the New*. Gainesville: U of Florida P, 1973. Print.
Buffett, Jimmy. *A Pirate Looks at Fifty*. New York: Ballantine, 2000. Print.
Casey, Edward S. *Getting Back into Place: Toward a Renewed Understanding of the Place—World*. Bloomington: Indiana UP, 1993. Print.
—. *The Fate of Place: A Philosophical History*. Berkeley: U of California P, 1998. Print.
Cash, Thomas H. Jr. "Ernest Hemingway and Death." MA thesis. University of Kentucky, 1951. Print.
Curnutt, Kirk. "Introduction: Hemingway and Key West Literature." *Key West Hemingway: A Reassessment*. Eds. Kirk Curnutt and Gail D. Sinclair. Gainesville: U of Florida P, 2009. 1–22. Print.
Derrida, Jacques. *On the Name*. Ed. Thomas Dutoit. Trans. John P. Leavey, Jr. and Ian McLeod. Stanford: Stanford UP, 1995. Print.
Dorsey, Tim. *Florida Roadkill*. New York: Harpertorch, 2000. Print.
—. *Torpedo Juice*. New York: Harpertorch, 2005. Print.
Hawk, Byron. *A Counter-History of Composition: Toward Methodologies of Complexity*. Pittsburgh: U of Pittsburgh P, 2007. Print.
Hemingway, Ernest. *A Farewell to Arms*. New York: Scribner's, 2012. Print.
—. *Selected Letters: 1917–1961*. Ed. Carlos Baker. New York: Scribner's, 1981. Print.
Homer. *The Odyssey*. Tran. E. V. Rieu. New York: Penguin, 1965. Print.
"Jimmy Buffett and Zac Brown Band." *CMT Crossroads*. 19 Mar. 2012. Television.
Kerstein, Robert. *Key West on the Edge: Inventing the Conch Republic*. Gainesville: U of Florida P, 2012. Print.
McGuane, Thomas. *Panama*. New York: Vintage, 1995. Print.
McKeen, William. *Mile Marker Zero: The Moveable Feast of Key West*. New York: Crown, 2011. Print.
Ogle, Maureen. *Key West: History of an Island of Dreams*. Gainesville: U of Florida P, 2003. Print.
Pottle, Russ. "Key West as Carnival: Hemingway and the Commodification of Celebrity." *Key West Hemingway: A Reassessment*. Eds. Kirk Curnutt and Gail D. Sinclair. Gainesville: U of Florida P, 2009. 285–298. Print.
Rickert, Thomas. "Toward the Chōra: Kristeva, Derrida, and Ulmer on Emplaced Invention." *Philosophy and Rhetoric* 40:3 (2007): 251–273. 1 Oct. 2012. Print.
Rowles, Burton J. "The Bonefish: Ghost of the Shallows." *Sports Illustrated* 2 Feb. 1959: 56–66.Print.
Schultz, Christopher and David L. Sloan. *Quit Your Job and Move to Key West: The Complete Guide*. Key West: Phantom, 2005. Print.
Sinclair, Gail D. "The End of Some Things: Hemingway's Decade of Loss." *Key West Hemingway: A Reassessment*. Eds. Kirk Curnutt and Gail D. Sinclair. Gainesville: U of Florida P, 2009. 59–76. Print.

Steinberg, Phillip E. "Bridging the Florida Keys." *Bridging Islands: The Impact of Fixed Links*. Ed. Godfrey Baldacchino. Charlottetown, PE, Canada: Acorn, 2007. 123–138. Print.

Stevens, Wallace. *The Collected Poems of Wallace Stevens*. New York: Vintage, 1990. Print.

Ulmer, Gregory L. *Electronic Monuments*. Minneapolis, MN: U of Minnesota P, 2005. Print.

—. *Heuretics: The Logic of Invention*. Baltimore: The John Hopkins UP, 1994. Print.

3 Miami Spatial Stories

Jeff Rice

When I was a child, my grandmother would play a game with me. "It's not Your-Ami," she'd say. "It's My-Ami." I, in turn, would insist that the object under discussion was "My-Ami." "No," I'd argue in response, "It's not Your-Ami!" This would go on for ten or fifteen minutes, until one of us yielded virtual possession of the city to the other. Like many residents of her age, my mother's mother came to Miami from New Jersey in the 1950s (my grandparents were originally from Brooklyn). The verbal contention regarding who owns Miami functioned for us as a childhood game, but it continues to play out in the physical space of a portion of land in South Florida as well. I grew up in Kendall, a southern suburb of Miami populated by approximately 80,000 people. Our mailing address, though, proved contentious as well since its destination was Miami, not Kendall. The question of where I lived—suburb or city—was always contentious. In Kendall, we imagined ourselves as Miami. "There are at least two Kendalls," notes Paul George while describing the area's contested borders surrounding the city of Miami (118). Kendall is named for Henry John Broughton Kendall, an English trustee for the Florida Land and Mortgage Company. There seems to be no real reason Kendall would be named for him other than that his name appeared on many banking documents during the nineteenth century acquisition of South Florida land for development.

One government website points to Kendall's presence in South Florida as a mystery and one of contentious residence.

> The great mystery of Henry Kendall is the eighteen-year period, between 1884 and 1902, during which he managed Sir Edward Reed's lands in South Dade. There is no evidence that he lived anywhere in South Florida and we know that he was quite active with his duties as a banker in New York and London at that time, particularly in the 1890s. Kendall was married, with five school-age children and maintained the family home in Hatfield, a suburban town 20 miles north of London, throughout his time in America. (Kenward)

I have not been back to Miami, or to Kendall, in almost twenty years. I don't care to go back, a declaration my wife, who loves the South and who has never been to a real beach, finds mysterious (as if I am keeping the city to myself). My desire to not head south again may seem odd, particularly since I have spent the last eleven years living in climates where snow is frequent in the winter. In 1967, Wayne Cochran, on the other hand, pledged he was "Going Back to Miami," a song about returning to the city for a girl (though maybe not his wife). Billy Joel painted Miami as a destination point after an apocalypse occurs in the not so distant future. In his song "Miami 2017," Joel imagined Miami as a refuge. In the narrative or diegesis Joel builds, Miami is never mentioned. But Joel describes how dangerous and contentious New York has become in this futuristic, dystopic scenario. The city's citizens, we are led to believe, will once again flee south, just as they did almost eight years earlier. Joel sings:

> They burned the churches up in Harlem.
> Like in that Spanish Civil War.
> The flames were everywhere.
> But no one really cared.
> It always burned up there before.

When New York and nearby New Jersey residents, such as my own family, flocked to South Florida after World War II, they were not fleeing a burning city. Instead, they were participating in a mass migration in search of better jobs, cheaper housing, and warmer weather. "In 1959," Jeffrey Gurock writes, "approximately forty-three percent of Miami Jews came from New York City, a proportion that slightly exceeded the percentage of American Jews living in New York after the war" (107–108). My family, who came from northern New Jersey, Brooklyn, and Philadelphia, were among those Jews who left New York for Miami in the early 1950s. Some of those Jews were recent residents of New York; they had, a few years earlier, fled their own devastation, the Holocaust of Nazi Europe. So, too, had Billy Joel's family arrived in New York from Europe. My grandfather fled the loss of a New Jersey chicken farm so that he could start over in Miami selling insurance.

In 1980, I was ten and living in Kendall when Liberty City burned and experienced the devastation of a riot. Insurance salesman Arthur McDuffie's death at the hands of several police officers, who were not convicted of the murder, set the city ablaze. Our sixth-grade classes at F.C. Martin were canceled because of the general fear of danger, a danger sparked by a possible race riot in the African-American neighborhood where the school was located. If McDuffie was guilty of anything, it was likely the suspicion of anyone who doesn't appear to "belong" to the majority's social club (African-American man riding a motorcycle seemed out of place to the patrolling police). "I wouldn't mind being followed by a cop," a Miami party-goer says in the early minutes of Alfred Hitchcock's 1946 *Notorious*. "Of course I'm a marked woman," Ingrid Bergman's character responds; she is a German outsider who has just watched a Miami court convict her father of treason (a suspected Nazi).[1] "I'm likely to blow up the Panama Canal any minute now." If Miami had "burned up there before" or even blow up, to echo Joel, it hadn't been for twenty years at least, dating to some point in the 1960s when American cities burned in response to other racist beatings or to the 1968 assassination of Martin Luther King Jr. During the political turmoil of the 1960s, Wayne Cochran was not concerned with racial inequity. He wasn't fleeing New York's devastation, like Joel's anonymous protagonist, but merely trying to get back to his baby. We may never know where McDuffie was going when he was stopped and beaten, and we may never return to the moment he allegedly fled police. But his brutal beating eventually led to "more than 1,400 riot related arrests" and "$125 million in property damage and losses" (Skolnick and Fyfe 182). Going back to a baby, heading south, these responses pale in comparison to the damage racial discrimination generates. Asked by *The Miami News* to respond to the 1980 rioting, Muhammad Ali, a former resident of Liberty City in the 1960s, too, fell short of grasping the totality of McDuffie's murder, but noted that, "This is a heavy thing. It's difficult. It makes my fight comin' up with Holmes looks [sic] so easy" (Brubaker 8A). After the riots, Thomas Boswell, Ira Sheskin, and Carroll Truss interviewed residents of Liberty City and other African-American neighborhoods in order to understand local responses to the event. Two thirds of Richmond Heights and over three quarters of Liberty City respondents noted that "it's almost impossible for a black to get a fair trial in Dade County" (9). In other words, the prevailing attitude was that only those with ethnic membership to a select, white club could get justice.

Miami's Jews, as well, learned the contentious nature of such clubs when they arrived to the city in the early part of the twentieth century. "No Jews, No Dogs" signs often greeted them at parks, restaurants, hotels, apartment buildings, and other locales. Possibly, this is why the Jewish Joel, who features Miami in a dystopic future, cannot yield his love for New York, where most of Miami's Jews fled from. Miami was racist. New York, Joel sings, is a state of mind.

> Some folks like to get away.
> Take a holiday from the neighborhood.
> Hop a flight to Miami Beach or to Hollywood.
> But I'm taking a Greyhound on the Hudson River line.
> I'm in a New York state of mind. ("New York State of Mind").

Racism, as well, is a state of mind even when it materializes in actual practice and locations. "'Until the late 1930s, Jews were barred from almost all oceanfront hotels above Lincoln Road; it was not until World War II that a law banned display of restrictive signs such as "No Jews or Dogs"'" (qtd Lavender). In the February 1966 issue of *The Crisis* magazine, a profile of NAACP National Life Membership Chairman and Jewish philanthropist Kivie Kaplan related a Kaplan anecdote about experiencing Florida racism. On a business trip to Central America, Kaplan stops over in Miami Beach. "When I got back they wanted me to go sightseeing before we left for home. Among other things they showed me a hotel with a sign out front that said, "No dogs or Jews allowed" (White 116). These signs return to contemporary memories of northern migration to South Florida. Daniel Patterson, writing in the food magazine *Lucky Peach*, remembers Rascal House (the later manifestation of the classic Jewish restaurant Wolfie's) via the infamous sign.

> The city was barely born when the snowbirds, as they came to be called, began to arrive. Slowly at first, and then faster after the First World War, East Coast Jews and others developed the beachfront, and Miami became a winter hangout for well–heeled New Yorkers. Though the "No Dogs or Jews Allowed" signs stayed up for many years, the diaspora of aging first–generation refugees whose members were still fresh with the horrors that they had left behind, were able to make a community for themselves. They built hotels and businesses, synagogues in which to worship, and delis that reminded them of the food they had grown up with. (115)

The first known Jewish settler to Miami was Brooklyn-born Isidor Cohen, who arrived in 1893. When Cohen's son was born, the *brit milah* (circumcision) was reported in *The Miami Metropolis*. As Marcia Jo Zerivitz reports and quotes from the paper:

> "Interesting ceremonies attending circumcision of Miami's first born Hebrew child yesterday." Normally the *brit* is held on the eighth day after birth, but it took three weeks for Rabbi Julian Shappo to arrive by boat from Key West to perform the ritual. (Zerivitz 14).

I was not circumcised in Miami, and I have never seen a No Dogs, No Jews sign, but I did eat at both Wolfie's and Rascal House when I was a kid. The Wolfie's sign was iconic to Miami residents, and a marker of our occasional trips to Miami Beach (often after Rosh Hashanah services at Temple Israel). Wilfred Cohen founded both restaurants (holding on to Rascal House until 2008). As Jan Whitaker writes, Wolfie's hosted

> big and little gangsters and bookies with a yen for chicken livers, pastrami, and cheesecake. In the 1970s, mobster Meyer Lansky, pursuing the simple life of a philosophical, Chevrolet-driving, book-borrowing library patron, was often spotted noshing in Wolfie's.

Circumcision marks the "club" Jewish men join when they enter into the covenant with God. Wolfie's marks a club for Jews' gastronomical "home away from home" (Patterson 116). When not eating chicken livers or pastrami, a circumcised, Jewish male represents his ethnicity via circumcision. When Isidor Cohen convinced a rabbi to travel three weeks in order to perform Miami's first circumcision, he engaged in an act of representation; Jews could now be represented as native people in the Sunshine State, a claim that would be countered by racist signage in the early twentieth century. Typically, Florida is represented as tourism, vice, and sunshine. Just as typical, elderly Jews are represented as transplanted New Yorkers. These topoi provide the basis of any number of narratives we tell about the state or its principle city, Miami. In some ways, then, there is a diegetic covenant with a city like Miami, one that frames the city as a commonplace so that our circulated stories feel familiar and comforting. But even as my introduction of overlapping stories suggests, there is more to narrative than commonplaces. There are patterns. As I begin to write about Miami, I realize that the narrative I'm telling is neither historical nor linear, but instead, it is a series of patterns.

Spatial Stories

I've wanted to write about Miami for some time. Its history of Jews, migration, race, music, and other items fascinates me even if I have no desire to return to the city I lived in for almost fifteen years. That is, I want to write about Miami not because I am nostalgic for the city or hold it dear to me in some sentimental way, the way my wife does Austin, or someone else might do another city. Instead, I want to write about Miami because it merely captures some part of my imagination. My reasons are likely connected to an internal representation I hold but cannot fully express. I don't maintain one image of Miami (popular or otherwise). My-Ami drifts from reference to reference, from pattern to pattern, from affective moment to affective moment. As Roland Barthes might ask "How do you describe something that does not represent anything?" (61). It might be that such an idea as the one I have called Miami to myself and to others only can be expressed, not represented. Expression, I might add, marks a point of invention, of coming up with an idea, of delivering that idea. Pattern formation is one method for expressing or inventing ideas (as opposed to how topoi might inform argumentation). With patterns, we find some type of insight—from the banal to the extraordinary. With patterns, we are capable of expressing outside of literal representation.

In the memory I have of some placed called "Miami," I can create or express what Michel de Certeau calls a spatial story by revisiting Miami as a series of associations or patterns I return to for the purpose of invention. The spatial story, de Certeau writes, "distributes places" (130). Rather than totalizing Miami as one place, I want to distribute it as a number of places, sites, times, images, moments, and so on so that I can spatialize it as a narrative of distribution, rather than as a grand narrative which attempts to capture the city as a whole. The purpose of this spatialization would be to invent another Miami, one that I feel, but struggle to represent. In that sense, I am trying to explore a non-representational space in my writing so that the totalized space does not dominate my or anyone else's imagination. What I invent materializes in this writing. In a distributed Miami, there is no place that centralizes my representation of the city I grew up in. I move through fragmented, networked moments spread out over various media and time periods.

In that sense, I am exploring a way to write about the city I grew up in, a way that does not, as Fredric Jameson requires, always historicize, but instead fleshes out patterns and associations as a narrative. Mine is not a history of Miami. Mine is not a Miami (or Your-Ami) others could have experienced in the same manner. In the age of new media, associations replace logical argumentation as a method of persuasion. These associations may appear as networked moments, fragments, and isolated details juxtaposed into a larger narrative. In a series of associations that begin with this preamble of movement, race, and death, I am not trying to persuade a reader to believe in something called Miami, Florida. Instead, as Gregory Ulmer might note, I am trying to present a feeling as text. Miami evokes in me a feeling I cannot adequately represent without resorting to the patterns the city yields. The basic premise of Ulmer's digital diegesis is the concept of the felt, the moment of feeling that weaves together a variety of ideas (*Internet Invention* 36). Miami, for me, is a train of associations, thoughts, and movements. It is a type of feeling, not a representation nor an argument. I feel that the city is My-Ami. That feeling begins with a riot that occurred when I was ten and then leads into a pop song.

Figure 1. The feeling of Miami: 1974.

In 1963, James Brown, known for declaring more than once that he's "got the feeling," begins a live performance of his single "Night Train" by introducing his list of cities the night train visits with the declaration, "Miami, Florida." The song "Night Train," and in particular, this shout-out to Miami, is what Mark Winegardner's gangsters hear in the novel *The Godfather's Revenge*, as they are about to be killed by the mob (488). The mob and Miami have a specific and commonplace connection: 1963 Miami. Four days before being assassinated, John F. Kennedy visited Miami. Four days later, Kennedy would be shot dead in Texas, and there would be no rioting. 1963 is a year that I know well. 1963 was the focal point of my book *The Rhetoric of*

Cool, which critiques my discipline's (rhetoric and composition) commonplace understanding of the field's rebirth narrative. A commonplace indicates a site of already known knowledge (such as Miami is a site of sunshine and fun). For some time, my field pointed to 1963 as a site of already known knowledge. To immediately invoke Kennedy's assassination in a discussion of 1963 would be to call upon a familiar point or meaning as well. In my book, I did not write about the Kennedy assassination. Instead, I focused on a club-like mentality that viewed writing in narrow terms, one that opted to historicize this narrow vision as contemporary pedagogy by neglecting other spaces of meaning already in circulation in 1963, among them pattern formation. A rigid, temporal-historical reading, I showed, failed to account for or represent other, associative, temporal moments.

Miami's commonplace might be sunshine or tourism. The commonplace moment from 1963 is Kennedy's assassination. Few speak of Kennedy's Miami visit outside of conspiracy theorists who claim Kennedy was supposed to be killed in Miami by the mob (or in some cases, conspiracists claim, by the Jews). When Kennedy spoke at the American Hotel in Miami Beach in order to address the Inter-American Press Association, he mentioned extending a hand to Cuba.

> No Cuban need feel trapped between dependence on the broken promises of foreign communism and the hostility of the rest of the hemisphere. For once Cuban sovereignty has been restored we will extend the hand of friendship and assistance to a Cuba whose political and economic institutions have been shaped by the will of the Cuban people. (Kennedy)

Kennedy's failure to overthrow Castro in the Bay of Pigs is often credited as the secret behind his assassination; a betrayed mob took its revenge. Had I known about the visit or the conspiracy when I was writing my book, I might have included it in *The Rhetoric of Cool* in order to exemplify another missed, compositional moment (i.e., conspiracy as a form of writing). *Digital Detroit*, my second book, deals with the concept of secrecy (a form of conspiracy) as central to networked rhetoric (in one chapter, Detroit's Maccabees building is explored for its historical basis as a secret society and not for its Jewish name, a name it shares with the Jewish fighters the holiday of Hanukah celebrates). The secret of Kendall's name, I might argue, equates to the secret of Kennedy's assassination at the level of a pattern (and not of causality). Both are moments of writing whose mystery evokes desire for invention (i.e., what happened, why did it happen, how did it happen). The devastation felt after Kennedy's death is, no doubt, equitable to what Billy Joel describes occurring in 2017. As Joel sings about the night the lights went out on Broadway:

They say a handful still survive.
To tell the world about.
The way the lights went out.
And keep the memory alive.

Despite the nation's feeling of loss in 1963 and its memory of Kennedy, his death remains a secret. What is the secret, I ask, of Kennedy's Miami visit as a moment of spatial writing, even if that moment is not historical writing but rather the practice of invention? In a traditional, logical proposition that could easily be argued, the secret might be summed up as a formula: 2017 - 1963 = 54. Whatever fifty-four means, it could help serve a type of writing whose focal point is not just juxtaposition (a rhetorical principle I proposed in *The Rhetoric of Cool* and evident in the moments I am bringing together here), but mystery, secrecy, and conspiracy. When the railroad came to Miami in 1896, the city of eight hundred people called itself "The Magic City" (George 119). Uncover the meaning of fifty-four, a logical argument might propose, and you have performed, instead of a historical writing about a city, a secrecy writing, a magic writing. After all, the 1954 movie *The Miami Story* offers a temporal narrative of the mob as a city diegesis. Fifty-four already is found within the supposed argument.

Yet, that reduction might not suffice. In one circulated photograph of Kennedy's Miami visit, Kennedy is riding in an open convertible (as he will do in Dallas four days later) and a woman extends a hand for him to shake.[2] The handshake, among other things, suggests the presence of secrecy, as in secret clubs whose meanings are often based on how one shakes a hand for entrance (or the steady hand that prepares the circumcision). In Miami, we might call this the "old boy's club" mentality, a way of thinking that stretches from Carl Fisher's development of the city in the early twentieth century to politics and criminal activity. In the book of short stories *Miami Noir*, Tom Corcoran's contribution, "One Man's Ceiling," describes a group of gangsters who set up in a two bedroom apartment in Kendall and call their home "The Old Boys Club." (119). Famous gangsters, such as Al Capone and Meyer Lansky, led old boy's club lives and lived in Miami in not so secret lives. Lansky, it is said, openly walked the city's streets and favored the pastrami at Wolfie's. So, too, it seems, did actor Mickey Rourke who claims that he would eat at Wolfie's after amateur boxing matches he participated in as a kid. Sometimes, Rourke claims, he would see Muhammad Ali at Wolfie's as well. "They used to run on the golf course down there, and then they'd go to Wolfie's and have eggs and shit." (Walken).

Gangsters may not have created boxing in Miami, but according to the movie *Muhammad Ali: Made in Miami*, the city and its image of organized crime played a pivotal role in Cassius Clay's transformation into the alter ego Muhammad Ali. In 1964, Clay surprisingly beats Sonny Liston in Miami Beach. Shortly afterward, he changed his name to Ali. Some people have questioned whether the fight was a fake or legitimate (i.e., a conspiracy so Liston could bet on himself and pay off a debt to the mob). In one particular photo from Miami's FifthStreet Gym where Clay trained prior to the fight, Clay raises his hands as a sign that, in the club-like mentality of boxing, he is the greatest. Ali's secret was ego. He used his ego ("I am the greatest") as a weapon of intimidation. At the weigh in for the Liston fight, Ali made his ego clear and yelled, "I predict that tonight somebody will die."[3]

During his first afternoon in Miami in 1968 (as detailed in *Miami and the Siege of Chicago*), long time Ali admirer and fellow egotist, Norman Mailer strolls the convention hall of the Republican convention and imagines an old boy's club whose members include John Wayne, Barry Goldwater, Roland Reagan, and Richard Nixon. Mailer, as egotistical as Ali, imagines himself as the centerpiece of any club he writes about. "That evening at the Fountainbleau," he writes, " on the night before the convention was to begin, the Republicans had their Grand Gala, no Press admitted, and the reporter by a piece of luck was nearly the first to get in" (31). Mailer found himself within a specific club mentality of politics, but also of being on the "inside" of knowing the metaphoric handshake of access. Jackie Gleason, too, represents this Miami club mentality (in the 1968 movie *Skidoo,* Gleason played a retired, mob hit man). A transplant to Miami, the non-Jewish Gleason moved to Miami from New York just as the northern migration of the 1950s ended. Gleason juxtaposed golf and entertainment as old-boy networks that would promote his 1960s celebrity status and TV show. In an October 5, 1962 *Life* feature on Gleason, the celebrity is seen on the golf course, waving his hand in his canonical "And away we go" gesture. And in a 1969 report published in the *Montreal Gazette,* Gleason is quoted as telling a crowd of thirty-five thousand teens who gathered at the Orange Bowl about another special club, that of Christianity and wholesome living. Gleason tells the teens that "he believed their movement against filth and obscenity would mushroom across the nation, and 'perhaps across the world'" saving everyone for eternal life after death (Balfour 43). According to some sources, Miami was an alternative name (from the Chippewa) for the American colonists' preferred name for the people they encountered and later killed. It meant "naked." Vice was in this space from the start it seems—from Native Americans to Gleason's brimstone warnings.

Mailer enjoys the old boy's club convention center and the political vices it offers. While training in Miami for the Liston fight, Cassius Clay is denied the right to try on shirts at Burdines (an act which would have briefly exposed him as naked), and thus is exposed to the old boy's club mentality of 1960s racism, a racism that, as city founder Carl Fisher desired (and city signs confirmed), once forbid Jews from living in the city. Fisher's land "deed covenants stated 'Homes will not be sold to any individual who has one-quarter Hebrew or Syrian blood'" (Zerivitz 55). One story suggests that if Jews "were what [Fisher] considered 'upper crust,' special considerations were given to them at his golf courses" (Kleinberg 43). This issue of clubs, ethnicity, and exposure begs the question: why was Kennedy left naked (exposed) as he toured Miami? Kennedy, of course, was not a part of James Brown's imaginary night train, but rather traveled in an unprotected motorcade. Exposure, too, is a mystery, for what it leaves out, for what is missing in the narrative we try to tell about a city or some other representation that cannot accommodate the felt moment. A narrative about Miami Jewish migration to the south is not complete without what is missing: Fisher's and other's denial of equal rights. A narrative about Ali might not be complete without what is missing: trying on a shirt. Such a narrative or even argumentative gesture would flesh out what is missing in order to offer critique or analysis.

These patterns, so far, reveal Miami's narrative in opposition to dominant forms of expression, such as the critical argument. In argument, no matter what we try to prove, something is always missing (it cannot be adequately exposed). I can argue *against* problematic racial representation or even secrecy in Miami, but to do so leaves out what the patterns show. Even if I argue that signs and department store policy represent Miami racism, the argument leaves out the other moments and patterns I've come across so far. Argument is always missing the lost secret to pattern formation (fifty-four or otherwise). Argument, as it promises truth and meaning, cannot lose the secrets patterns reveal. One revelation is the return of James Brown in my Miami spatial story. In the *Miami Vice* episode "Missing Hours," James Brown plays Lou DeLong, a figure who mysteriously appears during an alien encounter and claims to represent a group called Astrolife. At one point in the narrative, the character Trudy, still searching for her missing husband, sings to Brown's "I Got the Feeling" as it plays in the background. Astrolife is a club for UFO conspiracy theorists. Astrolife, as the Brown character argues, promises members "to get the total truth." That total truth—what is out there—continues to intrigue and shapes how we write about given spaces. What more is there to this text or space, we ask? What does this city mean? What else is out there about this city that I can say or write? Our project in the Humanities has been indebted for too long to hermeneutics, the interpretative gestures designed to satisfy such questions about textuality. The responses we create as to why or how we interpret are often not satisfying. Who killed Kennedy yields to conspiracy and doubt. My-Ami or Your-Ami is a debate that cannot be won. With interpretation or argument, we act as if we know what some totality or total truth means, or that we can argue for or against some force and thus change policy. Our work in this type of writing more likely resembles a minor headline on a 1962 *Miami News* front page: "Ho, Hum Time at Canaveral." Argument or interpretation as *the* method of expression is ho-hum. Boring. Uninspiring.

Figure 2. Screenshot from Missing Hours

"With the launching of Walter Schirra this morning," the article notes about the astronaut's launch, "manned space flight made the transition from science fiction to routine fact—dangerous and pulse quickening, but still routine" (Volker). Argument. Interpretation. These, I note, are routine gestures in any kind of writing. The fantastical (such as launching into outer space) is what drives my narrative. My exigency, explored briefly in this chapter about the Florida city I grew up in, is secrecy; it is the Miami secret as fantastical, writing moment. No matter how I imagine the feeling I have for Miami, it remains a secret, something I cannot prove, much like the game regarding whether it's My-Ami or Your-Ami. The answer is: I do not know. In that lack of knowledge, I do not imagine a totality called Miami. There is no totality, as de Certeau or Barthes might say, at stake in a series of associations of Miami that work off of one another. While interpretative gestures or argumentative gestures as moments of exigency may feel dangerous—as Lloyd Bitzer famously declares in "The Rhetorical Situation's" first sentence–they are now nothing more than routine. They are ho-hum moments of rhetorical expression. Arguing for or against representations have minimal effect. I can argue that Miami is racist for denying Ali the right to try on a shirt or for murdering a man riding his motorcycle, but that argument still does not satisfy anything other than confirmation of the known, interpreted event. Interpretation is no secret. It is a commonplace method of expression. We are more familiar with interpretation than the patterns a given space might generate.

Space should evoke the unfamiliar. Florida, despite the fact that I grew up there and should know it, can be unfamiliar to me as I follow its spatial patterns. According to one source, Jackie Gleason's Miami Beach home was designed to look like the very unfamiliar shape of a spaceship. "His eight hundred thousand dollar circular Round House, designed to resemble a downed UFO, was the perfect place to store his incredible, arcane collection [of UFO material]" (O'Donnell 49). South Florida radio station WSHE's call letters (the rock station of my youth) began with the sound of a spaceship landing (stolen from Edgar Winter's "Frankenstein"). A spatial (or space-ial) imagination, generated by the stories it tells, is fantastical, is as if from outer space. While not from outer space, the hurricane, the storm that hits Miami every few years and is somewhat echoed in the Billy Joel song I began with, was first identified as Guabancex, the Taíno god (celestial, out of this world) of storms. The experience of surviving a hurricane can feel out of this world. The eye passes over a house or neighborhood or city, and an eerie, unworldly calm settles before the storm begins again. Andrew is one of the best known hurricanes to hit Miami. During one of my few returns to Miami in 1992, I arrived after Andrew had ravaged the city. I had come to help hand out food in Homestead. While Haitians and Americans stood in line for assistance, we received many first hand reports of the damage.

When I was nine, Hurricane David provided an out-of-this-world experience: my first sense of danger. David, I thought then, was my grandfather's name, the failed chicken farmer who had moved to Miami, along with many other Jews, after World War II. In anticipation of David, we boarded up windows and stocked supplies (canned food, batteries, candles) in case the worst occurred. Most of the homes in our golf-course community put plywood over their windows. Supposedly, Hurricane David interrupted the filming of *Caddyshack*, a movie about golf, at the Rolling Hills Country Club in Fort Lauderdale (at one point in the film's diegesis, Rodney Dangerfield tells his Asian golf partner, "I think this place is restricted, so don't tell them you're Jewish") ("Hurricane David"). The danger with hurricanes, academic writing might tell us, is like writing itself; hurricanes are subjected to the demands of causality and proof. Once predicted, they need to prove the value of fear often created throughout the days leading to landfall. When they don't, the anticipation for danger becomes deflated. When David failed to generate the damage most forecasters predicted, Hurricane Center director Neil Frank was criticized "for suggesting that landfall might be in the Miami area" when only the eye (center) passed over (Barnes 245). Hurricanes' trajectories are difficult to predict, Frank responded. So, too, are narratives' trajectories when patterns guide the spatial stories we tell. I have followed a series of trajectories: golf, racism, devastation, and handshakes. Miami's secret has not been solved. My story is difficult to predict.

What is the secret of a hurricane landing? What is the secret of a place such as Miami? If there is a secret to Miami, it might not be, then, a totalizing gesture like the equation that yields the number fifty-four, but rather something akin to Mailer's insistence that the writer is the center piece of any type of reporting. For me to write about Miami, for instance, I cannot ignore growing up in Kendall or that despite whatever I may write or say about Miami, I am likely to be the centerpiece of that discussion. My narrative always includes me. I am the reference of every image, Barthes declares about representation in *Camera Lucida*, an indication that no representation can escape his presence. He is a part of his object of study, whether that study is textual or photographic. My rationale for being the centerpiece is neither argumentative nor causal nor even egotistical. I am the eye of this chapter but not for egotistical reasons. I feel that I want to perform this type of exploration because I cannot separate myself from the representation I compose. I feel that I am a part of any Miami narrative. My rationale, therefore, is a felt one (emotional and textual weaving). This is the secret or conspiracy of writing. What will associations lead to in a given writing? I don't know, so I weave them. The weaving generates feeling. "This life feeling creates a space, an opening in the world, giving a sense of something 'more' (possibility, potentiality) that unfolds into an experience of freedom beyond or within necessity" (*Avatar* 27).

I feel, for instance, that Miami's patterns evoke the sense of something more. Something more than a place. Something more than a city. Something more than a childhood. I feel, as well, that I need to conclude by remaining with a detail of this particular Miami disaster and dangerous moment, Hurricane David. Miami, as the totalizing narrative often reminds us, is the site of numerous hurricanes, some deadly and devastating. In 1979, Hurricane David stormed through our suburban neighborhood and flooded our streets and canals. Muck rose out of the water and rested in the roads turning the cul-de-sac into a bed of sludge. At one point after the storm as we walked through our streets, I put my hand to our subdivision's canal, for some reason thinking it was empty, and I felt dirt, water, mud, and dead animals floating over its edges. We lived in a subdivision owned by a country club (now called Killian Palms Country Club—the palm indicating the extended secrecy of the handshake). At one point, the center, or eye, of the storm passed our neighborhood. I got out of bed in the middle of the night and saw the water rise and flood the street as it, no doubt, had done many times before, during many previous, devastating hurricanes. Standing at the window, I felt exposed. The storm could destroy our home at any minute. Against the security of the iron bars on my bedroom window, the bars my parents had instructed me how to open in case of flooding, the bars I needed to open so that I would be exposed to the outside andso I would not die in a flooded house, I placed my hand. This final gesture is my secret, repeating the hand pattern, extending from a childhood memory to a spatial moment to a city's historical fragments, and motivating my writing. The challenge, as I am faced at this moment, is to shape that pattern into this spatial story here as well as in future ones I will compose, explorations of the patterns and moments of any diegesis that resists interpretation and favors invention in its place.

Figure 3. The Miami home (as it now looks) where we lived before Hurricane David (courtesy Google Maps)

Notes

1. Thanks to Craig Saper for pointing out that Notorious opens in Miami.
2. http://goo.gl/LXcsRX
3. See http://www.youtube.com/watch?v=zaTbr5TrnHA

Works Cited

Balfour, Malcolm. "Gleason Predicts Increasing Decency." *The Montreal Gazette.* 25 March 1969: 43. Print.
Barnes, Jay. *Florida's Hurricane History.* Chapel Hill: U of North Carolina P, 2007. Print.
Barthes, Roland. *Camera Lucida.* New York: Hill and Wang, 1981. Print.
—. *Image, Music, Text.* New York: Hill and Wang, 1977. Print.
Bitzer, Lloyd. "The Rhetorical Situation." *Philosophy and Rhetoric* 1 (January, 1968): 1–14. Print.
Boswell, Thomas D., Ira Sheskin, and Carroll Truss. "Attitudes, Causes, and Perceptions: The 1980 Black Riot in Dade County (Miami), Florida." *The Florida Geographer* 20 (1986): 1–15. Print.
Brown, James. "Night Train." *20 All Time Greatest Hits!.* Polydor, 1991.
Brubaker, Bill. "Ali's Plea to Old Neighborhood." *The Miami News.* 20 May 1980: A1–8. Print.
Corcoran, Tom. "One Man's Ceiling." *Miami Noir.* Ed. Les Standiford. New York: Akashic Books, 2006. Print.
De Certeau, Michel. "Spatial Stories." *The Practice of Everyday Life.* Berkeley: U of California P, 2002. Print.
George, Paul S. "Kendall." *Miami's Historic Neighborhoods.* Ed. Becky Roper Matkov. San Antonio: Dade Heritage Trust, 2001 (118–122). Print.
Gurock, Jeffrey S. *American Jewish Life, 1920–1990.* New York: Routledge, 1998. Print.
Jameson, Fredric. *The Political Unconscious: Narrative as a Socially Symbolic Act.* Ithaca: Cornell UP, 1983. Print.
Joel, Billy. "Miami 2017." *Songs in the Attic.* Sony, 1998.
—. "New York State of Mind."
Kennedy, John F. "Address in Miami Before the Inter-American Press Association." *The American Presidency Project.* n.d. Web.
Kenward, Scott F. "In the Beginning: The Birth of Kendall—Part 1." *Village of Pinecrest Florida.* Florida State Government. Web.
Kleinberg, Howard. "Miami Beach." *Miami's Historic Neighborhoods.* Ed. Becky Roper Matkov. San Antonio: Dade Heritage Trust, 2001 (118–122). Print.
Lavender, Abraham D. *Miami Beach in 1920: Making of a Winter Resort.* Charleston: Arcadia Publishing, 2002. Print.
Mailer, Norman. *Miami and the Siege of Chicago.* New York: Signet, 1968. Print.
"Missing Hours." *Miami Vice.* NBC. November 19, 1987. Television.
Muhammad Ali: Made in Miami. PBS. WLRN, Miami. 2008. Television.
O'Donnell, Patrick. "Star Crossed: Hollywood's Dark Stars of the Way Out 1950s." *Monster Rally.* Ed. S. Michael Wilson. West Orange: Idea Men Productions, 2008. Print.
Patterson, Daniel. "We Waited as Long as We Could." *Lucky Peach* 4. (Summer 2012): 114–118. Print.

Skolnick, Jerome and James Fyfe. *Above the Law: Police and Excessive Use of Force*. New York: The Free Press,s 1983. Print.

Ulmer, Gregory. *Avatar Emergency*. Anderson: Parlor Press, 2012. Print.

—. *Internet Invention: From Literacy to Electracy*. Boston: Longman, 2003. Print.

Volker, Al. "Ho, Hum Time at Canaveral." *The Miami News*. Front Page. 3 Oct 1962. Print.

Walken, Christopher. "Mickey Rourke." *Interview Magazine*. Interview Inc. 16 January 2009. Web.

Whitaker, Jan. "Famous In Its Days: Wolfie's." *Restaurant-ing Through History*. 27 March 2011. Web.

White, Maurice F. "Kivie Kaplan: Man with a Vision." *The Crisis*. Feb. 1966: 115–119. Print.

"Hurricane David." *Wikipedia*. The Wikimedia Foundation Inc. Web.

Winegardner, Mark. *The Godfather's Revenge*. New York: Putnam Adult, 2006. Print.

Zerivitz, Marcia Jo. *Jews of Greater Miami*. Charleston: Arcadia Publishing, 2009. Print.

4 Florida Trouse

Charlie Hailey

The flower is always in the almond.

—Gaston Bachelard

You may not find a house in every place you roam. But when you own a Spartan you always have a home.

—Spartan Aircraft Company

Bambi

After Hurricane Andrew, we moved to Homestead and lived in an Airstream trailer with an autographed portrait of Divine. The photo was inscribed to my mentors who were repairing the cycloned house they had designed and built. The trailer was a Bambi, Airstream's smallest model, less than 13 feet from hitch to tail lights. It was parked next to the main house whose occupants had ridden out the category-five storm as its center heaved down Hainlan Mill Road on its way across the peninsula. They had emerged from the house's bunkered, concrete-block ground floor—what some have called South Florida's only basement—for a moment during the eye's azure calm, but these reinforced walls could not protect the inhabitants, my mentor's clients, from the storm's emotional impact. They sold the house to its builders and moved to California.

There we were four months later, ready to rebuild, living in a silver bullet lodged among Dade County pines laid down like pick-up sticks, having timbered westward ahead of the eye then back eastward and northward in its wake. Our Airstream was parked less than a hundred yards from the main house, but this distance seemed like a mile when we fled its aluminum skin for the house's block-wall stability. It was 1993's Storm of the Century, and we awoke to winds that were sure to send the travel trailer footballing through the jungle. As we ran, half-naked, through banana leaves and spider webs, we traversed not just a rain-pelted landscape but a conceptually-charged space between Bambi and basement.

Relations between house and trailer are direct and indefinite, archetypal and atypical. Both serve as dwellings, and both can be defined as home. But when juxtaposed or paired, their physical separation accommodates a space of paradox—between permanent and temporary, between host and guest, and between big and small. Administrative and economic distinctions also parse the house-trailer relation. Life-safety rules codify differences in the construction of site-built and manufactured housing units, and appraisal practices further distinguish the property values of house and trailer. Florida offers a unique environment for this house-trailer pairing. The peninsula's moderate climate means that a trailer's domestic life might readily—and comfortably—extend into the landscape, that trailer and house might both be planted in a semi-tropical garden's salubriousness, and that trailer might eventually become house. Florida is alternately sympathetic and antagonistic toward its trailers. Its climate allows for year-round living in and around their limited volumes. But this weather is also capricious, and it supports the storms that lift and destroy.

No one saw the Storm of the Century coming. We heard the winds, felt the trailer wobble, and ran for the main house. The next day, what Hurricane Andrew had not destroyed in 1992 and much of what Homestead's residents had rebuilt was damaged by the storm. Blue tarps were ripped, rooms were again flooded, and trees were leveled. In the empty lot next to the Redland Tavern, itinerant construction workers returned to tents and trailers. This ad hoc version of the post-disaster relief camp constitutes another line in Florida's house-trailer genealogy. After Andrew, disaster relief officials inaugurated the FEMA trailer to provide temporary housing that would essentially become a permanent house for many. Trailers in eponymous places like FEMA City near Punta Gorda already languished well past their planned eighteen-month lifespan, and criticism peaked with their continued deployment after Hurricane Katrina in 2005. Images of FEMA trailers next to gutted houses have become a common post-disaster photographic trope, underscoring ironies of tragedy, response, and unplanned permanence. Economy outweighed design in the production of these trailers, which are taciturn foils to their muted counterparts. Their small windows gaze impassively at the site-built residence, their white corrugated aluminum casts unflattering light on the wreckage, and above-ground PVC pipes patch into septic tanks. Rogue ventriloquists of the domestic experience, many of these trailers continue to speak long after disaster.

Figure 1. Spartan on house lot

In spite of its winds, Florida's trailers stay put. This long history of intransience extends back to the municipal camps of South Florida. In the 1920s, city boosters initially embraced northern tourists who traversed sometimes perilous crushed-shell roads for the state's semi-tropical paradise, but they soon realized that the "sun-hunters" could also be "time-killers" who overstayed their welcome (Roberts, 8). In the following decade, Florida and California offered more auto-camps than anywhere else in the country, with the greatest concentration in Tampa and Miami. And many of the trailers were more than seasonal retreats. After World War II, retirees and tourists were joined by returning troops, many of whom had trained in the state's expansive military bases and planned to settle in its moderate climate. The nation's housing industry struggled to keep up, and trailers provided an immediate response.

Near the center of the country, J. Paul Getty extended his wartime hiatus from the oil industry and rapidly converted Spartan Aircraft Corporation into post-war production of trailers—he called them "mobile homes"—that would meet the needs of returning servicemen as well as the country's burgeoning recreationalists who wanted trailers that could be both house and home. Decades later, one of these Spartan trailers came to rest in Florida's tidal swamp. Despite its location in an out-of-the-way region alternately called the Nature Coast and the Real Florida, this trailer was no longer the ingenuous mobile vehicle. It now bore the responsibilities of a housing market and more recently a housing crisis. More broadly, its house-trailer ambiguities raise questions about dwelling itself, particularly when living is understood as process rather than product. Bambi would become Manor, and the Florida *trouse* matured as an undeniably real part of the region's cultural landscape.

Spartan

RE: "Concrete Block home with a spartan trailer entombed."

—Real Estate Appraisal Forum

In September 2008, a "newbie" contributor posted an online question to AppraisersForum.com to begin what would become a lively, if unconventional, discussion thread for AF's website. The above quoted subject line reads more like a tabloid headline than an anxious homeowner's post to the online real-estate forum. Its capitalization adapts sensationalist style to highlight the house's conventional, ostensibly more permanent, construction in concrete block. The lower-case "s" in "spartan" exchanges the trailer company's proprietary status for the adjective's latent qualities of thrift and prudence, tempering—for the moment—the shocking reality of this domestic monster. Then comes the real hook: "Entombed." House and trailer are not merely connected; they are bonded by burial practices, sepulchral rituals. The trailer becomes a body interred within the charged meanings of house and home. What does it mean when homeowner becomes real-estate undertaker?

> *I have a home in Florida 10 minutes from the Gulf of Mexico which is concrete block with a Spartan travel trailer entombed in the middle.*

After seven years in the dwelling, "Bigpup" was selling a concrete-block house built around a tag-along trailer manufactured by the Spartan Aircraft Corporation, but the new buyer's lending institution would not issue the loan because of the trailer's presence. Same house, trailer, and appraiser, but different bank, leaving the seller to query the Forum if this change of heart turned on the "current housing craziness." Follow-up responses corroborated not a current attitude but more fundamental guidelines for lending that have implications not just for buying and selling but, more deeply, for living. The thread's arc is also telling. Two immediate posts from a longtime, five-starred conversant made clear lending policy and appraisal technics. Later posts turned attention to the trailer itself, and the final posts took a nostalgic tone, ruminating about the trailer's vintage status and observing penchants for restoring these "birchwood beauties."

> *The travel trailer parts that are left are the front, the back, and the ceiling. The rest has been remodeled and there is a roof over the entire house.*
>
> *Can you add pictures of this house? I'm trying to picture it, and having a hard time . . . Thanks!*

The homeowner tends to the implications of this illicit burial and, to an extent, oversees the trailer's decay. The post summarizes what remains of the trailer—its front, back, and top—but the overall dwelling remains hard to visualize. The house wraps and deconstructs the trailer. Accretion and erosion. The shell within the shell is broken to conform with necessities for living within a much less forgiving, less flexible, concrete skin. The trailer's decomposition also appears to be the house's continued development and expansion. In the process, what was once a germinal vehicle has become an integral part of the dwelling's structure, and what might nominally be considered mere construction is more closely aligned with imagination.

The modification of trailer toward house is common, particularly in Florida's environment. Residents add onto, cut away from, and build around their trailers. Wheel space—the zone between chassis and ground—becomes ready-made crawl space. Its surface often patterned with brick or stone print, skirting affirms this translation of void to solid. It simulates a foundation. Trailer hitches also provoke connections between ground and trailer. In Florida, municipal camp residents frequently cultivated gardens around this point of contact. Like so many home-made welcome mats, intricate shell gardens spelled out residents' names as their makeshift design radiated from the pipes, blocks, and posts that supported the tongue and leveled the floor. Other trailers have come to rest under sheds, trellises, or more tenuous lean-to roofs. These ready-made umbrellas add a layer of protection from the elements; and if the roof is gabled, it provides another step toward the image of home. Residents also apply more direct accretions. Stairs, ramps, porches, and rooms barnacle onto the trailer's shell. Single-wides might then become double-wides, not by factory-issue but by self-build.

Transitions from trailer to house are really translations. They exchange one medium of living for another. Languages of mobility and mass production come to define something more permanent and personal. Changing the trailer affords an opportunity to rethink the house. What was internal consequently breaks previously established boundaries of domesticity. Now exposed, desires for space become concrete with incremental additions to the trailer, and the image of home is realized in a new composition of residential materials. The vehicle no longer approximates domesticity. Its bricolaged composition is home.

> *We bought this home almost 7 years ago from our very conservative Credit Union and they told us that as long as it could not be moved it was fine. The appraiser noted the travel trailer and all went well.*
>
> *We have the house for sale and the same appraiser noted the trailer inside and the banks are having fits. They ask questions about how old the trailer is (1960) and I don't think that can make up their minds whether to finance as a trailer or a house. Needless to say, the poor buyer cannot get financing.*

The imagined house is often at odds with the appraised house. One answer to Bigpup's query provides the technical framework for the new buyer's denial—"no matter how nice the construction of the wrap, it's still a trailer." Even though it no longer moves, the continued presence of the trailer proves highly problematic within appraisal models. Even though its residue is ostensibly benign and even though the term "trailer" is invoked innocently, evaluating the house is problematic. The trailer's existence also triggers a critical re-assessment of the house as a manufactured home, but the manufactured housing industry long ago disowned the term *trailer*, considering it

Figure 2. Spartan advertisement, 1953

"outdated, derogatory slang," often associated with "trailer park" ("Manufactured Home Fact Sheet"). In 1956, ten-foot-wide trailers were first officially called "mobile homes." Even if Bigpup's trailer were still an unadulterated unit and even if Getty's early assurances that all Spartans were truly "mobile homes was accurate" this particular dwelling—dated to 1960—missed the deadline for HUD's minimum standards, which went into effect on June 15, 1976. After that, *mobile* home officially—and permanently—became *manufactured* home. If the entombed trailer did constitute a manufactured home, its evaluation would summon HUD's codes and FHA's guidelines for loans, neither of which a traditional mortgage vendor wants to violate.

Appraisal logic indicates broader attitudes about housing. With the "Spartan entombed," appraisers saw either a trailerinahouse or a housearoundatrailer. If it is a travel trailer, it can't be a house and an owner cannot have a mortgage. If it is a house, then it should not include the trailer's latent mobility. Resisting quantification, ideas of home are inadmissible. Travel trailers are meant for the road, and mobile homes are meant for the lot, for year-round occupancy. The trailer undermines the permanence and codification of house. Neither manufactured home nor site-built residence, the house-trailer eludes classification and eschews standardization. Despite a common purpose of dwelling, the pairing's mutual exclusion is a lender's tautological nightmare and, following a logic that trailers cannot be houses, houses must not be founded on trailers. Without imagination, assessment is simple. This house has buried the trailer, the homeowner is its undertaker, and the appraiser its mortician.

> *Is this a part of the housing craziness that is going on now. Should we just wait until things calm down in a couple of years?*

One expert's response to Bigpup's query hints that this previous transaction itself, rather than a problem with the current loan, is more indicative of the housing crisis. It is likely that the credit union originally approved the loan with its own internal standards and with a plan to keep the mortgage servicing in-house, apart from the constraints of other underwriters. The house-trailer eludes quantification and easy explanation, but its modest scale and implied affordability would not appear to strain the average homebuyer or the typical mortgage system. Unlike many of the loans issued for outsized housing stock in volatile markets, this idiosyncratic house fits. But it still fails the test. Even though a homeowner might attest to its livability, the appraised house must satisfy an investor and a system that will never see it. That distance creates a crisis of valuation. Language, in this case, neutralizes value, and the latent narrative—the truly spatial story—of the dwelling cannot be told. When appraisers report a trailer, lenders only see a problem.

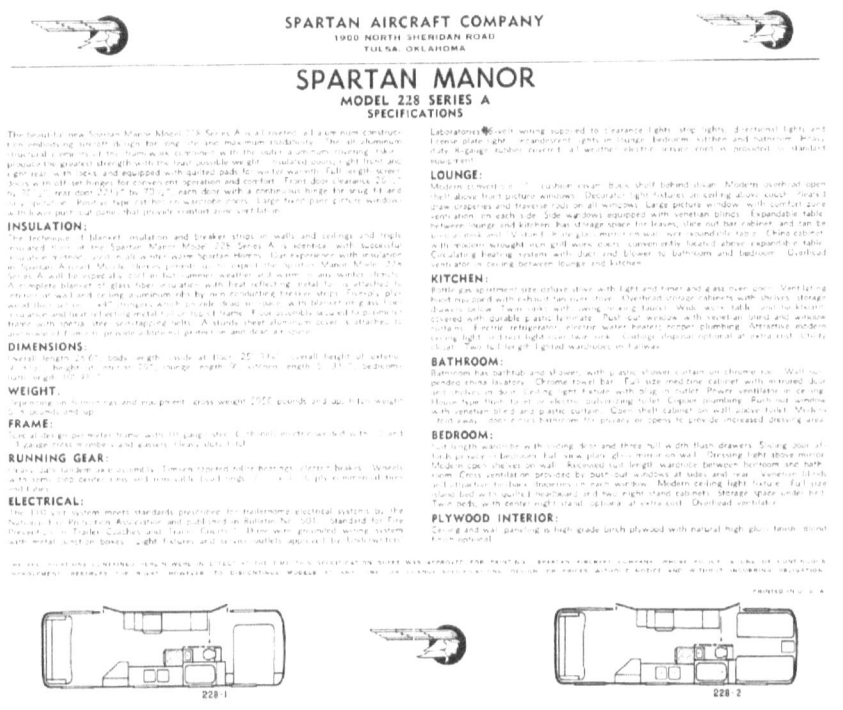

Figure 3. Spartan Manor specifications, 1954

From the outside you would never know until you come onto the screen porch and see the front and side bus window.

Is the trailer still a trailer? And what does the hidden trailer reveal about the house? As Bigpup noted, only fragments of the trailer remain. The house's components stand in for what has been removed from the trailer. This exchange of materials evokes the legendary paradox of Theseus' ship. Its parts repaired and replaced over many years, the ancient vessel maintained its original purpose, remained true to its basic form, but retained few, if any, of its original components. Greek philosophers argued whether this construct was still Theseus' initial ship. For Aristotle and for the historian Plutarch, who recorded this story, it was the cause that remained the same. In the paradox, purpose and identity persist when materials and even form change. In this respect, it is still Theseus' ship. Here, comparable cause yields similar effect, and purpose determines value. Unlike Theseus' ship, the trailer is not the same trailer—it is really no longer a trailer at all; but like the celebrated vessel, the overall dwelling is still a dwelling. Taken together, house and trailer sustain a way of living, and the two cannot be untied.

The trailer cannot hide. It is a burden the house must carry. Greek folklore also tells the story of a Spartan youth who steals a fox and hides the animal in his cloak. Even as the fox claws wildly at his skin, the boy does not divulge his secret. Plutarch's account of this tale emphasizes the Spartan's display of fortitude, and the hidden fox, which cannot ultimately be concealed, is an emblem of endurance—a moral code's obduracy. This story does not end well. With the boy unwilling to surrender, the fox scratches, gnaws, and finally feeds on its host's entrails. Boy and fox are inextricably linked by a paradoxical moral code, just as house and trailer are entwined in a fateful embrace, where the line between guest and host is blurred. To remove the interior is to kill the vessel. The moral of Bigpup's story is not about what the house hides—buyer beware—but what the trailer discloses—home endures.

Just as the Greek tale is not about the boy's act of stealing, the house-trailer narrative is not about concealing the trailer but about revealing domestic life. In the post, Bigpup described how remodeling has absorbed much of the trailer, which is not visible from outside the house. The Spartan is discovered only after you arrive on the porch and move through the house. Here, the contradictory relation of house and trailer unfolds in the actual experience of space—whether it is the inspection, the walk-through, or a tour of the house during a neighbor's visit. From what can be gleaned in Bigpup's account, these apparent contradictions do not prohibit domestic life. In fact, the absurdity of a trailer entombed in a house reveals dwelling's capacity to occur between transience and permanence and between one vessel and another.

The Spartan company, which began as a producer of military aircraft, was named to invoke mythologized perseverance and strength of character. After the war, when it shifted production to trailers, its name's bellicose associations might have seemed antithetical to domestic comfort. The translation of war, power, and business clout into visions of home can be complicated but not irreconcilable. Spartans were courageous, simple, and moralistic warriors, and postwar dwelling would also require persistence. Many of those seeking housing were newly returned soldiers, and the company's legacies of heroism—many of its employees were excellent test pilots—permeated its product line. And austerity did not prohibit domestic freedom, nor did it necessarily prevent luxury. Spartan's advertising copy proposes that its combination of "value and distinction" is unique, and the early foundations of this corporate identity included aircraft both for combat training and for corporate travel. This was a new code in which valor met comfort, sunlit idylls illuminated thrift, and convenience meshed with opulence.

SPARTAN HOMES find their way with their proud owners to the Lands of Healthful Sunshine and Pleasant Surroundings. Go in your SPARTAN HOME and live. . . . Live happier, live more care-free, really live.

It will be your friendly Spartan Dealer's pleasure to show you the luxury and convenience found only in SPARTAN HOMES. Lifetime exteriors and easy to clean, easy to use interiors. Investigate and be a proud SPARTAN OWNER.

Manor

Now they'll know the joy and comfort of living in the world's finest modern mobile home. . . . They'll have the value and distinction denoting the superiority that only Spartan builds into its mobile homes.

—Spartan Aircraft Company advertisement

Bigpup's Spartan was probably a Manor. In the post to AppraisersForum, the model is not specified, but the production year is 1960. Only two trailers from that year match the travel trailer's eight-foot width—the Manor and the Royal Manor. In terms of length, the Manor is just short of thirty feet, and the Royal Manor is thirty-seven feet, within three feet of foreclosing its trailer status. Defining "travel trailer," Florida's Statutes explicitly limit its overall length to forty feet: "Travel Trailer means a vehicular portable unit, mounted on wheels, of such a size or weight as not to require special highway movement permits when drawn by a motorized vehicle. It is primarily designed and constructed to provide temporary living quarters for recreational, camping or travel use. It has a body width of no more than 8 ½ feet and an overall body length of no more than 40 feet when factory-equipped for the road."

Figure 4: Spartan advertisement, 1955

Their ten-foot widths attesting to Spartan's increasingly larger vehicles, the other 1960 models index both sophistication and playfulness: the Villa,

Imperial, Carousel, Executive Villa, Crescendo, Sparlane's Riviera, and Sparcraft's two lines—the Statesmen and the President. From what Bigpup describes, the Villa is too wide; the Imperial, the Executive Villa, the Crescendo, and the Statesman are all too long, reaching fifty-one feet; and the Carousel is too stylish with its distinctive Art Deco design. The Sparcraft President, the heaviest and the longest, offers more than five hundred square feet of stately living area, but its six and a half tons would have made for a difficult journey through the sandy, swampy ground of Florida's coastal area. I have assumed the dimensions of Bigpup's trailer are those of a trailer, and I imagine the relative mobility of the Manor more easily traversing the bristling—and, in the 1960s, still very remote—landscape of the Gulf coast.

> *With his return from the hostilities, wanting to immediately occupy the site and the peace it offered, the painter acquired a sophisticated caravan and installed it on the grounds.*
>
> —Architecture d'aujourd'hui (1952)

> Modern as tomorrow.
>
> —Spartan Aircraft Company advertisement

At mid-century, an architect built an iconic modernist house around another Manor. After returning from World War II, painter Sidney Wolfson bought a Spartan Manor in its first model year. Early in the spring of 1946, he towed the trailer to his property in Pleasant Valley, New York, put it up on blocks, and lived there for three years before he hired German émigré Marcel Breuer to design a house around what had become his country studio. Wolfson's trailer extended more than thirty feet, weighed more than two and one-half tons, and—perhaps most strikingly—cost more than four thousand dollars, not much more than the site-built houses under construction at Levittown one hundred miles downstate. J. Paul Getty and William Levitt both anticipated postwar housing shortages, the former betting on trailers and the latter on a production line of houses.

But combining house and trailer on Wolfson's site created something even more progressive. Breuer brought field stone in contact with the trailer's aluminum skin—its factory-smooth polish still mirroring its surroundings—to raise house and trailer on stone plinths, allowing both to share geologic and stereotomic solidity and to float above the Valley's gently rolling topography and waving grasses. Breuer, the Bauhaus architect, would have admired the trailer's industrial production but might also have remained blasé about its overall design, having his own ideas and designs for mobile living. The Spartan's manufactured materials—derived from aircraft technologies and industrial techniques for bending plywood—nonetheless resonate with the architect's own kit-of-parts domestic palette. Postwar production of plexiglass also allowed for the curved glazing at the trailer's front—exchanging a fuselage's air-tightness for the earthbound joys of natural lighting. The sleek industrialized exterior both confirms and obscures the well-appointed interior.

Completed in 1950, the house design was first published in *House and Home*'s inaugural issue, where it is the third house in the opening sequence. This early 1952 article posited the idea that such creativity might "rescue the American home from the antiquarian." Aiming their comments at professionals, the editors laid out the magazine's task in terms of how to build into the American house "all the satisfactions that make a house a home," from early design through closing finance (*House and Home*, 107). They also proposed that the housing industry owed American families "more than shelter." Houses should offer "the good life" with pleasure and utility. After admiringly describing Wolfson's penchant for sleeping, cooking, and eating in the trailer, the article offers something of a disclaimer, noting that the owner's preference for the trailer is not the "main point" of this story, "though it might suggest trailer-adjuncts to other owners as an emergency measure" (121). These housing complexities echo the financing troubles that would hinder Bigpup with the entombed Spartan five decades later.

In the same issue, an article titled "New mortgage crisis confronts reviving defense program" questions the livability of temporary defense housing and proposes trailer typologies as alternatives. Its authors call this option "mobile expandable prefab" and argue that such units begin "to bridge the gap between trailers and permanent housing," using as an example the recently unveiled model from the Knox Corporation for a "mobile house," with eight-by-thirty-two-foot dimensions that closely follow the Spartan Manor's frame (39).[2] A larger model, with four hundred square feet, was available for FHA Title I financing and cost $4,990—a price slightly higher than Wolfson's $4,200 trailer purchase six years earlier. The article notes that in December 1951, the Housing and Home Finance Agency spent nearly half of its defense housing funds to purchase 2,815 trailer and "temporary housing units." Because of its climate and its military bases, Florida became a target area for HHFA's goal, which according to the article was "to make sure temporary housing was so temporary it would not remain to blight post-defense communities" (42). The agency sent the "prefab demountable" units to the more "rigorous climates [where] trailers would not do," and most of the trailers were parked on the military posts. The trailers came to Florida, and many G.I.'s followed.

The ironies found in the naming of the company's two main model lines—the Spartan Manor and the Spartan Mansion—are the paradoxes of domestic value and the valuation of house. If *spartan* is frugality and thrift, *manor* connotes extravagance. Where *spartan* is laconic, *manor* is expansive: austerity and self-restraint placed against the expected lavishness of manor house and mansion. But the two terms also intersect at unexpected points. A shade of meaning suggests that *spartan* also connotes an over-use of the sententious to the point of pomposity that might befit gentry. Not unlike the refrains of 1950s jingles, Spartan's advertising campaign deployed maxims that ring with the pretentious moralizing of hackneyed terms like value, distinction, superiority, finest, modern. *Manor* can also correspond with *spartan*. From Latin *manere,* etymological roots of manor and mansion lie in a proclivity to stay in one place, whether for one night or for a longer duration. This remaining suggests a fortitude that would be familiar to the Spartan ethic. *Manor* is also tied to *demesne,* which connotes possession rather than ownership and suggests that we might claim what we view. These ideas of domain and an extended terrain have been coded into Spartan's promotional copy—wherever you go, you will find home. Even in your itinerancy, you have a domestic realm that is yours. *Manor* can make room for the economies and necessities of the snail's shell.

Trouse

Now, I write this from the trailer. A 1954 Spartan Manor. We debated buying either a Spartan or an Airstream. Some might say Spartan trailers are mobilized austerity to the Airstream trailer's Athenian artistry. But Airstreams have become known as "mainstreams"—following a commodified arc from relic to fetish to fashion—and it is the Spartans that are idiosyncratic and rarefied. Moreover, North America's laconophilia readily translates to its often thrifty trailerites; and today even a Spartan can teach us a few things about living within our means. After living in Florida off and on for twenty years, it was time to buy a trailer. We had lived in the Bambi, and we were ready for the Manor.

My papers rest on the telescoping dinner table, and I spy a hummingbird's dipping flight through the wide panorama of curved plexiglass, now crazed and cracking from almost six decades of sun. Spartan called this living area the observatory. Wrapping around the side, its signature front windows resemble the cockpit fenestration of the company's original aircraft designs. They also approximate the residential picture window. This common mid-century aperture served as much to display private domestic space to a voyeuristic public as it also allowed occupants—though infrequent visitors in their own well-appointed interiors—to look out. But the trailerite is not unlike the pilot, and the Spartan's picture window is an ideal viewport for looking inside out. Now, docked to its residential host, it offers a backyard perspective on our own daily life. It watches us from within our own foreground. Ostensibly it is a guest house, but it is really a self-made domestic probe. When I step onto its deck, which is really its porch, I look through the main door's porthole—1954 was this feature's last model year—to see not only the warmly illuminated birchwood interior, but also the main house reflected in the mirror that hangs along the trailer's opposite wall. House and trailer collapse in this circular vision that elides aluminum skin and brick wall.

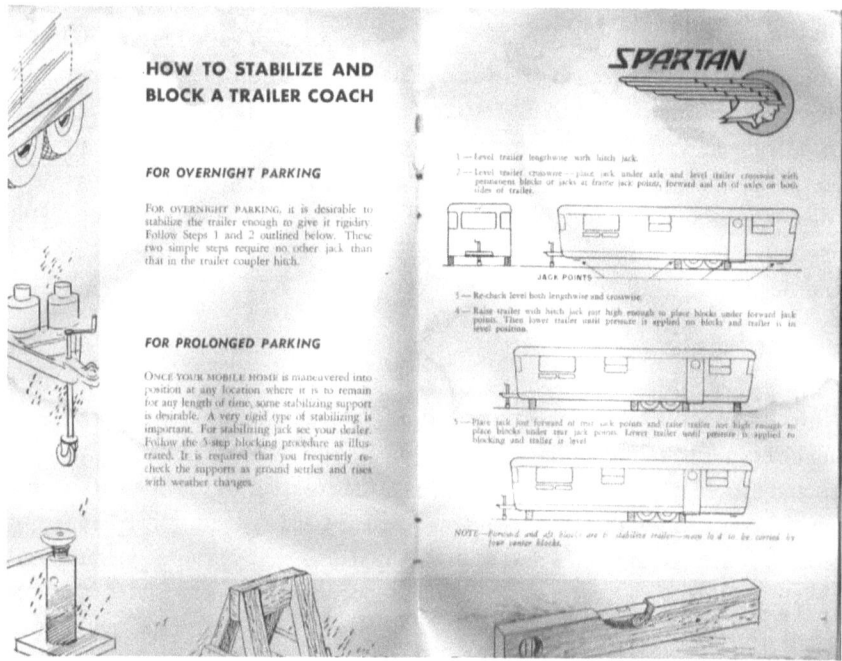

Figure 5. How to stabilize and block a trailer coach

We found the trailer in a hunting camp on an island in the Ocklawaha River. It was not easy to reconcile the juxtaposition of this wild place—Pine Island's residual Old Florida still traversed by black bears and panthers—with the conservative housing of the Villages and the rest of central Florida's burgeoning sprawl. On our way back home, the trailer stalled in the yielding sand of the island's antiquated causeway, but then floated easily on the freshly paved and lithely suburban roads. The last time the trailer moved, it would have been bears and bobcats—not retirees and golfcarts—all the way north to Gainesville. The Air Force veteran, who owned the Manor, opened all of its awning windows for a daily airing and administered to it from the utility building that served as a home away from home during storms and sub-freezing temperatures. Even out here, he knew of Breuer's project and asked if we had similar plans for his trailer. Our trouse would be neither docked nor entombed. A new porch only lightly tethers trailer to house.

On October 27, 2006, "trouse" was added to the lexicon of Urban Dictionary, a user-defined and web-based reference for slang and colloquial speech. While Bigpup lived contentedly in the concrete-block house that entombed a Spartan, one of the Dictionary's contributors with username "malp" typed in the inaugural entry: "term utilized in the real estate appraisal industry to describe a trailer which had been added onto and may or may not resemble a site-built home" (Urban Dictionary). This entry was supplanted as the primary definition with another user named Space Shuttle Sunglasses denoting trouse as a "blouse that can be worn as pants." A subsequent entry expanded the term to include music that falls between house and trance. Trouse's domestic synthesis of trailer and house had spawned unlikely fusions of sound and fashion—recall the standard British designation of close-fitting breeches, as a singular form of trousers.

The construction of the term "trouse" in Urban Dictionary's mock-serious forum is not unlike the similarly populist construction of house from trailer. One of the cyber-dictionary permutations invokes simulation and a home-made theory of representation: "An add-on built around a trailer, with the intended end-result looking like a 'real' house. Usually construction goes incomplete, as most trailer-dwellers lack ambition and money and the end result is a trouse." The latter part of this disparaging commentary unfairly substitutes social frame for technical inventiveness amidst necessity and economic exigencies. The usage example, now trading social for professional, suggests a DIY project gone wrong: "The end result was a Trouse, with random holes in the floor and walls since Jason had no clue what he was doing." Bricoleur's vision falls prey to amateur's ineptitude. In the older entry's usage example, the trouse has fewer aspirations to site-built house and instead augments the manufacturing of the mobile unit: "Hey, they added a second floor to their double-wide and now they have a trouse." Less successful in terms of Urban Dictionary's thumbs-up and thumbs-down rating system is Bully Seaman's entry that defines trouse through its non-portable elements in which additional construction anchors the trailer to its site for what seems to be an aesthetic success: "Hey Mandy, your tweaked out neighbors built onto their trailer. What a nice looking trouse." The process of defining "trouse" parses the varieties of domestic experience.

> *This is a really cool structure, an example of the 'SLV Hybrid' school of domestic architecture. Our ex-neighbor built the house around an old trailer—a common practice around here, like the practice of building homes around old boxcars—adding large living area, small kitchen, and bathroom.*
>
> —Urban Dictionary

We live by accretion. If we cannot trade up, we have to build out. Hermit crabs trade shells, while mollusks add calcified layers. Architects have experimented with expandable houses, such as Avi Friedman's "grow home" with flexible spaces that can accommodate "add-in" as well as "add-on" strategies, but planned domestic extensions can rarely match or keep up with self-built responses. DIY captures not just necessity but also desire. Building outward from a trailer follows the arc of this more propositional and reactive approach. Evolving incremental growth operates in both personal and mythic time. It draws from archetypes like trailer as hut, tree as roof, and wall as wind break. It also makes rooms for more intimate and immediate improvisation: cut a window here for viewing spring flowers, add a canopy there for cleaning fish protected from the noonday heat, and add a screened deck along this side for private meals after the sun has set. The longer it stays in one place, the more a trailer's shell is likely to be broken. Finite form yields to indefinite practice. There are no prototypes for the trouse.

> *The crypt underneath the manor was beautiful, and in perfect preservation.*
>
> —D. H. Lawrence

I am reminded of the crypt in D. H. Lawrence's recasting of Wingfield Manor, where Mary Queen of Scots was allegedly imprisoned. The manor's crypt serves as an illicit meeting place for the lovers in his novel. Our trailer followed the crypt's eccentricity. Though above ground, the trailer was thrilling in its sheer presence as well as its vulnerability and exposure. Dragging in the Manor, we were now going about things back to front. We brought a trailer to the house. In one sense, this is not permissible. Our Spartan Manor is a little too close to the neighbors, a little too visible from the street, and a lot too permanent. Lawrence might enjoy the trailer-ruin's "perfect preservation" as well as its exhibitionism and its marginal programs. The trailer is a conceit. Our house, however modest, required extra space only for peripheral programs of writing, hosting guests, and accommodating our children's sleepovers. In another sense, it demonstrates how the trailer is a labile component of living in Florida. The mobile home is not the twentieth-century brick that architect Paul Rudolph believed it to be, soon after he completed his design tenure in the state. The trailer *is* Florida's version of Bachelard's garret, Heidegger's hut, and Lawrence's crypt. It is the place not just to dwell but the place to dream. The flower is lodged in the almond, just as domestic code is embedded within the trailer. The Florida trouse can trace its germination to climate, but growing such a house leaves traces of something our state's built environment sometimes lacks—those domestic places that eschew quantification and offer residual escape.

Works Cited

Bachelard, Gaston. *The Poetics of Space.* Trans. Maria Jolas. Boston: Beacon Press, 1994.
Florida Statutes. Section 320.01(1)(b)(1). May 1992. Print.
Friedman, Avi. *Grow Home.* Montréal: McGill-Queen's UP, 2001. Print.
The Editors. "Cornerstone for a New Magazine." *House and Home* 1.1 (January 1952): 107. Print.
"La Maison du 'Trailer.'" *Architecture d'aujourd'hui* (September 1952): 13. Print.
Lawrence, D. H. *Sons and Lovers.* New York: Modern Library, 1999. Print.
"Manufactured Home Fact Sheet." MHProNews. MH Marketing Sales Management, 15 Jan. 2012. Web. 31 Aug. 2012.
"Concrete Block home with a Spartan Trailer Entombed." *AppraisersForum.* n.p. 8 Sept. 2008. Web. 12 May 2011. Web.
Rouquier, René. *La Boule de Verre.* Paris: Séghers, 12.
Roberts, Kenneth Lewis. *Sun Hunting: Adventures and Observations among the Native and Migratory tribes of Florida.* Indianapolis: Bobbs-Merrill, 1922. Print.
Spartan Aircraft Company. "We just bought our first home." n.p.: 1955. Print.
"trouse." *Urban Dictionary.*UrbanDictionary.com. 18 Jan. 2011. Web. 29 June 2012.

Florida Narratives

5 Tampa at the Sunset of Western Civilization

Todd Taylor

I descend from the ice people. My parents grew up in rural Indiana, which is the coldest place I have ever known, even colder than the top of a stormy ski lift, to me, because Indiana is all farmland, and how can spring planting grow in ground that's this cold on Christmas Day visiting my grandparents? In Florida, where I grew up, farms were season-less, humid, outdoor greenhouses where they use orchard heaters to protect the oranges when it dips below freezing for four hours in the middle of one night every other year. I'm sure it is technically much colder in North Dakota, Nebraska, and Maine than in Indiana, but I didn't reverse migrate to those places to visit family left behind. So, as far as my Floridian view of the world was concerned, Indiana was as cold as it gets. To warm up a little after college, my parents left their John Mellencamp small towns and moved to Buffalo, but I only have a couple snapshot memories of that place, as we left there in the summer just before my third birthday.

Yes, my parents contributed to the great state-income-tax-evasion migration from the Midwest via a couple of early career stops in the Rust Belt to the Promised Land: Florida—more specifically Central Florida, which is one of the three de-nativized zones in the Sunshine State. The northern part, from the Panhandle to Jacksonville, contains most of the true natives—that is, the non-indigenous natives, because no one is quite sure where the indigenous have gone (they're not playing ball for Florida State . . . wait a minute . . . I think there's a reservation near a truck stop on a turnpike somewhere). The northern tract, which follows the traverse of I-10, is (un)affectionately known as LA, or Lower Alabama. It's perhaps one of the few places where the term "cracker" is sometimes self-applied. The first de-nativized zone begins south of the farmlands around Gainesville and Ocala—this is the Central Florida Triangle, from Orlando to Tampa to Melbourne.

In case you didn't know, Florida is the only large-population state other than Texas without a state income tax. So, the post-war, super-secure middle classes from Illinois to New Jersey retired to Florida for the warmth and relaxation (in terms of climate and taxes) in huge numbers from the 1960s to the late 1980s. This migration of capital combined with the tourist dollars meant that the state could provide modern schools and highways without overtly taxing the pensioners a penny. A fantastic formula! No need for greed or corruption since the money just grew on trees—or on the cheap, fragrant land of former orange and pine trees now making room for retirement villages, golf courses, and the supporting strip malls. No urban decay or race riots in Eden either.

The Midwestern boomer-parents like mine set up shop, converting the swampy lakes from south of Ocala to south of Orlando into an analogue of a perpetual Indian summer on Michigan shores, including the familiar abundance of indigenous names and absence of indigenous faces. The tax advantage scheme was working great until the 1980s when every other place on the planet did the math and *realized* that every precious tourist dollar is a triple prize in that: (1) a tourist dollar could be taxed more heavily because the payers have no vote in the matter, (2) it moves capital into the state instead of exporting it, and (3) it pays for infrastructure instead of local tax payers having to invest. Since Florida's lion's share of the national and international tourist industry has declined, the state found itself in the new century with a dangerously rising tide but without paddles of revenue to negotiate. Tickets, food, lodging, and gas purchased in obscure places like Branson, Missouri continue to chip away at Florida's former vacation monopoly.

The other two de-nativized zones are from Palm Beach to North Miami (migrants from the Northeast) and Miami itself (migrants from Cuba). My colleagues in this collection will examine these other places, but this chapter is about Midwesterners who left their icy homelands for the suburbs of Central Florida, and, in my case, Tampa.

My parents' exodus from the tundra to the Promised Land began in 1957. In the spring of my dad's senior year, he strolled down to the gym at Indiana University in Bloomington with a C average in mathematics. The maître d' walked him across the lacquered floor of all those glorious, sweaty, winter, indoor basketball triumphs over to the tables of the insurance companies, who were waiting for the math majors. Each company offered him a job, and he took the best paying one. My parents and each of their senior friends carefully arranged their half-dozen weddings at the Indiana country clubs across successive weekends after graduation throughout June and July—the same white dinner jacket working for each event. The job offer letters understood, and the start dates accommodated the communal loss of virginity. They honeymooned in my aunt's apartment in Manhattan with a heavy Chevy full of china and silver, never worrying for a moment about theft in that neighborhood. These were the earliest days of computing and data processing, which was great timing for a C-average math major. My mother, an A+ French major, did the same job as Dad at first, although her income could not be included on their starter-home mortgage application because she was neither a nurse nor a teacher.

After a decade of duty in the Rust Belt, Dad received an offer from the Medicare-fueled Blue Cross and Blue Shield explosion among the retirees in Florida—a world away from the cold and calamity of the urban northeast in the late 1960s. We left Buffalo for a beach rental on my third birthday, while they were pouring speckled terrazzo and installing shag carpet and foiled wallpaper in our new suburban, all-electric home. There was an orange tree in the front yard next to the air-conditioning unit. The thick St. Augustine grass could not grow in the shade of the tree, so I could bury my GI Joe and Major Matt Mason in the sandy soil there, whereas the rest of the lawn was irrigated fully, fertilized and pesticided bright green, and, consequently, webbed tight. On the fresh Dover-white concrete driveway: a sensible Dodge Dart for the commute to work, home for lunch, and back again to finish the day and the Buick LeSabre V8 land yacht for driving the kids to the A&W with curb hops, the drive-in theater, the beach, Sunoco for a full-service fill-up after church on Sundays (thirty-six cents per gallon), and Disney World.

My executive father was invited for and took the whole family to a Disney World preview a year before it opened, where he purchased a package for the debut holiday weekend, which was Thanksgiving, 1971. At the preview in 1970, I was a terribly confused six-year old. I couldn't get the concept that we weren't at the real Magic Kingdom—I had seen Cinderella's Castle every Sunday night on TV's *Wonderful World of Disney* show, but I couldn't understand what or where California was. At the preview, I got a stuffed Pluto to placate my frustration, and I remember being fascinated by a giant model of Disney World and EPCOT under a plexi bubble, fantastically preserved from the atmosphere around it, including the fallout from the riots and assassinations, the summer of love, and the police action in Southeast Asia.

We stayed in the Contemporary Hotel at Disney World that holiday weekend, and I remember being particularly fascinated by the monorail running through the hotel and by the space-age, spongy polyester Vellux blanket I had neither seen nor imagined before, sleeping like Major Matt Mason, and drinking Tang in the morning. If you missed it, you can't imagine how astronaut-obsessed we were back then as we began to win the space race with the Apollo missions launching from Florida's east coast, which the Buick LeSabre also took me to witness. The traffic jam going into Disney World on Thanksgiving 1971 was twenty-two miles long. The Highway Patrol cruised the emergency lane with megaphones instructing everyone without tickets and reservations to turn around and go home, which was not our problem. We had a cooler of drinks, four adults, and two kids comfortably spread across two bench seats, with those pesky lap-belts tucked down in the cracks to keep them out of the way. It was too hot to lie down under the glass on the rear deck board behind the back seats, although that was my favorite road trip spot once the sun went down.

I grew up in Disney World. I can still tell you what's located in every corner of every alley in the park. I can tell you which attractions previously required E-tickets. I remember when Space Mountain opened and 20,000 Leagues Under the Sea closed. I never cut a line, but learned exactly how to time and sequence my assaults. I lost track at age seventeen at my number of visits—two dozen at that point. If stickball was a definitive American art form you learned in the Bronx and jazz was what you got in New Orleans and hot dogs are what you knew in Chicago, then negotiating the consumer/entertainment "system" was the education I learned in Disney World (and later in public school in Tampa). In England, you might call it queue management; in this part of America, it was called beating the crowd (from within). On the other hand, those first few years of Disney World were fantastically and truly mind blowing. At seven years old you don't notice the pneumatic sounds, creepy jaw-hinges, and jerky joint action of the animatronic robots—those country bears and that hall of presidents are *better* than real: they're *magic*.

On the tram ride (I can still smell the diesel) from the parking lot to the "transportation centers" that then shuttled you to the Magic Kingdom, the drivers would of course first remind you to make note of location and keep everything safe and secure, and then their routine included the factoid that *all* of Disneyland, California could fit inside the parking lot of Disney World, Florida. This made you feel proud and wise to have chosen this vacation destination and to be a Floridian (in my case)—and, of course, it soothed you about the epic, time-consuming odyssey to actually get into the Magic Kingdom.

My home back in Tampa was dredged from brackish wetlands, which would have been a bad thing back in the Midwest, but here it meant that the resulting right-angled canals gave access to boating, although we never had a boat. Why get on a boat to snake through the mosquitoes and the mangroves into Tampa Bay when every other house on the street had a fresh, clean, cool, chlorinated swimming pool and lots of cheap labor to maintain them? Although it seems a couple of people sharing our backyard canal liked to fish. When we moved into this particular house aquatic in 1977, you could see the bottom of the canal about twelve feet down at mid-tide. You could see streams of mullet and sunfishes, frequent dolphins, and the occasional manatee. By the time I graduated high school in 1983, there was no visibility and only the occasional dolphin would slide through—who knows if the mullet are still down there?

The front yard was a cul-de-sac in the shape of a gentle bowl, which was essential for collecting the tropical rains and throwing the runoff into the canals. Aside from the indulged lawns and designer palm trees, everything else in the front was concrete or asphalt, which was heaven for me because my life from 1977 to 1980 was skateboarding, and this masonry bowl was decent light work until Saturday when I made the weekly pilgrimage to the Skatewave on Hillsborough Avenue. I learned from my skateboard magazines that the Skatewave was based upon a design of a skateboard park in Anaheim, California, which was also the home of Disneyland. I'll never forget my first glimpse of the Skatewave in Tampa, my face wedged into the chain link outside in the parking lot: it was exactly the same breathtaking euphoria that I experienced at that model of Disney World under a plastic dome, because very soon this fantasyscape would be all mine to wallow. The American Dream realized, at least the white male adolescent 1970s version of it.

Was it Piaget or Vygotsky who went on about the stages of cognitive development, from being immature and self-centered to recognizing that there are other people and other worlds out there? That's what skateboarding culture did for me in the late 1970s, and it was jacked instantaneously through the precious *Skateboarder* magazine I would receive every month. What they were doing out West in California was so far ahead—it was *radical*. They had punk rock, but we only had pop, metal, and disco. They could surf or skate, whereas there were no waves at all on the West Coast of Florida, and the ones in Melbourne weren't even worth the trip because they were so tiny and inconsistent. Eventually Florida would have pro riders like Mike McGill (from the Skatewave Saturdays), Allen Gelfend, Rodney Mullen, and Kelly Slater who would influence skating and surfing, but it all started on the *real* West Coast in California, not the trailing one in which I was stuck, in Tampa.

They say that the fundamental story of America, on a genomic or subatomic level, is the impulse to initially adventure and then eventually settle after the setting sun. Westward ho, the wagons! Heading west from Cinderella's castle, you travel from Fantasyland and through Liberty Square until you reach Frontierland—the same route followed by white American settlers, except that the endgame was not the Country Bear Jamboree or Fort Wilderness but Southern California. The mid-century SoCal tract-home suburbs are at the end of the road of Western Civilization. It's where the wagons stopped and the chosen people entered into *their land,* with its perfect, sunny, low-humidity climate; sunsets over the ocean; exploding post-war economy; dammed up rivers to convert the desert into a fruitful Eden and to provide the hydroelectricity to illuminate suburbs and power the television tubes.

Florida, as it transformed rapidly in the 1970s and 80s, was California's little brother, perhaps from a different and more humid, sweaty, and provincial father. Little brother grew up in the shadows, wanting to be so much like his internationally trend-setting idol, even though his Disney World was much larger than the Anaheim original—an over-compensation, no doubt. There is a pronounced California Style—in fact, many of them. Florida style, if it can be called that, is defined by retirees from cold paces. Tampa, as we now know it, was defined as the (mid)western wave of settlers finally ran into the sea and out of real estate upon reaching the coast. It was the moment in the 1960s and 1970s, when families like mine left their legacy farms and Rust Belts and settled in suburban Florida, that shaped the State's identity. Tampa, located as it is on the "other" American west coast, embodies these impulses and traits . . . inherently.

Tampa's first identity, however, was "Cigar City." Actually, it was a neighborhood in Tampa known as Ybor City where the cigars were rolled out in huge numbers for the international industrialist fat cats beginning in the 1880s but crashing hard during the Great Depression, of course. Ybor City was a wildly multicultural immigrant phenomenon, with workers from Spain, Cuba, Italy, the Caribbean, and even Germany making the cigars and forming an especially communal experiment with various ethnic clubs providing social support and infrastructure. Ybor City was abandoned after the Depression, although the world-famous, flamenco-dancing Columbia Restaurant has remained since 1905.

Returning home to live with my parents again after college in a trickle down economy, I used my degree to work at a Sicilian Creole restaurant in Ybor City. Vincent Martinez Ybor built his cigar business here because it's adjacent to the port of Tampa, which George Steinbrenner would eventually control. In 1990 Ybor City was a scary, dangerous place. The front entrance into Ybor is located at the convergence of I-275 and I-4, the latter of which connects Tampa to Orlando. Traffic at this intersection can be horrible, so locals will often take the back route, which pinched you between brutish industrial shipping-based hulks like Chilean Nitrate of Soda (which I still do not understand) and the civil rights era "projects" at the edge of downtown Tampa. Artists and eccentric entrepreneurs had just begun to squat and gentrify Ybor City, whose only two anchor tenants at the time were the Columbia and a sprawling, outrageous, and nationally known gay club called "El Goya."

In January 1991, Tampa hosted its second Super Bowl, and even though we could guarantee a lack of ice and snow, we couldn't control the rain. The entire weekend was clouded, which was horrible for the city, since the main tourist attractions at the time hinged on being outside in the tropical, winter-suppressing weather. Nine months out of the year you need a shower after walking from a parking lot into a building in this humidity, but December through February is so very nice in these parts. At the time, Tampa lacked adequate hotel space and a true downtown entertainment district; so the Super Bowlers, stuck in their scattered rooms until the game, reported back home that Tampa was not the place to go for a good time. In response to the Super Bowl XXV tourism backfire, the city took a look at the mostly abandoned Ybor City, which was on the wrong side of the tracks; underneath a broken cloverleaf of interstate; and wedged up against an industrial port, housing projects, and poverty, and saw a potential Bourbon Street party zone. This vision wasn't difficult to imagine, since the very same industrial-age masons who were building in New Orleans in the late nineteenth century were the ones who constructed Ybor City. The trade route connected New Orleans to Tampa and then out into the Caribbean and beyond. As you walk down Seventh Avenue in Ybor, you could mistake much of the architecture, especially the use of brick and wrought iron, for New Orleans because the same people designed and built both. If you glance behind the former "Sin Palace," the El Pasaje building on Ninth Avenue where Teddy and his Rough Riders once partied, you can see the prostitutes' tiny upstairs apartments linked by iron catwalks.

In order to get the Super Bowl to return, as it would ten years later, Tampa itself (and not the beaches across the bay) had to offer more fun, some of it indoors. The city handed out the liquor licenses, pumped up its version of a Mardi Gras parade (called Gasparilla), and sent the cops in to try to protect the weekend partiers and their parked cars in the still sketchy neighborhood of Ybor City. They disguised a city bus to resemble a St. Charles Street car, providing free shuttle from the downtown hotels to the party in Ybor. The streetcar route eventually converted the industrial rim into a tourist strip. The Florida Aquarium stands in place of Chilean Nitrate of Soda—because nothing says "urban renewal" like giant fish tanks. Next on the tour is a cruise-ship port, in case the drinks run out on board you can moisten up at the Ybor watering hole. Then there's the "Ice Palace" for the Northerners to watch professional hockey, a giant, convention-sized hotel (finally!), the convention center itself across from the complementary shops and restaurants, and eventually the brand new football stadium with a pirate ship in the end zone and a miniature Yankee Stadium for spring training sharing the same parking.

If you've never been to Tampa, you are likely to assume that it has nice beaches. This is not true, which is why they're called the Tampa *Bay* Buccaneers. The idyllic beaches on the Gulf of Mexico (and the Scientologists) are across the far side of Tampa Bay in Pinellas County. Of course, the waterfront along Tampa Bay is still nice property for the gentry, even though there's no sand or real public access to the shore there—not even a pier. First, there's the Victorian style and then arts-and-crafts suburban houses—historically the first bedrooms on the edge of downtown Tampa and the Hillsborough River. The Gatsby properties align Bayshore Drive with their non-industrial views into the heart of the water. Next, Macdill Air Force Base sticks itself out into the Bay, interrupting the aristocratic real estate momentarily, which picks up again on the far side of the Palma Ceia Country Club, where Judge Smails lives and golfs. Then it's Tampa International Airport, built in the late 1960s, featuring an iconic, post-sputnik hub-and-satellite-terminal design, which dates the moment at which Tampa and Florida turned from its sleepy, musty past toward a new profile as strip mall in a steam bath. It used to be agricultural and floral. Now, it's synthetic consumerism under the spell of tropical escape. It used to be locals with their boats, tackle, and farms. Now it's parrot-heads who can't tell port from starboard but can tell their IPA from a lager.

As the housing bubble was bursting in 2008, the home we used to live in was converted by a developer from a modest ranch house to a 5,900 square foot McMansion because of the dock and canal in the back yard and the cul-de-sac out front. In the 1990s, a different developer wrangled some "high density" housing next to our quaint little subdivision. They named the new apartment buildings things like "Audubon Village" and "Spoonbill Bay" in place of the salty wetlands where we used to go to do stuff we shouldn't as teenagers, as long as we could withstand the swarming, biting bugs. I can still taste the poison fog pumping from the rear of the county mosquito-control truck that toured the neighborhood as frequently as the ice cream man. I would run indoors to avoid the truck, when it didn't catch me on my skateboard returning home, but there were kids who would play in the mist. Since monthly indoor bug spray isn't optional in Florida, maybe there's no difference? Even Judge Smails's estate has roaches.

In 1980, my suburb was bused on still reverberating desegregation orders to a sparkling new Thomas Jefferson High School squished between downtown Tampa, the "ethnic" West Tampa neighborhood, and Tampa International. On the home stretch into the student parking lot, we self-driving tardy teenagers would actually drop below the speed limit out of self-preservation because visitors looking for the rental car return lots and desperate to make their flights were guaranteed to panic—it was bumper-car roller derby in the streets. My high school was roughly one-third black, one-third white, and one-third Cuban. TJHS was designed as a mall, with a large central corridor and wings branching perpendicular: L-Hall for language arts and M-Hall for social sciences. We had no stadium for football because apparently there was not enough money for us. This was *the* urban school, and we had to play our home games miles away at Plant High School, which was home to the Smails kids from the Palma Ceia Country Club.

I was student body president my senior year, which meant I was a technocratic leader as opposed to the senior class president who was elected by popularity. As such, I "testified" at a meeting of the Hillsborough County Commissioners in support of a temporary penny sales tax increase to build a stadium for our high school. The stadium was, of course, the sentimental sugar coating on a plan to fund much larger things, about which I was ignorant. When it came time for the vote, instead of simply saying "yea" or "nay," one of the commissioners whipped out a secret chart he had brought with him and suggested that we should not use the pennies to fund the projects but to eliminate property tax in the county for one year. My expertise in parliamentary procedure was offended, and this dude was totally out of order, essentially making a hostile amendment after the question had been called. He, of course, eventually voted against the defeated proposal. Soon after, he and another commissioner were convicted by federal prosecutors and sent to jail for accepting bribes from developers for the upscale neighborhoods expanding into the old cow pastures north of the city, since everything was already built up against the bay to the south. Years later, once those northern suburbs demanded a high school of their own, TJHS got its stadium simultaneously—or the very thinnest aluminum-riser version thereof. As student body president, I also once had the opportunity to tour the school with someone from the Ford Foundation who was there to award us a grant for achievement in an urban school based upon outstanding AP exam scores. The same thirty or so of us, largely bused in from the suburbs, had essentially the same coordinated AP schedule from first period to last. It was a school within a school.

In whispers, Tampa, at the time, was called "the wild, wild west of Florida politics." Like most places, I suppose, the good ol' boys in their non-collegiate fraternities ran the show. They owned all the expansion land for generations and the boom was on. The cattle barons morphed into developers. Tampa still has an annual "Gasparilla Pirate Festival," based upon a completely fictitious figure named Jose Gaspar. The manufactured event was launched and funded by "Ye Mystic Crewe" as a civic gift to promote identity and tourism. Like Mardi Gras in New Orleans, various "crewes" hold exclusive balls and parties leading up to the big parade. Like Mardi Gras and Las Vegas, over time the spectacle has become more integrated and family friendly, but, at its beginning, it was good ol' boys getting drunk in public and gambling in private inside their pirate ship-barge, the parade floats careening past the surnamed streets as the native sons launched largesse on the masses via plastic beaded booty, keeping the buccaneer spirit alive, not a fiction after all.

I remember watching the Florida legislature on the public access channel back in these days. I remember a bubba in a polyester blazer awkwardly wrangling with his tethered microphone from the chamber floor, addressing the speaker by first name, saying something with exasperation like, "Jim, I don't understand why we've got to bring up this open-container issue every year just to vote it down. I know I like to have a scotch in the car on my way home. [Incredulous, open-mouthed pause.] I know you do too!" The Mothers Against Drunk Driving Organization would eventually prevail on this account, even in party states like Louisiana and Florida. Or perhaps it was the insurance companies behind MADD that turned the tide? I recall a giant, expensive ad campaign in the mid-1980s producing a new tagline for Florida beyond "The Sunshine State." The Florida Department of Tourism came up with: "Florida, the rules are different here," featuring TV ads with beachy girls in swimsuits explaining the difference. That campaign died almost instantly, largely due to *Miami Vice* and the war on drugs, but the ethos lived on, as apparent from the 2000 presidential election.

The Hillsborough River extends north from downtown Tampa until making a right turn toward the east. It's not much of an urban river like the Hudson or the Chicago. There was a late colonial fort there originally to control the thoroughfare and the Seminole Indians. Magnate Henry Plant built a grand hotel on the banks of the river and at the end of his railroad line in the 1890s. It's now technically a museum and the home of the University of Tampa. The building features distinctive, silvery minarets, an architectural non sequitur years ahead of the international simulacrum at EPCOT. I wonder how the minarets survived McCarthy? One suburban development after another grows out from the intersection of the bay and the river by the Plant hotel, like age rings on a tree stump. It begins with Hyde Park to the west and Davis Islands to the southeast. Then it's Seminole Heights and Temple Terrace to the north. Each of these neighborhoods has gone through successive eras of boom, decline, and re-gentrification. In the movie *Goodfellas*, mobsters take a guy to Florida to feed him to lions, which, I assume, might be based on the Lowery Park Zoo in Temple Terrace and the local Don Santo Trafficante. The suburban rings eventually swelled out west until reaching Pinellas County at Dunedin Beach. To the north, the empty pastures previously home to only the University of South Florida and Busch Gardens became consumed by golfing communities inflated by the roaring 1990s.

That's where Tampa ends. In the bay to the south. At the beaches to the west. At the tennis clubs north. And to the east, there's the artery to Orlando. It was the artisans and masons from New Orleans that gave Cigar City its original flavor. Now it's the simulacrum and synthetic running downhill from theme parks in Orlando. A frighteningly articulate Ted Bundy blamed the anonymity of the interstate highway system for (his) moral decline, although "Ole Sparky" at the state pen in Starke got the last word on him. You probably knew this, but Eisenhower built the interstate system as a nuclear strategy, as a way to keep the missiles on the backs of trucks in perpetual motion. The Internet was also launched as a nuclear defense system. As such, I suppose it's the same story everywhere. There's no *there* there anymore. The last "authentic" Floridian I think I ever knew was Captain Tony Tarracino, owner of his infamous namesake saloon in Key West and mayor of that "republic" briefly. Captain Tony was a bootlegging gangster from New Jersey who escaped to Florida and ran a charter boat. He must have known Hemingway. He would boast about the skeleton of one of his ex-wives hanging behind the bar in front of his designated stool, and I saw him in action enough to know never to bring a girlfriend within fifteen feet of him, which was tricky because Captain Tony's Saloon is a tight fit. The rings of those suburban expansions eventually extended all the way down the West Coast until they choked off the southern exhale of the Everglades, where the movements in Orlando and Tampa finally washed down to the Keys, owned by the Japanese and compromised by cruise ships in the 1990s.

There certainly are still locals in Tampa and families living there for generations (who belong to Ye Mystic Crewe or not). You used to be able to tell a local as they packed up their vinyl, folding lounger and headed to the parking lot at Clearwater Beach at 3:45 under cloudless sunshine. By the time the car cooled, the daily downpour at 4:00 would drown the out-of-towners still at shore scrambling for their lives in the thunderstorm capital of the world. The tourists, mesmerized by the sea vista to the west, never saw the weather approaching from the other direction, although the fact that we have a domed, warm-weathered baseball stadium and a hockey team named the "Lightning" might be clues. The Everglades created some kind of natural thunderstorm factory as the warm air would suck up moisture all day, moving east to west across the middle of the state until it ran up against Tampa Bay and then, DUMP. We learned to ride the taillights of the car in front of us in a zero visibility daisy chain, making our way back across the causeway in the deluge to our Tampa, where the sun would be shining again in time for happy hour around the pool. But something ecological has shifted and you can no longer set your watch according to the 4:00 storm—the weather pattern has changed. Maybe it was the Army Corps of Engineers who drained the swamps Maybe it was the industrial sugarcane farms. Maybe it was suburban sprawl or climate change. Maybe it's all the same. I was reading just the other day about the need to hunt Burmese pythons to counter the epidemic encroachment of this alien species in Florida. It certainly has never been news to find an alligator in the sewers or streets in Central Florida like it is in New York. Locals like me are so accustomed to gators that they're no more interesting than a giant palmetto bug or garden lizard. They're profoundly lethargic when left alone and out of reach of your toy poodle, except during mating season. I can just see the divorced parent leaving the vacated house with faux stucco and tipping junior's aquarium into the swampy ditch that drains toward the retention pond behind the subdivision, a perfect habitat for nurturing a constricting monster. I remember the road signs across Alligator Alley in the Everglades begging drivers to be cautious about the Florida Panther: "only 29 left." As the numbers on the lottery billboards went up, others came down.

    I suppose it's a matter of how you define *native*. My good high school friend named Chuck still lives in West Tampa where he grew up. He moved into his Tío's house when he passed. Chuck's parents live around the corner. It makes more sense to walk rather than drive around their neighborhood, whereas the rest of Tampa is like Los Angeles, demanding automobilization. The West Tampa bungalows are cinder block on slab, like I used to have. The thermal mass keeps things cool in the heat and steady in the storms. I daydream about having a stone house again someday as I don't trust these brittle sticks of kindling I now live in. Tío ran a market in the neighborhood for decades; so Chuck always knew the best places to eat and his mom's food was so savory and delicious compared to the anglo-style food I had at home. It's the one thing I miss most about leaving Florida: Spanish/Cuban food in West Tampa. Otherwise, I struggle to locate a cultural center or signature on the West Coast of Florida. Tampa Bay has given the world Hulk Hogan, death metal, and Hooters. Even though bilingual families like Chuck's have been in Cigar City since its beginning, it's interesting how most sensibilities would probably consider it "new historicism" to label the families in West Tampa as "founders," although they were. They're the *there* there. Chuck could afford to move to a new house, but I know he never will, although we have never discussed the thought—there's no need.

6 Assembling New Port Richey, Florida

Cassandra Branham and Megan McIntyre

In its natural state, Florida may appear poorly designed: meandering rivers, shifting coastlines, and shore-hugging mangroves. Malleable, accessible, and seemingly inexhaustible, the Florida landscape can become anything that humans want it to be.

—Gary Mormino

Introduction

Until the 1940s, Florida was home mainly to those who were born here. In the aftermath of the housing booms that characterized the 1950s, 1960s, 1970s, and 1980s, however, the composition of Florida's population shifted fairly radically: "in 1980, Florida became the place where everyone was from somewhere else" (Mattson 35). This shift, as well as evidence of Florida's early character as home to Native Floridians, remains, and New Port Richey, part of Central Florida's Pasco County, offers a microcosmic picture of the heterogeneous character of modern Florida. What's unique about this place is not any one story, community, or population; what's unique about this place is that it seems to be home to some version of most of the stories that characterize the American experience. There's no better way to understand the strange amalgamation that is New Port Richey than to examine its annual Chasco Fiesta Boat Parade: members of the parade vary widely from million dollar pleasure vessels captained by professional crews to ancient pontoon boats used to navigate the marshes that surround the more populous areas of the county to small family fishing trawlers and the occasional rusty creation cobbled together—like a nautical Frankenstein—from the pieces of any number of no longer seaworthy vessels.

The boat parade emphasizes the heterogeneous quality of this place; however, this complexity is often elided by news stories that feature Floridians as miscreants; misfits; and, on occasion, serial murderers. This perception is reinforced by the strange news stories that often originate in the state, evidenced by a number of blogs and news stories dedicated to reporting Florida's strangest news, including the *Sun Sentinel*'s "FloriDUH," the *Tampa Bay Times*' "Bizarre Florida," and *The Huffington Post*'s "Weird Florida." Ranging from high-profile events such as the 2011 trial of Casey Anthony to more localized stories, including a West Palm Beach man charged with the unlicensed practice of health care after injecting silicone into the buttocks of two women in a motel room, Florida seems to have no shortage of oddities. Author Drew Curtis and newspaper editor Tom Scherburger attribute Florida's strange stories to the diversity of its residents, with Curtis suggesting it is "endemic of the population" (qtd in Ferran). Similarly, Scherburger calls Florida, "the land of refugees," because, "people will literally get on a bus with no job, no money and land in Florida looking for something to do." Author Paul Levine agrees, arguing that "Florida, being sort of the end of the road, is where all these cracked marbles kind of roll and now they come to a stop in the sand. When you're there, there's no place left to go" (Ferran).

The weird and wacky Florida described above represents only a single dimension of the Floridian experience. In an attempt to trace[2] additional dimensions, in what follows, we offer three narratives, and their accompanying photographs, which we believe offer insight into the diversity of lived experiences in New Port Richey and, by extension, Florida more generally. We believe these narratives—when taken as a composite assemblage—allow us to better represent the multiplicity of experiences that characterize life in the Sunshine State.

Our tracing is made possible, in part, through the work of Bruno Latour, particularly his articulations of assemblage, description, and narrative. These three concepts, of course, exist beyond his work, but the ways in which Latour argues for connections between these concepts and for the need to trace networks of actors provides an alternate way of exploring, understanding, even theorizing about a place. These intersections, and Latour's value of objects as equally vital and agentive, also allow us to consider the subjectivity of the place itself. In tracing this assemblage, we attend almost exclusively to common, banal experiences—commonplaces, to use Michel de Certeau's phrase. We argue for the value of commonplaces particularly based on de Certeau's argument that, in retelling familiar stories, we might discover seemingly insignificant details that provide some heretofore unforeseen element(s) of a place or experience.[3]

Assemblage Theory

First, we use Latour's work to argue for constructing a provisional network of somehow connected entities—an assemblage, to use his vocabulary. Such a network seeks to better represent the diversity of experiences by producing "a composite assemblage" instead of a totalizing whole (208). This is a useful concept for considering places because, as Tim Cresswell argues in *Place: A Short Introduction*, one of the goals of place theory is to reveal the world as a set of "attachments and connections between people and place" (11). Because of their provisional natures, places, like assemblages more generally, "are never 'finished' but always 'becoming'" (Cresswell 35). Latour further argues that any assemblage—any set of provisional attachments—"that pays the price of its existence in the hard currency of recruiting and extending is, or rather, has subjectivity" (218). The goal of our tracing, then, is to offer an account of the subjectivity of this place, to acknowledge the heterogeneity of the assemblage by calling attention to groups and experiences that both complicate and reinforce notions gleaned from any oversimplified, superficial examination of such a place.

The term assemblage, of course, is not unique to Latour's work, grounded as it is in Deleuze and Guattari's discussion of relations and deterritorialization (60–61, 95–101). Following Deleuze and Guattari, Manuel de Landa's work on assemblage theory emphasizes the need for approaches that can account for complex systems like economies and environments. De Landa also argues, in part, that the concept of assemblage is useful because it allows us to escape reliance on linear causality an "accommodate complex forms of causal productivity" (21).

In addition to de Landa and Latour's work in sociology, assemblage theory has growing relevance for geography. In their introduction to a 2011 special issue of the journal *Area* on assemblage, Ben Anderson and Colin McFarlane note the increasing importance of the term and suggest that its value as a theoretical concept lies in its emphasis on "emergence, multiplicity and indeterminacy" (124). The term, they suggest, "connects to a wider redefinition of the socio-spatial in terms of the composition of diverse elements into some form of provisional socio-spatial formation" (124). We would note that de Landa and Anderson and McFarlane, as well as Latour, value the assemblage as a way of understanding provisional yet productive networks of actors. This emphasis on the provisional and shifting nature of the assemblage, as well as on the heterogeneous nature of assemblages in general, allows us to reimagine places like New Port Richey as diverse networks of sometimes conflicting elements.

Beyond its value in terms of sociological and theoretical work, assemblage has important connotations in terms of the visual arts. The term is sometimes used interchangeably with "collage" and "montage," though "assemblage" art is nearly always characterized by the use of found objects. Assemblage compositions are also notable for their transgression of boundaries of medium and form and, according to artists Norman Laliberté and Alex Mogelon, the seemingly random quality of assemblage and the inherent transgression that characterizes such work makes it uniquely suited to addressing "the human experience in the second half of the twentieth century" and beyond (17). For our purposes, this sense of the word offers an important element of peculiarity that we believe also characterizes the connections between members of the assemblage that constitutes New Port Richey: it is not that the elements that make up an assemblage are remarkable in and of themselves; rather, because they tend to be found objects, the components of an assemblage are mundane. The peculiar, transgressive nature of such work comes, rather, from the presence of elements, perhaps with conflicting purposes or origins, side by side in a single work.

DE CERTEAU AND THE COMMONPLACE

Like the commonplace elements that characterize a visual assemblage, the narratives that follow, which focus on everyday experiences, provide insight primarily into the banality of life in this Gulf Coast city. There are no grand moments at play here; instead, there is a sense of ordinary-ness, an emphasis on the commonplace, especially as understood through the work of de Certeau. De Certeau's sense of the commonplace suggests that retelling common stories can reveal seemingly insignificant details that offer insight into the character of a place: "The significance of a story that is well known . . . can be reversed by a single 'circumstantial' detail. The 'insignificant detail' inserted into the framework that supports it makes the commonplace produce other effects" (89). Our goal, then, in retelling mundane experiences is to, through our tracing, uncover the "extra element" such a tracing reveals (de Certeau 89). Based on the narratives that follow, we believe this extra element may well be the simultaneous diversity and proximity of these experiences.

Following de Certeau, then, we do not wish to tell a new story, nor do we wish to portray the traditional as negative. Rather, our purpose is to complicate, through an emphasis on multiple banalities, commonplace experiences, and expected versions of life in Florida. As Rice notes in his chapter "Miami Spatial Stories," "there is more to narrative than commonplaces"; there is, in addition, "a series of patterns" (48–49). The narratives that follow depict a number of seemingly commonplace experiences, but when taken together, these fragments of life in New Port Richey also reveal strange connections and repetitions. We present the following narratives together in order to emphasize that these lived experiences, though quite different and representative, perhaps, of both sides of traditional binary relationships, also happen simultaneously. This concurrence is perhaps the unexpected element our tracing calls attention to: these narratives, these binaries, and these extremes all exist together in the same small city.

Narratives

Also following Latour, we rely largely on the act of description to provide one view of this complex set of interactions and actors.[4] In *Reassembling the Social*, Latour spends a great deal of time emphasizing the important role of description in the work of understanding the assemblage. "God," he says, "is in the details," and it's all details precisely because, in the name of avoiding reductionism, we must note with great detail how things are connected—how the network enrolls its members—but also how particular members are unique (*Reassembling the Social* 137). Latour recognizes, however, that description is perhaps the most difficult of all tasks for the academic: "to describe, to be attentive to the concrete state of affairs, to find the uniquely adequate account of a given situation, I myself have always found this incredibly demanding" (144).

Closely related to the act of description is the act of narration. Latour suggests there is certain equivalence between the two: "A good ANT account," Latour asserts in *Reassembling the Social*, "is a narrative or a description or a proposition where all the actors do something and don't just sit there" (128). However, we also recognize that the act of narration works as part of the construction of the place we wish to describe. In a 1993 interview with T. Hugh Crawford for the journal *Configurations*, Latour suggests that the object of his own study, that is the construction of facts through the work of science, represents "phenomena that have the characteristics of being narrative, collective, and outside. They are quasi-objects; they are not of our own making.

We build them collectively, and they are narrated. That is it: real, narrated, social" (263). The place we wish to trace—New Port Richey—is a similar beast, a quasi-object that is collectively, socially, narratively, and physically made through the interactions of the many actors that call the city home. Unlike Newman, who, in his chapter can clearly identify the dividing line, the "definitional sharpness" that separates one neighborhood or group from another (151), in some ways, New Port Richey resists such a separation: the lack of clear political and neighborhood boundaries creates a composite in which the parts are sometimes difficult to discern.

Latour's emphasis on narration and description connects nicely, we'd argue, to Michel de Certeau's emphasis on storytelling as a tour. In *The Practice of Everyday Life*, de Certeau notes the difference between the kind of knowledge gained from maps versus the kind gained by experiencing the place through the act of touring it and suggests that tourism reveals the heterogeneity elided by the totalization inherent in mapmaking (188–122). The detail accessible in taking and narrating the tour offers something different, something more: "The finely tuned ear can discern in the saying the difference introduced by the *act of saying (it)* here and now" (de Certeau 89). A specific account of banal Florida lives challenges the reification of simply mapping the character of the state.

Though census data suggests the county is largely Caucasian and lower-middle or middle class[5], we believe residents' lived experiences suggest a large degree of heterogeneity. This variety is made visible because, following Latour, we rely heavily on narration and description. In order to trace the assemblage that constitutes New Port Richey, then, we examine three neighborhoods. Though these short discussions can in no way do justice to the complexity of experiences for residents of these neighborhoods, we wish to demonstrate a sense of life in these areas. As Rice notes in the introduction to this collection, assembling Florida is not intended to "deliver a comprehensive vision" of the state (4); rather we offer, like many of the other contributing authors, fragments, moments, and stories. We also wish to suggest, by contrasting the geographical proximity with the experiential diversity, that, on its own, each of these neighborhoods is entirely commonplace. In combination, however, they demonstrate a strange truism about Florida: there is no single Florida. There are only Floridas, always already plural.

Shamrock Heights

About five miles inland from the Gulf of Mexico, nestled north of Tampa and St. Petersburg, sits New Port Richey, Florida. Only about a square mile total, navigating all that downtown has to offer takes less than thirty minutes on foot. From the historic Hacienda Hotel, whose famous guests once included silent screen star Thomas Meighan and famous attorney Clarence Darrow, to the Richey Suncoast Theatre, downtown centers on Main Street and Grand Boulevard, the latter of which cuts from US 19 along the Cotee River, through Sims Park and dead-ends a few miles past downtown. If you follow Grand Boulevard about a mile and a half past the Richey Suncoast Theatre, you'll encounter Trouble Creek Road, which stretches from the outskirts of Moon Lake, on New Port Richey's eastern edge, to the mangroves and brackish marshes that border the Gulf of Mexico to the west.

Just three miles from picturesque downtown, Shamrock Heights is just one of the many sprawling lower-middle class communities that make up New Port Richey, which was built as a bedroom community for Tampa businesses.

Figure 1. Street sign marking the turn from the subdivision's main thoroughfare onto Pirate Place

The town reflects this suburban mentality: sprawling neighborhoods and tract houses proliferated in the 1960s and 1970s and drew scads of families. By the mid-1980s, when Megan's parents moved from Logansport, Indiana to their house on Pirate Place, though, the newness of the neighborhoods surrounding New Port Richey had largely worn off: the black and cream house her family moved into was just one of the many aging tract homes on a street full of working class families.

From seven to nine, I took baton twirling classes at the Grove Park Community Center. Grove Park, also home to the only public pool accessible to residents of Shamrock Heights and its neighboring subdivisions, was the nexus of the neighborhood for many of my formative years.

Figure 2. Front facade of the remodeled Grove Park Community Center

The concrete cinder-block building, like most of the neighborhood, was built in the 1960s and reflected the neighborhood's sensibility: always busy and a little bit dirty. The one-building community center functioned as a dance school, community-meeting site, birthday-party venue, and home to nearly every other kind of neighborhood activity. In the spring of 1993, my baton troop was slated to march in the annual Chasco Fiesta parade. Three days a week for six months, my fellow twirlers and I, all girls aged seven to twelve, practiced throws, exchanges, and other tricks meant to wow parade goers. A few of the moms, including mine, designed and sewed silver lamé skirts and added white fringe to button-down, white shirts for the occasion.

Unfortunately, Florida's infamous weather had other ideas. On March 13, 1993 Florida's Gulf Coast was blindsided by what is still known by locals as the "No-Name Storm." This moniker has to do, in part, with the fact that, unlike storms that occur during the Atlantic hurricane season, the National Weather Service doesn't bestow names upon winter storms. The name is also a nod, though, to the devastating lack of warning: the Pasco County Sheriff's Office was forced to rapidly evacuate nearly 1,200 New Port Richey residents in the middle of the night (Fischer). The parade, of course, was canceled (for the first and only time since its revival in 1947).

My street fared fairly well: our next door neighbors had their roof rearranged, a few doors down, the Allan family lost their above ground pool to a wayward umbrella pole, and my parents awoke to find three inches of water in their bedroom. Shamrock Heights in general, though, saw quite a bit of damage. By my own rough estimates, nearly one-third of the houses in the neighborhood received some damage, three of which were total losses and, in the year that followed, razed by the county. The neighborhood, though, came together: my dad and some of the other men and women in the neighborhood went from house to house securing blue tarps over damaged roofs and plywood over damaged windows. The neighborhood also organized its own parade: when school let out in June, families built floats in lawn-mower trailers and smaller displays in children's wagons, middle school and high school marching band members broke out their instruments, and my fellow twirlers and I donned our lamé skirts and fringed shirts and showed off the tricks we learned.

Throughout my elementary school years, the neighborhood seemed to thrive despite the age of the houses and the declining income levels of the residents: new families with young children moved in, and my brother and I had lots of friends to play with. By the time I reached the sixth grade, though, the neighborhood had begun to change: the steady trickle of new families dried up and families began moving out of the neighborhood. One by one, houses became and remained vacant.

During the summer between sixth and seventh grade, I had my first experience with what would unfortunately become a common occurrence in the neighborhood. One Thursday morning near the end of July, I sat on the front porch of the house reading one of the books on my summer reading list—a biography of Abraham Lincoln, I think—when three police cars, sirens loud and lights flashing, screeched to a halt two doors down. Most of the officers, guns drawn, approached the house, but one of the officers headed straight for me. "You should be inside. Now. Lock the door and don't come out." As the officer rejoined his colleagues, I ran into the house, snatched the cordless phone from its base, and headed straight for my closet. I didn't emerge until my mom—whom I frantically called as soon as I was safely ensconced behind the folding closet doors—arrived home forty-five minutes later. Neighborhood gossip claimed that the couple renting the house while the owners were home in Ottawa had been making and selling a meth-like concoction to local middle and high school students.

Figure 3. Megan's childhood home, present day

> *Whereas my mom had once let me play out front until well after the streetlights came on, I was now under strict orders to be inside the house before the sun went down. My parents were scared, and that fear only increased as the number of drug arrests in the county steadily increased. The drug problem was a product, in part, of a steadily declining financial situation in Pasco County. As the cost of living in Pasco increased, wages remained stagnant. Despite the fact that both my parents worked full time, my family received government Women, Infant, Children (WIC) food assistance and free lunch at school.*

As it turns out, though, these problems were not unique to Megan's neighborhood or to the 1990s: according to the 2008 Florida Youth Substance Abuse Survey of Pasco County, over ten percent of middle and high school students in Pasco County admit to having abused prescription drugs in their lifetime, versus eight percent in Florida ("Florida Department of Children and Families") and less than three percent nationally ("Prescription Drug Abuse"). According to *City Data*, which compiles and analyzes crime data for cities across the country, both the violent crime and people crime indexes for New Port Richey regularly run twice the national average. In 2010, for example, *City Data*'s violent crime index for New Port Richey was 472.3 violent crimes per 100,000 people; the national average was less than half of that at 222.7 ("Crime in New Port Richey, Florida"). The same year, according to Florida's Department of Health, nearly sixty percent of children between the ages of zero and four years old in Pasco County received WIC food benefits, and New Port Richey accounted for roughly one-third of the WIC participants in the county despite being home to less than six percent of the county's population ("Pasco County Health Department").

This negative trend for Shamrock Heights, however, represents only a fraction of the lived experiences in New Port Richey and only a fraction of Megan's experiences with the town. At the same time that the neighborhood began to deteriorate, brand new schools opened, churches brought safe community events to Shamrock Heights, and Grove Park was renovated. These simple moves by community institutions (churches, local governments, and community associations) offer an oddly hopeful contrast to the neighborhood's growing drug problem. This can likely be said for any neighborhood or town facing such issues. However, the uniquely Florida twist, we'd argue, is that there wasn't a sense of oddity, then or now, surrounding the mix of hope and fear; of abysmal economic prospects and a multimillion-dollar makeover to downtown; of drug dealers, working families, and millionaires. The not-so-surprising story of suburban sprawl and residential decay merits our attention precisely because of its commonplace nature. Taken by itself, a narrative that describes the slow infestation of drugs and an increasing need for public financial assistance may not seem like anything new. But the geographical proximity of this ordinary suburban neighborhood to the posh Bailey's Bluff subdivision and the rural Moon Lake community—all of which exist within the limits of a single coastal Florida city—offers an intriguing picture of the disparate, yet oddly connected groups (the composite assemblage) that constitute the New Port Richey community.

Bailey's Bluff

Less than a quarter of a mile from Pirate Place, US 19 runs along Pasco County's western edge, all the way from the Hernando County line in the north to the Pinellas County line in the south. Before reaching the county line to the south, however, drivers must cross Gulf Trace Boulevard. The corner of US 19 and Gulf Trace is fairly unassuming: there's no traffic signal, only a sign for the Key Vista subdivision and an always busy McDonald's mark the spot. A right turn onto Gulf Trace takes drivers through a fairly typical upper-middle class subdivision, with its houses painted the soft peaches, blues, and greens that one finds in many of Florida's planned communities. If, however, a driver has the patience to wind through two miles of these candy-colored houses, she'll reach Strauber Memorial Highway, the last road before the Gulf of Mexico. Driving Strauber Memorial Highway requires a great deal of concentration, though; the road is narrow with sharp curves and no shoulder.

Figure 4. One of many dangerous curves on Strauber Memorial Highway

If a driver ends up off the road, it'll take a tow truck, a winch, and a prayer to recover her car from the sandy marshes and mangroves that line the road. But hidden, past the most dangerous of the curves and the oldest of the mangroves, sits the most exclusive subdivision in the county: Bailey's Bluff.

Only 110 houses populate this stretch of Gulf-front land, and the price tag to join the exclusive neighborhood can be steep: the houses on the water range, according to the Pasco County Appraiser's Office, range from $1.1 million to just over three million dollars. Like much of Pasco County, this neighborhood isn't exactly what you'd expect. Across the street from multi-million-dollar beachfront estates sit houses appraised at less than $150,000.

Figure 5. A two-story, 2200 square foot home sits next to a much small home on the water in Bailey's Bluff

These residents though—both those who occupy the cavernous mansions and those who reside in the 1920s bungalows and the 1950s cinder-block houses—consider themselves part of the same neighborhood: they belong to the same neighborhood association, take their kids to the same parks and beaches, and attend the same neighborhood events.

Figure 6. Bailey's Bluff Beach, home of many of the Bailey's Bluff Civic Association Events

However, the incongruity that this picture suggests may offer a microcosmic sense of how residents of New Port Richey understand the identity of their town. The banal moments, the fish fries, civic association meetings, and city-council debates, tend not to pit the rich against the poor but rather represent a kind of plurality of experiences that may be unique in their simultaneity: all these lives, all these definitions of the town and its people coexist.

The history of Bailey's Bluff seems to reinforce this odd heterogeneity: long before it was home to wealthy financiers and other scions of Pasco County society, such as it is, Bailey's Bluff was among the most important locations for early sponging companies, one of the first and most long-standing industries to spring up on Florida's Gulf Coast. From before the Civil War until around 1912, when the first of the major sponging enterprises set up shop further south in Tarpon Springs, Bailey's Bluff was home to the thriving "Sponge Harbor" that was populated by small single family homes owned by local fishermen and, in its heyday, supported more than two hundred sponging vessels (Cannon).

After the loss of the sponging industry, however, Bailey's Bluff largely disappeared from the public consciousness. An April, 1956 *St. Petersburg Times* article notes that until the county paid to pave the 3.5 miles between the Bluff and US 19, Bailey's Bluff was mostly "a lost paradise" ("Lost Paradise Comes To Light In Bailey's Bluff Development"). Despite the supposed rediscovery in the mid-1950s, public utility service wasn't available on Bailey's Bluff as late as 1978 ("Tax Increase Protested at Bailey's Bluff Fish Fry"). In the decades that followed, however, more than seventy families moved onto the Bluff. Some razed older, smaller structures and built multi-storied, multi-acre estates while others preserved smaller homes more reminiscent of the Bluff's early history as a small fishing village. Today, the eclectic mix of homes still lives, and it's something residents are proud of. Linda, now twenty-six years old and living in Central Florida, grew up on Bailey's Bluff and says she wasn't aware of how strange the socio-economic range of her neighborhood would seem to those outside the community: "I didn't think it was that strange that our house was three times the size of our neighbor's house. My friends were my friends. We were a close community. It just was" (Kooperberg, personal interview). In other words, Kooperberg's experience growing up in Bailey's Bluff seems, to her and to other New Port Richey residents, eminently commonplace.

Bailey's Bluff is not notable, we would argue, because it represents a place of drastic socio-economic differences, nor do we position this description of Bailey's Bluff after Megan's narrative about growing up in Shamrock Heights in order to emphasize some sort of lack in either of these neighborhoods. Our goal, rather, is to note the physical proximity of these spaces (less than five miles separate the two, an approximately fifteen-minute drive), the richness of both places, and the similarity between the perceptions of those who grew up there. For both Linda and Megan, there is nothing all that strange about the neighborhoods in which they grew up, nor is there anything particularly strange about the fact they both attended the same elementary school. For these two women, as Linda says, "it just was."

Moon Lake

On the other end of the spectrum—both geographically and economically—sits the Moon Lake section of New Port Richey. Housing in Moon Lake is a mixture of homes, manufactured homes, and trailers. In 1979, when Sandy's mother found out she was pregnant, her parents purchased a plot of land in Moon Lake, upon which her father and his friends built the home that her parents still live in today. The street was dirt, as were the majority of the streets in the neighborhood, and featured large potholes surrounded by sugar sand. Her family's house was one of only seven houses on the street, with heavily wooded areas lying in between.

Figure 7. Sandy's childhood home in Moon Lake

The road was eventually paved in 1995, but many of the roads in Moon Lake remain unpaved. Later that same year, Sandy's parents purchased the house and property located next door to their home, which is where she lives today. With the exception of three months spent living in Ohio and three months spent living elsewhere in Pasco County, Sandy has lived on the same street in the same small neighborhood for her entire life.

> *I will always remember the night I realized, really realized, that my neighborhood was different from the neighborhoods around us. On a hot, sticky Friday evening in the summer of 1988, my mom and I*

got home slightly later than normal. My mother taught third grade at Moon Lake Elementary, which I also attended, and we usually came home immediately after school. I don't remember why we got home late, but I remember that it was after dark. My dad wasn't home, but he was only about a mile away at the local bar, The Boondocks.

Figure 8. Boondocks, Moon Lake's popular local bar

It was, and still is, the type of bar where everyone knew everyone else. Everyone had a nickname. My dad was one of several Bills that frequented the Boondocks, and since my father was a mechanic at my grandparents' Mobil gas station on US Highway 19, Moon Lake's residents knew my dad as "Mobil Bill." I remember listening to my mother call the bar that evening, asking the bartender to "Please just tell Mobil Bill to come home. Immediately."

As we drove slowly down our street (which was the only possible way you could navigate the gigantic potholes in the poorly maintained dirt road, especially in the Ford Mustang my father, a bonafide car enthusiast, insisted that my mother drive regardless of its impracticality), everything seemed normal. Until we were only about three potholes away from home (we didn't have any neighbors until 1990, so I can't provide the traditional "X houses down" description common in neighborhood narratives). My dog, a black Chow-Chow named Pokey, was wandering around in our front yard. "How did she get out of the house?" my mom muttered aloud. I thought, innocently, that my dad must have somehow let her slip past him on his way out. When my mom pulled the car into the driveway and we could see that the front door was open, I was still convinced my dad was the culprit. I was wrong.

After instructing me to remain in the car, my mom rushed inside to grab the cordless phone. Returning to the car, she telephoned my dad and then the police department. "We've been robbed," she told me. My mother reported the robbery to the police, telling them she was alone in the driveway with her young daughter and a dog. To her surprise, the officer on the telephone calmly informed my mother that they would not be able to come investigate our home this evening because the police department only came to Moon Lake after dark in the case of an emergency. He did, however, recommend that we try not to touch anything so that the officers that visited in the morning could try to get fingerprints.

After my dad received the message, came home, and searched the house, I was finally allowed to enter. While I still remember the way the house looked—completely ransacked, not a drawer left untouched, the thieves had even taken my pink, plastic piggy bank full of silver dollars—what I remember even more is the feeling of bewilderment I was confronted with. Why wouldn't the police come to our neighborhood after dark? Were they afraid? Should I be afraid? I was. I slept in my parents' bed that night, something I hadn't done in years.

Because Sandy was a child, and a fairly resilient one at that, she soon dismissed her feelings of fear. As she got older and experienced more of the world, her feelings of Moon Lake's uniqueness remained, though. Yet, rather than being a dangerous place, perhaps Moon Lake can be better conceptualized as misunderstood, a tangible representation of Curtis and Scheburger's descriptions of the "diversity" and "refugee" status of many Floridians. In fact, Moon Lake's stigma as a dangerous community lives on, allowing Moon Lake to develop in very different ways than other areas of New Port Richey, such as Shamrock Heights and Bailey's Bluff, described in the previous narratives. It is these differences that we intend to highlight here, in order to represent the uniqueness that can be found in the banality of small-town life.

Moon Lake is one of the many rural areas that exist in Pasco County. As with many rural areas, residents of Moon Lake are often stereotyped as "white trash." Rebel flags are flown proudly in yards, and residents commonly say that members of the Ku Klux Klan reside in Moon Lake. In fact, in 1993, these Ku Klux Klan members adopted an area of Lake Drive, the main road in the Moon Lake Community, as part of the Adopt-A-Road campaign (Fox), complete with a sign proclaiming "This area of road maintained by the Ku Klux Klan." The placement of the sign was so contentious that the story made it all the way to the *Baltimore Sun*, who reported that vandals destroyed the sign so often that the state eventually refused to continue replacing it (Pelton). Although the signage portraying the presence of the KKK is long gone, local lore indicates that the KKK's presence is still strong in Moon Lake. Evidence of this belief is prolific in Internet forums such as a 2004 Tampa Forum for residents of Pasco County, in which one user, 95civex, writes, "o shit . . . moon lake . . . isnt that like kkk capital of FL" [sic]. This sentiment is echoed in a Tampa Racing forum, in which user cha0tic indicates his concern about moving to Moon Lake because of rumors that "the KKK and White Supremacist[s]" live in the area.

Figure 9. Front view of a gated compound in the eastern portion of Moon Lake

Unfortunately, despite efforts on behalf of the community to revive Moon Lake's image, the negative stigma surrounding the community remains (Fox). Present day concerns about the safety of Moon Lake can be found in a 2011 online forum on the *City Data* website, in which a user, who self-identifies as a realtor, describes Moon Lake as follows, "Moon Lake, on the east side, makes *Deliverance* look like a Sunday Disney TV Movie of the Week . . . To say the KKK WAS active in Moon Lake is probably incorrect. They ARE active . . . it is a vicious cauldron of suburban gangs, meth labs, prostitutes, murderers and rapists." While comments like this one, though certainly hyperbolic, represent a certain truth about Moon Lake, what they don't reveal are the positive elements of the community. For example, Moon Lake Elementary is a seven-time winner of the Five Star School Award, which is given to schools that exhibited "exemplary community involvement" ("Moon Lake Elementary School"), and is an "A" school despite its Title I status, which indicates the largely impoverished status of many of its students. Additionally, construction on the Moon Lake Christian Fellowship Church, a nondenominational place of worship, was completed in 2010, thanks largely in part to community volunteers (Fox).

As with the other narratives we have provided, what we wish to highlight is not what Moon Lake lacks, but rather what Moon Lake has, and the ways in which the experiences of Moon Lake residents are both similar to and different from the experiences of other New Port Richey citizens. Although outsiders may view Moon Lake as an area of lawlessness, residents of the neighborhood appreciate the fact that Moon Lake offers the opportunities of a rural lifestyle within the city limits. While Moon Lake is located on the edge of the city of New Port Richey, its close proximity to pre-planned subdivisions such as River Ridge and the affluent neighborhood of Water's Edge, which is located directly across the road from the Boondock's Bar that marks the entrance to Moon Lake, makes apparent the importance of the assemblage. It is not uncommon for manual laborers to share drinks and conversation with surgeons at the Boondock's, as it attracts residents from Moon Lake, River Ridge, and Water's Edge. Again, it is this proximity of diverse experiences that we wish to attend to through a focus on the commonplace. We recognize that none of these experiences are unique on their own, but when viewed together as an assemblage, we believe that the presence of these varied experiences within the same small town is an interesting element of the assemblage.

Conclusion

New Port Richey, like much of Florida, is in a constant state of flux; the assemblage of people, communities, businesses, and environments that connect to form our conception of this place shift, and as they do, the place itself changes. Note, for example, the history of this place: once home to large Native American tribes, Florida was "discovered" by the Spanish in 1513; it was, during the Revolutionary War, the site of battles between the Spanish and the British and later between American revolutionaries and the British, and Florida was the third state to secede from the Union during the American Civil War. As people, places, and events act upon Florida, the assemblage shifts to accommodate some new participants and exclude others.

Each of the neighborhoods we describe in this chapter are (to borrow a term from Grant's discussion of Town 'n' Country later in this collection) seemingly "non-places" because, though each neighborhood is identified as New Port Richey by the post office and the census, each exists outside the posted limits of the city. We would, however, contrast the political non-place occupied by these neighborhoods with Grant's "non-place" of Town 'n' Country, with its "absence of a history, its relative emptiness, and the generic appeal" (228). New Port Richey is certainly full—full of history, full of people, and full of contradictions.

In his recent book on modern Florida, Florida historian Gary Mormino argued that "reinventing Florida is an enduring cottage industry. Shifting images and associations cast and recast Florida as a haven for the elderly, the fruit and winter vegetable basket for North America, a citadel and arsenal, and the crossroads for the Americas" (9). Like Mormino's description, we believe our three brief narratives offer a compelling look at one of the oddities of Florida's identity: the state is a mix of the bizarre and the commonplace; it is both peculiar and pedestrian—at the same time. The concurrent existence of New Port Richey's multiple, sometimes conflicting identities, then, is the strange feature revealed by our tracing.

Notes

1. For Latour, "trace" has two important senses: the verbal form of trace represents both Latour's goal and his methodology for achieving that goal; the noun form represents the artifact through which we are able to understand the connections forged in and by networks. In *Reassembling the Social*, Latour asserts that his project is an attempt to redefine the work of the social sciences "not as the 'science of the social,' but as the tracing of associations" (5). The way in which Latour seeks to accomplish this redefinition is by tracing (*v.*) the traces (*n.*) that the work of assembling leaves behind (*RS* 23). All members of a network, all those who are enrolled and those excluded, leave traces behind through which we can identify them (8).

2. We also note the value of the commonplace for ancient rhetorical theory, particularly Aristotle's discussion of *topoi* as foundational and vital components of communication.

3. We recognize that Latour often positions description/narration in opposition to explanation and analysis: "Either the networks that make possible a state of affairs are fully deployed—and then adding an explanation will be superfluous—or we 'add an explanation' stating that some other actor or factor should be taken into account, so that it is the description that should be extended one step further." (*Reassembling the Social* 137). Because of time and space constraints, however, we cannot deploy a 'complete' description of any of the situations narrated in this piece; therefore, we sometimes rely upon explanation and analysis to fill these gaps.

4. According to the 2010 census, Pasco is home to over 460,000 people, approximately fourteen thousand of which reside in New Port Richey or unincorporated sections of the county identified as the greater New Port Richey area; 88.2% of county residents self-identify as white and approximately eleven percent of the population self-identifies as Hispanic. Approximately ten percent of New Port Richey's population over twenty-five years old holds a college degree.

WORKS CITED

95Civex. "Hernando/Pasco People." *TampaForums.com*. 5 Dec. 2004. Web. 9 Jan 2013.

Anderson, Ben, and Colin McFarlane. "Assemblage and Geography." *Area* 43.2 (2011): 124–27 Print.

Cannon, Jeff. "Tracing the History of Bailey's Bluff." *New Port Richey Patch*. 2 Oct. 2011. 7 Nov. 2012. Print.

Cresswell, Tim. *Place: A Short Introduction*. Oxford: Blackwell Publishing, 2004. Print.

"Crime in New Port Richey, Florida." *City-Data*. Advameg Inc, n.d. Web. 10 Nov. 2012.

de Certeau, Michel. *The Practice of Everyday Life*. Berkeley. Trans. Steven F. Rendall. Berkley: U of California P, 2004. Print.

de Landa, Manuel. *A New Philosophy of Society: Assemblage Theory and Social Complexity*. London: Continuum, 2009. Print.

Deleuze, Gilles, and Félix Guattari. *A Thousand Plateaus: Capitalism and Schizophrenia*. London: Continuum, 2004. Print.

Ferran, Lee. "Casey Anthony Case Latest in Florida's History of Unusual News." *ABC News*.20 October, 2008 Web.

Florida Department of Children and Families. Executive Office of the Governor. *2008 Florida Youth Substance Abuse Survey: Pasco County Report*. n.p., 2008. Print.

Fox, Geoff. "Pasco's Moon Lake Community Tries to Shed Reputation." *The Pasco Tribune*. Tampa Bay Online, 14 May 2010. Web. 26 Nov. 2012.

Kooperberg, Linda. Personal Interview. 10 Nov. 2012.

Laliberté, Norman, and Alex Mogelon. *Collage, Montage, Assemblage: History and Contemporary Techniques*. New York: Van Nostrand Reinhold Co, 1971. Print.

Latour, Bruno. *Reassembling the Social: An Introduction to Actor Network Theory*. Oxford: Oxford UP, 2005. Print.

Latour, Bruno, and T. Hugh Crawford. "An Interview with Bruno Latour." *Configurations*. 1.2 (1993): 247. Print.

"Lost Paradise Comes To Light In Bailey's Bluff Development." *St. Petersburg Times*. History of Pasco County, Florida. http://www.fivay.org/baileys_bluff.html. 1 April 1956. Web. 9 Nov. 2012.

Mattson, Gary A. *Small Towns, Sprawl, and the Politics of Policy Choices: The Florida Experience*. Lanham, Maryland: UP of America, 2002. Print.

"Moon Lake Elementary School." *Pasco County Schools.* Pasco County School District, n.d. Web. 12 Jan 2013

Mormino, Gary R. "Sunbelt Dreams and Altered States: a Social and Cultural History of Florida, 1950–2000." *The Florida Historical Quarterly.* 81.1 (2002): 3–21. Print.

Pasco County Health Department. *Pasco County Community Health Profile 2010.* 3rd ed. 2010. Print.

"Pasco County Property Appraiser." *Pascogov.com.* Pasco County Property Appraiser, n.d. Web. 3 Nov. 2012

Pelton, Tom. "Klan's Effort Stirs Debate." *The Baltimore Sun.* 10 March 1999: Print.

US Department of Health. National Institutes of Health. "Prescription Drug Abuse." *National Institute on Drug Abuse.* Washington: GPO, 2011.Print.

SparklingWaves. "Waters Edge, New Port Richey, Fla." *City-Data.* Advameg Inc., 29 July 2011. Web. 7 Jan. 2013

"Tax Increase Protested at Bailey's Bluff Fish Fry." *St. Petersburg Times.* 17 Oct. 1978. (7). Print.

United States Census Bureau. *2010 Census.* Washington: GPO, 2010. Print.

7 Ferris Wheels, Concertos, Sidewalks and Sassy Tongues: Negotiating Racial Performances in the Capital City

Lillie Anne Brown

When the door is closed, you must learn to slide across the crack of the sill

—Yoruba proverb

As a child of the 1960s, I was very much aware of the open resistance to any kind of integrationist policies designed or established for the security, console, protection and uplift of people of color. The Jim Crow South was a time when wayward, unsuspecting glances and quiet whispers from innocent adults or children could trigger violent confrontations between the looked-at and the looked-down-on, a time when adherence to recognized social tenets was fervently enforced. Non-conformity to prescribed political mandates could be costly, and an already-tenuous relationship between black citizens and white citizens, often exacerbated by the slow progress of social policies, had the potential of volatile altercations between warring groups.

Offensively repulsive terms—spewed with a fierceness as combustible as explosives with timed wicks—often became catalysts for confrontations and physical conflicts, and for African Americans the psychological bruising could be long-term and more detrimental than physical disagreements had the capacity to become. In Tallahassee, the state's capital, the racial and political dynamics between blacks and whites were discomforting, intense and unyielding. Friendly alliances could be found among various groups, but location was more an exception than a rule. Work ethics, pride and dignity were, in many communities of color, distinguishing features that governed families and made survival possible. The same qualities that helped define family values and principles could also, however, be unwittingly compromised in an effort to remain emotionally assured, economically solvent, and possessed of the knowledge and appreciation of one's cultural pride and heritage.

Racial politics in the capital city, as in most southern towns during the era, dictated that black citizens and white citizens operate under distinct social, political, and institutional engagements, and while Tallahassee served as the state's principal arbiter of political change for other cities to emulate, its own terrain was a constant battle involving acceptable as well as unacceptable conduct among its citizens. As the city developed into a regional marketplace, national retailers began constructing commercial businesses across the city on open tracts of land as well as on established sites. While many stores in the city, like J. C. Penny and F. W. Woolworth's, operated in smaller commercial units on North Monroe Street, one of the city's main thoroughfares, the retail giant Sears & Roebuck was prominently anchored in a shopping plaza facing Apalachee Parkway, the street leading to the state capital building.

Smaller chain stores, including Lerner's, Thom McAn's, and Neisner's were also successful businesses operating in the plaza, but Sears, with its vast array of goods and services, enjoyed a greater patronage among citizens. Along with its prominence and success, however, were staunchly enforced markers of segregation: in-store signs prominently positioned on bathroom doors indicating separate facilities for black patrons and white patrons. The store's "Whites Only" sign, artistically crafted, perfectly centered, and securely affixed, contrasted greatly with the eye-level "Colored" sign and its hand-scripted declaration and haphazard attachment. Although I had seen the signs on previous visits to the store I also had never thought to "disobey" a sign.

Once, however, on an afternoon visit to the store with my mother, around age nine or ten, I ventured from her watchful gaze and boldly entered the whites-only facility. While the sign on the door was direct, I had witnessed white children my age enter the facility and exit the premises unscathed, and I wanted, out of curiosity more than necessity, to know what mysteries lie in wait behind the door and what forbidden reserves differentiated each facility. After entering and briefly looking around, I walked out in disappointment because of the near-sameness of the two rooms. My emergence, however, was met with a sense of pride from having literally taken a step into a forbidden arena. In my innocence, however, I had not thought beyond the consequences of my actions, nor had I concocted a tale for my presence had I been subjected to an inquiry by an unsuspecting patron when, just a few feet away, a sign stating "Colored" was clearly attached to "our" door. Even though the store's policies were visible for all patrons to see, my impromptu decision to breach a prohibited space without fear of retribution, not only taught me a powerful lesson in engaging the unfamiliar and owning the moment, it also taught me, in a small way, the power of taking risks and stepping out of safe and protected spaces.

There were, however, no unknown moments or risks when it came to the distribution of textbooks in segregated elementary schools across the district. Black students understood the process very well: Worn and outdated books would be routinely delivered from white elementary schools to students at black elementary schools at the beginning of every school year. At Southwest Elementary, the primary school I attended, classroom shelves sagged under the weight of hand-me-down textbooks and used supplies. Casual inspection of a book's multi-line issuance label would reveal a row of children's first and last names as well as dates spanning several years of a book's usage. Students' signatures, mostly written in pencil, revealed snippets of their identities, including nicknames; undecipherable drawings; and bold, cursive signatures extending into the label's narrow margin. My examination of signatures posed more questions than answers: Why did Southwest students consistently receive worn-out books from other schools and, more importantly, why weren't new books ever delivered? Who made the decision that Southwest's students would get old books all the time? At Southwest, used textbooks from Caroline Brevard Elementary, a white school, became our primary learning tools.

Named after Caroline Mays Brevard, one of Florida's most distinguished educators, historians and authors, the school contained a student population similar—and a grade level identical—to Southwest's. "Caroline Brevard Elementary School," stamped in black ink throughout the textbooks delivered to Southwest, appeared above and below books' inside labels, on preliminary pages, and inside back covers. Occasionally, penciled "cupid" drawings of the hearts and arrows kind claimed multiple pages of the textbooks. The creations seemed declaratory in nature, indicating that "new" users of the books should be aware that previous students shared a special bond not only between couples but with the book as well. *Even the drawings are old*, I remember thinking. While many students at Southwest frowned and privately complained about the book distributions, silent protests did not change the facts or the circumstances of disbursement. Teachers continued to teach, students continued to excel, and academic objectives continued to be met throughout the year. Numerous school activities across the district were held annually, and as a participant in school-sponsored and district-wide spelling competitions over the years, I enjoyed the academic camaraderie and was oblivious to the school board's polities that mandated racial separatism among contestants. Elementary schools in the district were not, however, the only institutions affected by segregation in the capital city.

Young adults across the city marched in peaceful protest of the city's two segregated movie theaters, the State and the Florida, and downtown businesses, including McCrory's and other stores, where services were discriminatory against blacks. While the Leon Theater, Tallahassee's only movie house for black patrons, served as a kind of cultural babysitter for children and adults on Saturday nights, the city's lone public swimming pool for blacks, the Robinson-Trueblood Swimming Pool, unwittingly became a catalyst for change in the city's policies on integration of public facilities. Located in the historic Frenchtown Community, Robinson-Trueblood represented part of the movement by black citizens to end racial discrimination in the capital city. During the 1950s and 1960s, Frenchtown was seen by many black residents as the cultural hub of the city's black community.

Located northwest of downtown Tallahassee, its most well-known address, Macomb Street, runs through the heart of the community. During Frenchtown's zenith, businesses boomed and entrepreneurs flourished. Small restaurants blared music from jukeboxes and patrons of the community enjoyed an atmosphere of communal affection. Jazz musicians, including Ray Charles, an Albany, Georgia native whose family moved to Greenville, Florida when Charles was an infant, and brothers Nathaniel "Nat" Adderly and Julian "Cannonball" Adderly, Tampa natives who moved to Tallahassee with their parents, performed at the celebrated Red Bird Café. The Lawyer Smith Band, a group of talented African-American jazz musicians, engaged their craft at various venues in the community.

Figure 1. Protesting in front of the McCory's Store, 1960, State Archives of Florida

The Leon Theater, the city's movie house for black film-goers, claimed a small space among a handful of storefront businesses within walking distance of Macomb Street's main district. The theater was a safe and reliable entertainment site for generations of African-American children and adults who were prohibited from attending the city's two all-white movie houses, the State and the Florida theaters. At the Leon Theater, movie posters heralding films starring Sidney Poitier, Dorothy Dandridge and Harry Belafonte dotted the theater's small, dark lobby. "The Imitation of Life," an all-time favorite starring Juanita Moore, appealed to adults *and* children due to its dramatic story of mother-daughter estrangement and issues of colorism. Very few movie-goers left the theater dry-eyed after viewing the emotional wreckage between the two on-screen stars.

On any given day in the Frenchtown community—but especially on Friday and Saturday nights—the aroma of food wafting from restaurants seized the taste buds of visitors and residents of the district. Respectful camaraderie governed the region and residents served as watchful observers of occupants as well as businesses. Schools, churches, hair salons, barber shops, shoe repair businesses, and independent stores provided a space where community and kinship not only thrived but blossomed. Once an oasis of talent and cultural bearings, the district declined over the years, forcing the closure of several businesses and leaving the artistic sanctuary a shell of its former self.

During one brutally hot summer in the mid-60s, a few brave souls from the Frenchtown community tested the racial waters of the city's segregated recreational facilities by invading upon a revered turf: a whites-only swimming pool located in a community populated by white residents. While Frenchtown had its "own" pool, the Robinson-Trueblood facility, news of the "dark invasion" traveled swiftly throughout the city. Hysteria ensued among frightened and perplexed white parents, stunned swimmers, and city officials, furthering a frenzy among residents of a racially divided city. A post-swim inquiry of the incident by city officials prompted the immediate closing of each of the city's facilities and children across the city, black and white, would, as a result, suffer mightily during the remaining summer days following the Big Splash.

A number of black families, including my own, made weekend treks to St. Andrews State Park in Panama City, some one hundred miles west of the capital city, where a portion of the beach had been designated the "colored beach" for patronage by African-Americans. While black patrons at the St. Andrews State Park would most likely have had no objections to non-black swimmers invading "their" waters, strictly enforced legalities prohibited black swimmers and white swimmers from intermingling in others' waters.

At the Robinson-Trueblood facility, only the architecturally bare essentials were part of its structural design, and on any given summer day the facility almost always exceeded its capacity. Comprised of a small circular swimming pool for young children, a larger one for older swimmers and a building for showering, Robinson-Trueblood was intended to serve an entire city of black families. As a popular site for teenagers and young adults, it almost always served an overflow gathering during the summer's hottest months. Patrons dismissed its shortcomings, however, proudly taking pleasure in its presence as an iconic institution. It is where countless black children and adults learned to swim. It was also the only public facility in the city where black residents were allowed to train as lifeguards.

The pool's closing, however, spoke louder than the exploits of the young swimmers who dared take a chance. Following public outcry from black parents and local activists regarding city officials' decision to close each of the city's public swimming pools, the no-integration policy was eventually amended, allowing black children access to whites-only pools. Even though the policy was all-inviting, white patrons did not embrace the city's new policy. As a result, the city's all-black recreational facility remained in its previous state.

While whites-only facilities in the city flourished and enjoyed periodic upgrades, Robinson-Trueblood suffered through years of neglect and decay, eventually paving the way for its temporary closure. For many black residents, in particular those who lived in the Frenchtown community, the closure spoke volumes about the city's non-embrace of its most disenfranchised citizens. Its subsequent re-opening many years later, coupled with periodic summertime reunions of community members who were part of the its golden era, however, allows it to now serve as a stately keepsake and symbol of one community's pledge to maintain an institution. As one of Frenchtown's landmarks, Robinson-Trueblood now serves a new generation of children whose resolve affirms their forbearers' struggles. As one communal icon in the capital city struggled to remain afloat, however, another custom festered in its own tradition.

During the last week in October in the capital city in the 1960s, the annual North Florida Fair (NFF), a traveling carnival, came—as it currently does—to the city amid the jubilance of school children and older festival-goers. Assembled over several days on an expansive tract of land on the southern region of town, its set-up elicited excitement throughout the city. School children took note of the impending festival by saving weekly allowances, selling seasonal fruit and nuts to small, independent stores and vendors and performing chores for local residents all in anticipation of spending fun-filled days at the fair. The carnival's opening day—and subsequent days of operation—was a bonafide commercial draw for the city, for no other event promised such an economic boost as much as the NFF. Visitors traveled from adjoining states and surrounding communities to engage the festivities, and while the carnival may not have been the most cultured affair the city offered residents and guests, it was by far the city's most anticipated public event. Radio spots heralded its coming, colorful flyers dotted the landscape and city and conversations among schoolchildren centered upon the impending festivities.

On the afternoon of the first day of the five-day affair, a city-sponsored parade served as the carnival's base, providing as much excitement as the principal event. In the time-honored tradition of small-town parades, floats with young women in striking pastel-colored gowns, dancers and acrobats in sequined attire, marching bands with high-stepping majorettes, trucks and automobiles decorated with multi-colored streamers and banners identifying occupants and organizations and businesses dominated the parade. Over a nearly three-mile stretch, attendees of all ages lined portions of North Monroe Street, the procession's main boulevard, in anticipation of an afternoon of wholesome family fun.

Figure 2. Historic Frenchtown, photo by the author

The relentless interaction between parade participants and observers helped cement the atmosphere of the long-anticipated occasion as children eagerly awaited the arrival of the parade's "candy tossers," riders in mini carts who flung sweet treats far and wide for onlookers to retrieve. While the approach of mini cars was a predictable highlight eliciting certain behaviors from attendees young and old, the candy-tossing became, for me, yet another prohibitive occurrence, likening itself to similar—and familiar—restrictions imposed upon me by persons and institutions of authority. The forbidden this time, however, became the personal: my mother's stern, facial reproach at the outset of our first attendance of the annual affair. In an instant her piercing gaze barred me from sprinting into the street in retrieval of any treat hurled from festively-dressed drivers in mini cars.

As equal numbers of black children, white children, and adults scampered into the streets, I stood quietly on the curb, seething because I was prohibited from engaging, in what I determined to be, a small highlight of the parade. In the moment of my discontent, however, I understood the larger lessons of her upbraid, and I accepted them without resentment: You will not exhibit such unbecoming behavior for the price of a token indulgence literally hurled to you in public; you do not have to endorse that which is offered simply because it is propositioned; you must not compromise your standards because you are witness to others who do not share your knowledge of public decorum. Her own upbringing, informed by lessons in grace and deportment, helped dictate her approach to social and public decorum, and she was determined that I would follow suit no matter the occasion or the circumstances.

Two aspects of the parade, however, proclaimed the most divergent visual of the yearly event, giving prominence to dissimilar entities operating under the auspices of a single processional: the positional arrangement of marching bands and majorettes from black high schools and junior high schools in the city as well as the situational line-up of accompanying units comprised of African Americans. Situated last in the parade, all-black organizations, single corps, and marching bands from the county's all-black schools were positioned in the most conspicuous place in the line-up of parade participants: at the rear of the "show," animal; that is, behind the slow-walking horses and their respective riders. Horses, the organizers' unspoken rules proclaimed, deserved positional distinction more than talented students and musicians of color, and while "parade sweepers" were efficient, resourceful, and capable, their proficiency did not counteract the positional arrangement of the all-black units. Neither did it lessen the declaration such arrangements conveyed to the viewing public.

Despite their last-place assignment, the all-black units and marching bands provided stellar performances, eliciting cheers and applause from onlookers and parade enthusiasts. African-American parade-goers, supportive of the bands, organizations, and pedestrian units, remained to cheer on the participants despite the absence of many white attendees who had long since departed. The parade's most prominent all-black band, from Old Lincoln High School, performed exceptionally well for a grateful constituency, and while the marching band played standard parade marches by European composers throughout the performance, it also entertained the crowd with popular musical selections of the day, including songs by James Brown, the Temptations, and the Four Tops. The Old Lincoln High School band brought the distinctive sounds of Motown to the streets of Tallahassee, and while their position in the parade was questionable, their performances were a combination of pride and perfection. In-school performances by the band, including musical selections played at pep rallies, assemblies, and special occasions were well received by faculty, staff, and students throughout the academic year.

Figure 3. Old Lincoln High School, 1960, State Archives of Florida

Located two blocks west of the Governor's Mansion in Historic Frenchtown, Old Lincoln High School carried a proud tradition of academic, artistic, and athletic excellence. Opened in 1869, during the period of Reconstruction, it became the county's first public high school for African-American students. Recognized as an historical site by the Historic Preservation Society of Florida Heritage Foundation, it graduated its last class in 1967, following full integration of the county's public schools. Because it traditionally received students from the all-black Nims and Griffin junior high schools, its closure devastated the hopes of a new generation of students who had dreams of attending and graduating from one of the county's most venerable public institutions.

In 1974, however, a new high school was built and assigned the name "Lincoln." Many residents in the city believed the designation was an effort to appease black citizens who felt the closing of the original Lincoln was racially motivated due to re-districting policies which would affect white children living in proximity of the Governor's Mansion. The new Lincoln's location, structure, and student population, however, did not reflect the historical legacy of the original institution. In an attempt, therefore, to sustain the identity of the original school from the newly constructed establishment, the designation of "Old" was assigned to the original Lincoln.

With Old Lincoln's closing, the bulk of the remaining students were dispersed to newly-integrated high schools in the county, including James S. Rickards High School, which graduated its first fully-integrated class in 1968. While school integration was a new engagement for students across the district, affected students—explicitly, black children—were expected to adhere to the mandatory policy without benefit of in-school discussion groups, intercessional colloquiums, or advisory sessions. If such assemblies occurred, they were conducted primarily in the privacy of students' homes by parents of the children who would be making the transition from neighborhood schools to institutions located several miles from their homes and communities. As much as community leaders could, they tried to prepare students for "the change." Pastors and religious leaders at local churches centered many Sunday morning sermons upon the racial changes taking place in Tallahassee, the South, and communities across the nation. Change, however, did not preclude custom, and positional lineups in the North Florida Fair's annual parade were repeat conventions.

As all-black units from local schools entertained parade enthusiasts with exceptional music, showmanship, pride, and confidence, their positional assignments—obvious, unmistakable, and calculated—did not overshadow the skills and talents of the bands' directors and assistants. Nattily attired in crisp, tailored uniforms, they orchestrated their respective corps with diligence and pride. Though the units performed flawlessly and were enthusiastically received by remaining parade attendees, the positional arrangements proclaimed them "borrowers"—not title-holders—of the space in which they participated: Full residency, the arrangements declared, belonged to participants who annually shepherded the procession.

Elements of the secondary treatment of African-American parade participants in the capital city extended, unfortunately, to the school district's policy of "designated days" for black schoolchildren and white schoolchildren in the public schools who wished to attend the North Florida Fair during a specific school day: Black children and white children were forbidden from attending the fair on the same school day as an authorized policy implemented by the local school board. On Wednesdays of the week of the carnival, African-American children were dismissed from school at high noon to attend the fair; on Thursdays, white students were similarly dismissed from their respective schools. Even though teachers at the all-black schools still performed their instructional duties accordingly on the day of the dismissal, the focus of many students' conversations centered upon the early release. At Southwest Elementary, administrators adhered to the district's policy of designated days as a matter of social, political, and academic policy.

While I was certainly cognizant of the school system's racial policies of "designated days," I still anticipated joining a throng of friends and festival-goers in anticipation of the big event. Cursory discussions of the policies, intermittently exchanged between students and teachers leading up to the noontime dismissal, often resulted in resigned acquiescence. "Designated days" not only enforced the board's policy on segregation, it also produced a racial dichotomy all its own: Following the closing of all county schools during regular operating hours, black citizens and white citizens could mingle at the fair without designation, directive or adherence to school board policies.

While a number of black children in the district refused to participate in the NFF's activities in protest of the school district's policies, others elected to take part in the festivities despite the rulings that had shaped the event for years. Carnival workers at the North Florida Fair embraced a dissimilar agenda, choosing instead to focus the nucleus of the annual enterprise upon all things economic. When the county's assigned carnival days were eliminated circa 1964, following the Supreme Court's school desegregation ruling, the elimination was seen by many citizens in the city as a small movement toward making a community whole. The North Florida Fair's moniker, "the fair," always seemed oxymoronic: "Designated days" was discriminatory treatment of the county's most disenfranchised and vulnerable citizens. "The Un-Fair" seemed a more apposite term, not only for those who elected to participate in—or disengage—the event, but also for those who recognized racial issues in the city larger than the North Florida Fair but felt powerless to change them.

The Jim Crow South was a period of political angst and deliberate, unconscionable behavior, and television images of snarling dogs; hosed-down protesters; and pictures of brave black children walking amid vitriolic, jeering crowds of racist men, women, and children were strong and powerful visuals of an intolerant South. As I watched television reports and read the *Tallahassee Democrat*, the capital city's evening newspaper, I became increasingly alarmed by the brutishness of men and women whose sole agenda appeared to be the physical, emotional, and psychological destruction of people who looked like me. Though I was greatly disturbed by the images, I followed news of the civil rights struggle intently, hoping for a more defined understanding of the turmoil as well as a desire to know in what ways I, even at such a young age, could help alleviate the crisis. I was quite idealistic.

On my journey of understanding, I began an examination of social and political performances occurring within my own family and my responses to those performances within the context of southern racial politics. Although my working-class parents were not publicly engaged in the city's political movements, they were socially conscientious and encouraged their three school-aged children to become knowledgeable of social and political events occurring in the city and beyond. As products of a segregated South, as well as having witnessed racial events during their childhoods, they knew and understood the importance of tackling social injustices head-on and wanted their children to know and understand the history of African Americans' struggles, former and current. Toward this aim of fostering an understanding of social, economic and political issues in the lives of their children, themes of social and political consciousness as well as discussions of upward mobility permeated the discourse in our home.

In our small, blacks-only community, a horseshoe-shaped enclave dubbed "The Drive," parents had, as did parents in communities across the nation, noble aspirations for their children. Academic excellence and membership in certain institutions and social exchanges were important engagements for many children, and full participation in outside cooperatives was a fundamental expectation of children who lived in "The Drive." Towards the goal of cultural assimilation and a future of artistic appreciation, my parents enrolled me, the youngest of three children, in piano performance classes at a very young age. As a culturally edifying enterprise for young black girls of the era, piano-playing, specifically complex musical arrangements by master composers, was an artistic pursuit outweighing larger musical collectives and associated interests: Individual talent communicated initiative, independence, creativeness and a certain awareness of broader cultural expressions.

While young boys in the enclave joined various organizations in schools and in the city with a focus upon manhood, responsibility, and accountability, many parents of young black girls who wished for a more refined presentation of their young daughters were of the notion that piano-playing presented an open window of opportunity to a world of social assimilation and future advancement. Lessons in grace, deportment, and "carriage" were the defining imports that "learning the piano" would bring. From my earlier restrictions surrounding the county's North Florida Fair's parade, I knew that my mother's teachings on grace and deportment could be utilized in such an environment of social propriety.

My perspective, at the time of my enrollment in piano performance classes, was theoretically centered: (1) If one could, in the future, appreciate a renowned pianist's highly acclaimed repertoire, then the cost of the music lessons will have been worth the family's economic sacrifices and (2) Many African-American parents found it essential to prepare their children (mostly their young daughters) to be (and become) socially acceptable in "polite" company and to become part of a growing middle class of young African-American adults whose interests and talents were mutually inclusive. If these two objectives could be met, then a principal role of African-American parenting will have been achieved. "Other" communities might direct their young daughters and sons in alternative passages, but piano-playing black girls were, in many respects, representatives of social grace and imminent acclaim. Therefore, on Tuesdays and Fridays after school, for nearly eight years, I attended piano performance classes taught by an African-American husband-and-wife duo whose strict regimen of at-home practice sessions was a signature of their teachings. While each instructor possessed formal musical training, students' advanced lessons were the domain of the more experienced instructor whose primary occupation permitted evenings-only teaching. Children from prominent and working-class families from across the city assembled on various days throughout the week for individual lessons in theory, application, and related training. While most children at the institute got along well and became friends, subtle class divisions were clearly evident in personal relationships being established among students as well as in pedagogical approaches engaged by the instructors. As a quiet but keen observer of the social dynamics between the teachers and students, I learned early on that the economics of class and the hue of one's skin—though all of the students were black—were factors that often determined one's treatment and level of instruction by the team-teaching duo.

At the institute, a student's skin tone appeared, to me, to take root in the instructors' approach to teaching and their interaction with students: The lighter a student's skin, I observed on numerous occasions, the more accommodating and favorable a student-performer's treatment by the instructors. I recognized that quite often a student's economic background, irrespective of talent or skill, helped determined the level and complexity of the instruction. While I did not understand the social politics of colorism, my premise centered upon a hue-conjecture regarding the female instructor's nearly-white appearance and her preferential treatment of students who mirrored her appearance. My contention sustained my tenure at the school. While questions of the instructor's "true ethnicity" governed students' private conversations, her ability to "pass for white," *if she wanted to,* centered the debate.

If a student, in my observation, was dark-skinned and came from a lower socio-economic class, the instructional duo's temperament was none too pleasant. In such instances musical compositions had to be of the highest performance to be the recipient of a compliment. I was a student performer caught in the middle: While my economic background was working-class, my skin was light, so even during twice-a-week sessions when my performances were not stellar I was given a temporary pass, rarely incurring the instructors' wrath and displeasure as many of my darker-skinned classmates did. I recognized the unfairness of it all and aligned the treatment to the school district's North Florida Fair school district's policy, with a nod toward an old, African-American adage: "If you're white, you're alright; if you're brown, stick around; if you're black, get back." In the eyes of the instructors, their behaviors told me, I was safe, and no harm or harshness would befall me: I was a cut between being "alright" and being able to "stick around."

While some students at the academy might have been unaware of issues of intra-racism, the instructors failed, in my perspective, to conceal their positions and preferences, operating instead under the guise of stellar musical performances by their students. As I witnessed the game of colorism being played, I began to grasp issues of race and class that not only confronted young children, but also critical matters that defined and contributed to behaviors in adults. In the circumstances of the light-skinned/dark-skinned dichotomy at the music school, however, the staff operated without shame or concern of students' internalization of the treatment or its attendant consequences. I never voiced my observation, but internally I felt compassion for the students who, through no fault of their own, were treated unkindly by adults who knew the power of their authority.

For the duration of my attendance at the school, I practiced the instrument without much prompting and performed annually in venues around the city alongside other students whose parents sat quietly, but proud, in the audience of black parents. My mother was almost always the sole attendee from our family, owning primarily to my father's work schedule and my siblings' disinterest in the annual productions. As student-performers' musical repertoire advanced, compositions became more complicated. As I performed formal and complex musical compositions by Beethoven, Chopin, and Mozart at formal sites around the city, my brother, a saxophonist with the Old Lincoln High School band, was engaging a different musical genre.

In addition to playing in the high school band, he was also part of the "Intruders," an all-male jazz performance group which played at school functions and small local venues around town. While reception to my musical talents was commendable by family and friends, the public reaction to the jazz-playing group of young African-American musicians was more embracing. In contrast to the formal compositions by my fellow student pianists, the jazz group's repertoire was more culturally-influenced, containing arrangements by members of the group as well as compositions by well-known

African-American jazzmen, including John Coltrane, Lee Morgan, Duke Ellington, William "Count" Basie, and others. The dissimilarities between the classical piano structures and jazz compositions were as distinct as the North Florida Fair's "first" units and its positional units.

The *Intruder*s, whose name mirrored a 60s soul music group from Philadelphia, also featured female dancers and singers whose voices echoed contemporary urban sounds heard on radios, in dance halls, and at private parties. Because the revue's base location was Old Lincoln, the group enjoyed a reputation throughout the Frenchtown community as serious high school musicians. Throughout their partnership, enthusiasts acknowledged the troupe by supporting their performances throughout the city and requesting their presence at appointed functions. During the period of my musical performances, however, I became acutely aware that two distinct objectives claimed the basis of my enrollment in the music academy.

While both my parents wished for me to learn the instrument, making tremendous monetary sacrifices toward the lessons, their eventual purchase of a piano represented the ultimate financial sacrifice: With such an acquisition, I could practice without going outside the family home. The new piano made an imposing figure in the living room of our Elberta Drive home: a literal testament of the creative and artistic possibilities that awaited a little black girl in the segregated South. My enrollment in piano classes was, for my mother, her aspiration for me to become part of a larger social network, while my father's desires, though not articulated during my years at the academy, partly centered upon my "playing for the church." Although their objectives and purposes, driven by independent aims, were both honorable, the nucleus was identical: They wished for me to engage a larger presence outside the immediate community and to become part of an upwardly mobile class during an era when—not because—segregation was the law of the land.

Their desires, born of a tradition that children must "do better" than the generation before them, meant—in part—that "playing the piano," whether at recital halls in the city or churches throughout the community, was not only a statement of empowerment and class aspirations, it was also a personal declaration that social movement was an attainable goal. Although they were products of the rural South, my father's large family trumped my mother's single-child family and helped shape his worldview, political, and social perspectives.

A quiet, disciplined man who served a segregated military during World War II, he became, after attending vocational school in Tallahassee upon his honorable discharge from the United States Army, a well-respected house painter in the city with a large clientele that included black customers and white customers. A native of Campbellton, a rural community sixteen miles north of Marianna, in Jackson County, Florida, he and my mother (a native of Jackson County) purchased a home in Tallahassee via his military veteran benefits. As the third oldest of twelve children (and the eldest son), he was held to a higher level of responsibility on the family farm than his younger siblings, and in acquiescing to the demands of a strict father he learned principles of respect, discipline and self-sufficiency.

Although he rarely speaks of his military experiences, given an opportunity he recounts tidbits of events that articulate the horrors, overseas and stateside, of segregation. Memories of his WWII experiences, exacerbated by racial occurrences as a young man in rural Jackson County, remain quietly tucked away, resting just below the surface of the turbulence of the mid-1940s. Family gatherings occasionally elicit small recollections of his military tour of duty in the military, but rarely do talks move beyond perfunctory conversations. Generous prodding, often at the appeal of family members, seldom extends the discourse. Part of his silence can be obligated to his character; his work ethics command the solitude as well.

As a young boy on the family's expansive acreage, he was charged with tasks beyond his physical capabilities, including the handling of over-sized plows and other equipment used for maintenance of the farm. The psychological challenge of knowing that primary duties of the farm most often fell to the most senior male child in the family was a daunting task. Carefree afternoons rarely found their way to the homestead, for domestic duties and obligations had to be carried out efficiently as well as timely to ensure the most economically profitable results. Exhaustive work governed the day and copious restrictions normalized the nights on the farm. My father, who processed his limitations within the family's hierarchy, internalized the restraints, carrying them beyond the family farm into a marital life of discipline, resolution, and hard work.

His success as an independent painter largely depended upon the satisfaction of customers who then recommended his services to others. Owing to the legacy of an authoritarian father, his work ethics as well as his principles of perfectionism became a recognized trait allowing him the provision of steady work throughout the city. With a young family to support, he worked tirelessly—and without complaint—in an effort to sustain a level of economic stability, and the dividends from his (and my mother's) work ethics resulted in a comfortable home environment for a family of five. Prior to his employment in the same capacity at one of the city's academic institutions, his work as a painter was noted and his reputation as an honest and reliable worker was well known throughout the capital city.

During the span of his years as an independent businessman he would receive calls from white clients (usually male) seeking his services. The calls would generally come late in the afternoon, and I would usually be the first person to take the calls. As a young girl gaining associations outside my immediate family community, I eagerly anticipated the ringing of phones in our home, in expectation of personal calls from prospective friends. Most often, however, the calls were for my father, which, for me, upon answering the phone, resulted in an edgy exchange between me and the caller due, not only to my father's unavailability but also to my ritual retort:

"Is Frank there?" the caller would ask in a distinct, southern drawl.

"Frank? Frank, *who?*"

"Frank . . . Frank," the caller would repeat, a bit more prominently, with an obvious tone of irritation.

"Who?" I'd ask, with equal significance. "Who is it that you'd like to speak with?"

"Frank," the caller would say, annoyingly, a third time. "Is Frank there?"

"*Mr. Gray* is not at home," I would reply with a distinct emphasis on both title and name. "If you'd like you may leave a message for *Mr. Gray,*" I would finally offer.

When I answered the phone, white callers who addressed my father by his first name would often appear taken aback by the impromptu inquisition and, I presume, by the fact that the voice on the other end was that of a young girl who dared to speak with such impudence.

The informal requests for my father were offensive to me, and I was determined to wage a youth battle to rectify the injustice. How disheartened I would be, near the end of the exchange, however, to learn that my lessons in etiquette and deportment had not been received. I regarded the exchanges with the callers as safeguarding the integrity of my parents' home by lending my voice to a noble cause: the preservation, honor, and dignity of a proud and respected man, his home, family, and profession. In address of my father by his first name, white callers' sense of privilege, entitlement, and dismissal were in stark contrast to calls made by African-American clients who asked for "Mr. Gray." Their request, accented by the decorum of a title, spoke, to me, of a kinship born of a cultural sameness. In my youthful reckoning, my father's African-American clients understood the weight and significance of respectability politics.

Once, upon delivery of a message to my father, I lamented my displeasure of white callers' disrespect and the paradox of my parents' teachings regarding the address of adults by title and surname. His response, quietly and calmly delivered, was unexpected and disappointing, for in my naiveté I was of the notion that he would honor my exasperation, buttress my distress, and make note of it to future callers. "I make my living as a painter," he said, following my anguished declaration, "and if people call and ask for me by my first name, it is not something that you need to be worried about. Painting is what I do. When people call, just take the message." With that unruffled mandate, he turned and resumed his activity and future references on the subject of first-name phone requests, perceived indignations, and interrogations became a mute topic. Over the years, the phone scenarios repeated themselves, but I voiced no opposition to my father, opting instead to heed his instructions while also acknowledging that no lessons in etiquette had been delivered from him to the callers.

In the moment of his response to me, however, I began to understand the social and economic politics of his journey from the rural countryside of Campbellton to his experiences in a segregated military and, finally, to his work as a painter. Economics, I came to realize, trumped *my* vision of perceived slights and *his* response to those perceptions: If white callers were greeted, in the midst of employment offers, with interrogations, formalities, and offensives—especially from little black girls—business opportunities and contractual enterprises would end without notice or a regain of the enterprise. In the face of personal and public injustices, perceived or otherwise, silent acquiescence was, if not a "safe" route, then most certainly it should be a carefully modulated one.

A deeply-rooted Southerner, he knew the power of conciliation and had learned to navigate the political and social landscape that confronted him on a daily basis. His experiences growing up in the rural South presented an agenda larger than one child's idealized response to how one should be addressed. His words, "I make my living as a painter," equalized his presence in the workforce and affirmed his position as a provider for his family. He understood the harshness and brutal realities of the segregated South, but he also recognized that one must sometimes ignore indignities in order to move forward. For many men of his generation, economic survival became the agency over real or imagined indignities and humiliations.

His calm and reserved temperament, in the midst of tempestuously delicate situations, not only helped shape his response to racial conflicts waged on Southern soil but on foreign territory as well. He moved subtly, with a survivor's instinct, between discomfort and endurance, surrendering at times but also acknowledging conflicts that demanded his interference or injection into the fray. In the midst of the battles, however, he held his own in—and during—times and situations which may have toppled a lesser man.

The capital city of Florida was, like many southern cities in the 1960s, immersed in the conflict of a changing South. Institutions fostering racial separation, from schools to movie theaters to businesses to public facilities, maintained strongholds throughout the city, operating profoundly and prominently under the "separate but equal" doctrine. During the 1960s, racial tensions gripped the city, sometimes quietly, other times piercingly, and citizens working in unison to bring about social and political change beneficial to the community were sometimes met with defiance. Downtown Tallahassee was infused in protest marches, and places of worship, including Fountain Chapel AME Church as well as churches in the Frenchtown Community, served as headquarters for civil rights protest meetings. Community leaders and committed citizens, young and old, strategized about ways in which racial equality could be achieved and social activism could be peacefully engaged. As students at Florida A&M University claimed their rightful places on sidewalks and at lunch counters in peaceful protest of racial discrimination, organized demonstrators continued to maintain a powerful presence in locales across the city.

As the city's segregationist's policies slowly began to shift and integration policies were implemented, verbal tensions between black students and white students occurred with frequency in newly-integrated public schools. Following the assassination of the Reverend Martin Luther King, Jr., in 1968, the capital city was saturated in fear, anxiety, and racial discord. School assignments grew out of the racial tensions and minute incidents large and small expanded into larger episodes as anxieties and apprehensions increased. King's death—and the reactions to it—became the common denominator among disenfranchised citizens mired in the economic, social, and political vulnerabilities of the time. Steeped in racial volatility, Tallahassee sweltered in raw, unvarnished anxieties, soothed slowly and eventually by respectful dialogue and calls for peace by citizens who understood the urgency and assented to work for social and political change.

While the city's movement from all things separate and unequal began in measured cadences, its position as the state's public mirror could be ascribed as the foundation of the city's political occurrences. As the phase-out of "appointed days" was met with the elimination of whites-only recreational facilities, inferior academic tools, positional line-ups, and segregated public schools, political shifts occurring across the city rested primarily upon the continued advocacy of citizens in the implementation of policies dictated by a changing South. While larger and more socially progressive cities across the nation were not immune to issues of racial discord, class divisions, and respectability politics, Tallahassee's evolution was, as were many southern towns, cautious, guarded, and systematic. As the South began a slow walk toward justice, peace, reconciliation, and equality, so, too, did Florida's capital city.

8 Sort of on the Grid: An Eccentric Map of Growing Up Jewish in the Miami Suburbs, c. 1975–85

Steve Newman

10333 SW 120ᵀᴴ Street, Miami, FL, or, Positively 124ᵀᴴ Street

Figure 1: S. W. 120th Street today: Relatively unchanged since the 1970s

Florida shows us that a grid is never merely a grid, and I say this having grown up in a very rectilinear corner of the Sunshine State, the Miami suburb called Kendall. When we moved to 10333 SW 120th street shortly after I was born in 1970—the numbers indicating just how far we were from the ordinal center of Miami, the intersection of Miami Avenue and Flagler Street—there were tomato fields surrounding the house, or so I was told. Before that, according to one of the few histories of Dade County, the area known as Kendall "was slow to develop as no homesteads were available," though there were plenty of "panther and rattlesnakes" and as late as World War II a Seminole Indian village not far from my house (Taylor 39–40). This surprises me, since when I was a kid we had to head pretty far west to see Native Americans, into the still-extant Everglades proper to visit the tatty Miccosukee Indian Village where they wove baskets and wrestled alligators for small clumps of tourists and school kids. There were dairies and fruit-tree groves in Kendall, though they could be planted only after dynamite softened up the unyielding limestone left by a recently retreating sea. But Kendall didn't stay undeveloped for long, and by my childhood, the tomato fields had been replaced by more houses as suburbia kept creeping west and south. There were, of course, streets that did not adhere strictly to the grid. Dixie Highway (US 1) carved its serpentine path all the way down to the Keys, and there were the grace notes of various developments, cul-de-sacs and the like, just as their names confidently spoke of lakes and chases and runs as if they had been made by glaciers rather than excavators. (Our development was Pine Acres, which at least had some truth in advertising; identical half-acre lots with a couple of loblolly pines in most yards.)

So, like Sean Morey's Key West, my neighborhood was built on the bones of limestone. But it had little else in terms of bone structure, either geological or cultural; no coastline, no sprinkling of islands, no wrecks of pirate ships, no Papa Hemingway, and not much recorded history. Yet, with little to stop the grid as it spread toward the Everglades, Kendall was at once sharp and fuzzy, a function of the horizontality David Grant unpacks in the Tampa suburb of Town 'n' Country. In Kendall, you always knew where you were by the numbers, but you weren't sure what that where was in relationship to any other geography and surely didn't know what that where meant. That took time and attention, and in what follows I'm going to spend a bit of both on my under-storied neighborhood before going further afield and then heading to the mythical heart of Jewish South Florida, Miami Beach, among other places. Many contributors to this volume draw on the fertile work of Michel de Certeau, and his "spatial stories" (Rice) and "commonplaces" (Branham and McIntyre) certainly figure into the essay that follows, which does not pretend or want to offer a totalizing picture of Jewish South Florida in the seventies and eighties. Rather, it essays, it attempts to gather and re-frame a series of personal traversals across spaces shared by others (school, synagogue, or the office of the Mayor of Miami Beach) and structured by ideas of class, religion, and masculinity. It will, I hope, lead to a knowing nod among those familiar with this time and place or analogous ones or to pleasurable surprise to those unfamiliar.

Where I begin is at home, amidst the "[n]umbered streets and street numbers . . . [that] orient the magnetic field of trajectories just as they can haunt dreams" (de Certeau 104). Since my neighborhood lacked the strong proper names that ground the itineraries of de Certeau's walkers, it put more pressure on its dwellers to actualize their own paths through the grid. As Pierre Mayol puts it in the less-cited volume two of *The Practice of Everyday Life*, the neighborhood, grounded in the primal space of the home, is "a signature attesting to an origin, the neighborhood is inscribed in the history of a subject like the mark of an indelible belonging inasmuch as it is the primary configuration, the archetype of every process of appropriation of space as a place for everyday public life" (12). It is also a primary space where the need for recognition from the other outside the family along with the charged moments and conflicts that emerge from that need.

For me, SW 124th Street was a dividing line between two types of Jews, Jews from middle-class families like mine, and wealthier Jews that my friends and I, Jews and Gentiles alike, referred to by that ugly acronym—JAPs, Jewish American Princes and Princesses. For all the kids I knew, Jewishness was not primarily a religious identity, though we loosely observed Bar and Bat Mitzvahs and the High Holy Days as set forth by the Reform or Conservative synagogue we belonged to (and some didn't belong to a synagogue). Being Jewish was about spiting Hitler by supporting Israel and having a successful career (usually the father, but often enough the mother, too). Out of that striving came the material success and concern for status, bodily appearance and resultant envy/disgust that informed the tag "JAP," and, as Riv-Ellen Prell notes in her valuable study of the stereotype, it was no accident that the term emerged just as Jewish women were entering into the professions in record numbers (203). JAP was more often applied to girls but not exclusively so, and when used to stigmatize boys, it was to tag them as spoiled, "easily threatened [and] weak" (Prell 194). Of course, this phenomenon was not limited to suburban South Florida, but I would argue that it was more intense there. For one, its historical thinness meant less weight given to the traditional structures, Jewish and otherwise, that would have restrained the habitus of JAPpery. Miami invited self-invention, one of the "golden cities" along with LA, the "clean, spacious, open, horizontal places" that allowed Jews "to start anew" (Moore 3). For another, Miami was a place of the body not the mind (Whitfield 85–6), and this fed into the investment in adornment and physical beauty that led to more than a few nose jobs among the Jewish girls I knew.

Figure 2: The house next door to Eric's, close to identical.

Back to the neighborhood for a more concrete example of what I mean: Toward the end of fifth grade, I followed my best friend Eric Sonnenschein home from school, heading south rather than north from Leewood Elementary on 124th Street. (*N. B.* All names have been changed except for family members.) I had a plan; my plan was to kick his ass. He had been my best friend since first grade, but something had changed since he had moved to a striking modernist house of concrete, jagged angles and soaring interior spaces (and a pool!) that had been built just south of 124th Street, next to a Jewish dentist's house, his daughters at the zenith of JAPhood, his DeLorean parked out front (last time I checked, it was still there). Eric suddenly started caring a-bout what shirts people wore (Izod was the standard), what jeans (Jordache) and what shoes (Adidas). He started hanging around with JAPs we had hated before and suddenly started laughing at their inside jokes. He didn't sit with me at our normal table at lunch, and I was obviously not welcome at the table he now sat at. In the Gifted program, he worked with his new friends on logic games.

Eric was clearly in line for a beating. I circled around him and took up a position in the shadow of some Australian pines, my stomach awash in that sick feeling you get when you think you're going to get in a fight. I think

Eric saw me but pretended not to, though he did quicken his pace a bit. As he turned on 105th Avenue, I sprung out and told him what I was going to do and why. He raised his hands to protect his face and yelled, "If you hit me, my dad will sue you for assault and battery! He'll sue you and your whole family!" This made me pause. I knew his dad, Stan, was a lawyer. He must know the law. Could my family and I be sued if I hit him? Would we be fined? Go to jail? As I was puzzling this out, Eric ran past me; he was always a quick runner, and he had gotten even faster after reading a book that instructed him to keep his arms low and to his sides. (He had also trained himself to set the fifth grade record for the high jump, in part, by reading a book on the Fosbury Flop.) I was too disgusted to try and catch him as he disappeared down his long driveway and into the lush, subtropical landscaping around that damned house. We reconciled not too long after, and he remains one of my best friends; when I called him recently to see if my memory of this incident was accurate, he added that his father actually had consulted with a friend in the DA's office to see if charges could be filed for assault.

Expanding the Grid and Tough Jews at the Shabbos Table: Uniontown/Ann Arbor/Bogota

Looking to punch somebody in the face, especially your best friend, just because he snubbed you might not seem like something a nice Jewish boy would do. And I was a nice Jewish boy; a couple years later, I would even have a plaque to prove it, declaring me the winner of Temple Israel's "What Being Jewish Means to Me" Essay Contest. But I had been raised by my dad to respond to certain provocations with your fists. He grew up in the Western Pennsylvania coal town of Uniontown and the steel-mill and glass-mill town of Washington, his family having emigrated in the early 1900s from the shtetls of Hungary and the Pale of Settlement (no German-Jewish airs or rabbinical lineage that I know of). When I was a kid, Dad would occasionally refer to the fights he had with the "Hunkies" (a slur for Christian East European immigrants) when they called him and his friends dirty Jew or the like. My dad's pugnacity wasn't just a function of growing up Jewish in a small town. It also had a lot to do with *his* father, my Grandpa Lester, who looms large in the family mythology. While a traveling salesman, he spent a couple nights in jail for thrashing a man who owed him money for a sale and greeted Lester by trying to brain him with a two-by-four. Grandpa Lester certainly knew how to use his fists; a light heavyweight, he had great success boxing around Pennsylvania, Ohio, and West Virginia. Before that, he won a football scholarship to the University of Michigan, where he played right guard before being kicked out. There are lots of tales why that happened—

failing classes, or caught in flagrante with a coed in the bushes or unwittingly selling Communist newspapers, etc. There are also lots of stories of his strength and volcanic temper, among them his throwing a fully-set Shabbat table through the dining-room window because of his anger at my grandma's disappointment at his late arrival. He was what you would call a tough Jew, though not a Tough Jew in Rich Cohen's sense of the word—not a gangster. When my dad was in grade school he told Lester about being called "a goddamned Jew" by a high- school kid at the local store; Lester tore out of the house with my father close behind, fearful that his dad would destroy the kid. But all Lester did was rip him verbally.

I loved hearing stories about Grandpa Lester, but I never met him—he died of a heart attack years before I was born from smoking two packs of Lucky Strikes a day and from the stress of a coming IRS audit. He passed on to me through my dad a hot temper, though not, I'm sorry to say, any of his athletic skills. As he was taught by his father, Dad taught me and my older brother Keith that if someone really insulted you, and especially if you thought they were going to hit you or if they *ever* insulted our mom, we should "hit first, hit fast, hit hard, and hit repeatedly." Since my dad was and remains my model in so many things, I took this advice to heart along with a tetchiness at exactly the sort of JAPpiness Eric was guilty of. My dad's family wasn't wealthy; Grandpa Lester was a butcher and then a not very successful traveling salesman. My dad played some football in high school, too, though he wasn't a star, and he and his brother Art were in a gang called The Shifters (think *American Graffiti*), though they weren't into stealing cars or knife fights. My dad was revolted by anything approaching ostentation, especially from fellow Jews, since that somehow reflected poorly on us.

From this rough-and-tumble description, you might think that my dad grew up to be a stevedore or a pipe-fitter. Nope: English Professor. We got to Miami by way of graduate school at Ann Arbor; my dad helped to pay his way through school by working summers on a road crew swinging a sixteen pound sledge, and working at Kroger's. Early on, he abandoned the goal of medical school shared by so many Jews of his age; that his parents did not squawk about it points to the fact that Jews of their background were just proud to have a son in college and that a certain dream of refinement mattered to them. He wrote his dissertation on manners in Jane Austen and joined the faculty of the University of Miami where he spent his entire career. We would have never thought of living near the campus in Coral Gables, one of the toniest and WASPiest sections of South Florida. Even setting aside the expense, the housing brochures sent to my dad made it clear that our kind wasn't welcome. Here are two choice passages my dad remembers: "The owner's investment is protected by an invisible system of checks and balances," which sounds an awful lot like redlining. And then this dog whistle, in the key of Those Ostentatious Jews: "Families in the Gables have a new car in the front of his house and a boat in the back, but neither is mink-lined or gold-plated." Of course, a mink-lined, gold-plated boat wouldn't have been acceptable to us either, but that was no excuse for a brochure that discriminated against and didn't discriminate among Jews.

On the surface, then, my dad wasn't all that different from Eric's, who had gone to Harvard for his B.A. and J.D. But while our dads were both Jewish professionals, a story Eric recently reminded me of indicates how they differed profoundly. When we were about six, sitting in the multi-story tree house in his pre-south-of-124th street backyard, he bragged that his dad earned something like fifty thousand dollars (about two hundred thousand dollars today) and I told him mine earned something like forty thousand dollars. A couple of days later my dad commanded me to inform Eric that his salary was actually a fraction of that. The difference was as much about where our dads ended up as how they came up. By immersing himself in Jane Austen and the rest of the canon, my dad had vaulted right past new money and into a disgust with it. He had no truck with Jews who spent lavishly on cars, clothes, and vacations to Aspen, calling them in in a rare recourse to Yiddish rumbling contemptuously from deep in his throat, *"grubber yung"*— that is, crude. Nor did he have patience either for the old money snobbishness behind those Coral Gables brochures. At Ann Arbor, he was a member of Students for a Democratic Society, though he had dropped out of SDS before they morphed into the Weathermen and started blowing things up, and his radicalism had mellowed into an ardent liberalism. Jeff Rice's chapter reminds me that Muhammad Ali was based down in Miami in the 60s; he was a hero in our house as much for his politics and his verbal and pugilistic brilliance.

Though they did live in a much nicer house and though Eric's dad did drive a Datsun 280ZX, our two dads were actually pretty close politically. It was just that their postures toward the world did not mesh. Where my dad was raised and raised us to fight, Eric's passed on his pacifism. Where he pushed Eric to win academic prizes, my dad and mom told me that what mattered was what I learned and what I loved, But however much books were treasured in our house, my dad and brother would have snorted at the idea of reading one to learn how to run or jump, the sort of over-cerebral Jewish behavior that led to the stereotype of Jewish boys and men as soft geeks. I remember one time at a Y-Indian Guide meeting—we were the Menominees; I don't recall any Miccosukees making their way into this Native American fantasia—when Eric's dad and another Jewish dad said they had fulfilled the requirements for the hiking bead by walking around Dadeland, the gargantuan mall that was one of our few landmarks. My Dad shook his head in disbelief as the other fathers shook theirs in disgust, perhaps thinking that there was a good reason for that "C" in YMCA. I wanted to disappear. Looking back on it, though, I think that these two dads knew full well that this was not the kind of hike they were expected to take, but they were unapologetic about who they were. And they were as good as any paddling a canoe.

This mismatch between my dad's cultivation and Miami's gaudiness was heightened by its lack of high culture: It was not until the mid-1980s that it had a highly-regarded symphony or ballet; few visited the thin art collections in its sprinkling of museums and galleries (no Art Basel back then); the Art Deco renaissance didn't happen until the late-1980s and that was as much about beautiful people as architecture; and the University of Miami itself had a reputation, fairly or not, as a place for wealthy kids who couldn't get into better schools. I don't remember any mention of a literary scene, and I had no idea that Isaac Bashevis Singer lived part of the year in the Miami Beach shtetl of Surfside, even though he was the author of *When Shlemiel Went to Warsaw*, a book of Jewish children's stories I had loved for my mom to read to me. My parents often groused about the unwillingness of Miamians, Jews and Christians alike, to contribute money to high cultural institutions. Again, Miami was a city of the body, not the mind; everybody who headed to the beach saw that famous Coppertone billboard on Biscayne Boulevard of a little pigtailed girl getting her bathing shorts pulled down by a little black dog: "Tan, Don't Burn!"

I got caught up in this body-centered world, too, and the line separating Tough Jew and the body-conscious JAP isn't easy for me to draw in retrospect. Following my older brother, who teased me when I was ten for being chubby, I began lifting weights on our patio early in my teens. To the concerned puzzlement of friends like Eric competing for the highest class ranking, I took a non-honors class, weight training, all through high school. I became fixated on bench-pressing three hundred pounds, so much so that Eric and Tammy (a more serious fixation who would later briefly become my fiancée before she wised up) took out an ad in the school paper senior year, declaring me the only member of the 299½ Pound Club. I was tempted but never resorted to steroids. The back acne and hair loss that afflicted some of the guys in our grimy high school weight room or strutting on the beach freaked me out, as did their mood swings. Too slow to play running back or wide receiver and too small to play any other position in football (our high school team had a sprinkling of Jews way more athletic than I was) and too uncoordinated to have ever made a go of soccer (lots of Jews there), I joined the wrestling team. I wasn't much of a wrestler—too defense-minded, to my coach's dismay, as well as slow—but I was one of only two Jews on the squad, which made me feel like I was keeping up the Newman tradition of Jewish toughness.

So this is all to say that when I confronted Eric at the corner of 124th Street and 105th Avenue, that time and place had been shaped by Uniontown in the 1940s and 1950s and Ann Arbor in the 1960s. But suburban South Florida had its own way of bending light. It allowed for cutting loose from old ways and embracing a more hedonic existence. On the other hand, its open spaces also served as a screen for projecting memories of its immigrants' places of origin. Far out in the southwestern suburbs, there seemed to be even less to push against, as if the landscape were a transparency that let the past bleed through only slightly refracted, displaced Yankee fans and anti-Castro Cubans all the more rabid in subtropical exile, Jews from New York and Philly all the more Jewish in some ways.

My Miami was shaped by two other spaces, one quite far from the grid of South Florida, and one very much within it. One was Colombia, the other our Shabbos dinner table, and what linked them together was my mom. The first was a place of voluntary self-exile that altered the shape of my home: She was born in Bogota, and she brought to our family the Shabbos rituals that were not part of my dad's experience. If my dad faced anti-Semitism in Western Pennsylvania, you would be right to figure that it was worse in Colombia in the forties and fifties. She recalls being with her father one day when he was called a dirty Pole and told that if he were kicked out of the country he'd have no place to go. You had to be particularly careful around Easter because of the blood libel; no sane Jew would venture out without tucking away the Star of David or any other sign. Her brother, Idel, was forced out of the company he worked for when the management found out he was a Jew. He later immigrated to Israel, and I remember that when he called, my mom would talk to him in a mix of Spanish, English, and Yiddish that would echo through the house. She immigrated to the US at sixteen, arriving in Pittsburgh in 1960 to stay with her Aunt Miriam and Uncle Lazar, not knowing a word of English.

My mom's dark features make her look Latin American to some people, but I have the round face and lighter skin of my paternal grandmother (the Lisowitzes) and was born with blond hair and blue eyes to boot. "My little shaygitz" she used to call me and kiss me. I was 30 before I learned that *shaygitz* was the male equivalent of *shiksa*, but there was no sense of anything but affection when she used the term on me. My un-Semitic and un-Hispanic looks meant kids would say things around me that they might not normally. But I heard way more anti-Hispanic slurs than anti-Semitic ones growing up; I can remember only one instance of the latter, when a friend spoke of somebody bargaining for a baseball card as "Jewing him down." I slugged him in the arm and told him I didn't want to hear that again. But I heard "spic" frequently enough, especially in the wake of the Mariel Boatlift of 1980, in part because nobody ever suspected my mom was Colombian. I didn't really identify with Hispanic culture, and I didn't have close relatives there except for my crotchety grandfather who didn't even come for my brother's Bar Mitzvah or mine. Still, my liberal Jewish upbringing and my limitless capacity for indignation moved me to lash back at anyone who talked trash about Hispanics.

Tolerating and accepting others, excluding JAPs, was a frequent topic around our Shabbos table. Dad often reminded us that "you were strangers once in the land of Egypt" is the most frequent verse in the Torah. But Judaism in our house was about *tikkun olam* (repairing the world), an ethics rather than a theology. It was about a reverence for books and learning even if the Torah was not our central text. And it was about a way of carrying yourself, proud of all our successes, as if we had some special claim on Einstein. and ashamed if anyone Jewish ever got caught doing anything wrong (Meyer Lansky; Ivan Boesky). My dad found the idea of The Chosen People repugnant, but distinguishing ourselves from Gentiles was important. Hanukkah bushes were a no-go, and my mom was not pleased when our elementary school had us sing Christmas Carols at the school assembly.

On Shabbat, my dad would often put a folk album on the turntable; the song I remember best was "Tumbalalaika" by Malka and Joso, a duo from Canada. We would eat in the dining room rather than the kitchen; the sight of my mom gathering her hands to cover her eyes to *bentsch licht* would quiet my brother, dad, and me, and the Shabbat candles would play off the strands of hexagonal crystals that dangled from the chandelier. My dad would lead *kiddush,* the small silver kiddush cup that I now use high in his hand, and then we'd distribute pieces of the raisin challah. My childhood was punctuated with my dad's frustrations that this or that bakery couldn't ever remember his standing order. He gave Winn-Dixie a bunch of chances but they just couldn't get it right; but what would you expect from a store with "Dixie" in the name? He finally settled on Publix, which usually came through, though if they didn't we would hear about it as he made a joke of re-enacting his exasperation. I can't think of another Jew I knew in Kendall who observed Shabbat even in this minimal way.

Grandma's Places: Eastern Shores, 3423 NE 167ᵀᴴ St, North Miami Beach

There was another house that anchored my Jewish South Florida—my grandmother's house in North Miami Beach. It was in a neighborhood called

Eastern Shores; in the 1950s a developer transformed a mangrove into a series of vertebrae surrounded by water:

Figure 3. Aerial photo of Eastern Shores: From http//www.buysouthflorida.com/eastern-shores-miami.php; permission granted by Scott Patterson, P.A.

She lived there from when I was about 5 to 13, a sprawling ranch with a screened-in pool, and even grander homes around it, many with yachts tied up beside them. I loved that house, from the *japonisme* of the pieces in the foyer to the silver wallpaper in the guest bathroom imprinted with vintage cars; I loved the living room best, with its thick white shag and a big piece of lucite on a coffee table encasing a violet sea fan and orange coral. (It sounds like her interior designer was kin to Todd Taylor's in Tampa.) Grandma Jean had moved to South Florida in the mid-1960s after Grandpa Lester's death to work as a secretary in an investment office headed by the son-in-law of her sister Sally who had come down with her husband Saul to open a fruit and florist's shop on Biscayne Boulevard. Although Grandma lived on Miami Beach and she overflowed with love for her grandchildren, *bubbe* wasn't the right word for her. That was more Aunt Sally's line; her chicken soup and mundel bread were to die for, and she was the sweetest soul anybody ever met. Grandma Jean had little time for *haymishe* touches. She was a force of nature enhanced with a platinum blond wig and false eyelashes, beautiful on the *zaftig* side—the wig gave her a Marilyn Monroe look—smart, sharp-tongued, and brassy. She worked for some years as a social worker, which may not sound like much to some, but it was a job that normally required a Master's degree. She had gotten the position with only a high-school education thanks to a sympathetic boss and a sterling performance on the civil service exam. She was very proud that her two boys were doctors, even though not of the medical kind; my Uncle Art had a doctorate in education and taught at the University of Florida for forty years. But her frequent mentions of the brief professional development course she took as a parole officer at the University of Pennsylvania made me believe that she ached about what she could have been had she been born decades later.

By the time she moved into the house on North Miami Beach, she had been widowed twice more, and she was now living with a man I called Uncle Murray. Murray was a tall, handsome, well-tanned man in his late fifties who favored button-down shirts that showed off his ample, whitening chest hair, with a Star of David on a gold chain nestled in the middle of it. It was his house: He had made his fortune as the inventor of a photographic process that became the standard in industrial design. He had an autodidact's energy and insecurity; I always remember that he would ask me how to spell words like "idiosyncrasy." Hyperverbal the way faculty brats often are, I usually got it right. For a correct answer, he gave me a quarter or sometimes a half-dollar or even a silver dollar. With an inventor's love for gadgets, he was one of the first people to buy the home version of the primitive video game Pong, another point in his favor. So he was just fine in my book, although my parents found him a bit, shall we say, *grubber yung*.

Along with her grandchildren, Grandma loved many things—Scrabble, paste jewelry (which my daughter now plays with), and dashing men. But perhaps what she loved most was throwing parties. My mom was not a fan of these gatherings, and my father dreaded their too-muchness. The crowd was mostly Jews in their fifties and sixties, the accents tending toward Brooklyn and the volume toward very loud. I remember men in white shoes and white belts and plaid jackets and bejewelled women in bright dresses. Some of them sported furs in the Miami "winter." At some point during the party, they would gather around the double-decker organ that my grandma played not all that well; "Those Were the Days My Friends" was a favorite, and many would sing along. The menu was largely Jewish; my favorite appetizer was her sweet and sour meatballs. Dinner was often brisket or, better, lamb with mint jelly. Lots of mint jelly in my case. I would sit at the table, where Grandma presided, and try to make out what I could of the adults' conversation, which often turned to politics. Grandma was a liberal Democrat to the bone; she loved to tell of riding with Jack Kennedy and Jackie from the Pittsburgh airport to an event in Washington, PA. Jack was charming, but she thought Jackie, wise to her husband's philandering ways, was giving her the fish eye. At her dinner table, I would occasionally hear someone speak of *schwartzes*, but she would smack down anybody who said that word; I had been raised to do the same. Israel and its marvels was a favored topic: Grandma was a regional president of Hadassah, the Women's Zionist Organization of America. As for marrying Jewish, it was clear that this was expected, but it was complicated by her brother Bobby having married my Aunt Del. Like everyone else in the family, I loved Aunt Del, so much so that I swore to myself that I was not going to let religion get in the way of loving or even marrying someone. I did end up living out that credo both in my first, failed engagement and in a second one that to my great good fortune has worked out, though my wife converted after our marriage.

Grandma's Places: City Hall/Millionaire's Row: 1700 Convention Center Dr/5555 Collins Ave

When I was around ten, Murray and my grandma broke up; she kept the house. After that, she began working in the office of the Mayor of Miami Beach, ascending to the post of personal secretary to Alex Daoud, the first Catholic mayor of Miami Beach, whose unprecedented three-term winning streak was cut short by a conviction for bribery. I loved visiting her in the looming concrete bunker of the new City Hall, where upon seeing us she would put down the phone and spring up from her huge desk of blonde wood, call all of us by name ("*Ste*-ven!") and embrace us. She quit City Hall once she met her fourth husband, Bob, a lovely gentleman of the old school who had founded a company that supplied cold storage for hospitals and industry. She moved into his apartment at 5555 Collins Avenue, on Millionaire's Row. It was during this time that she started taking us to The Forge, a ritzy restaurant on Arthur Godfrey Road with a famously extravagant wine list. During one of our meals, we were told by a waiter that The Eagles had eaten there the week before and ordered a five thousand dollar bottle of wine. The Eagles! After Bob's death, she began serving as a sort of unofficial rabbi for her condo; she led weekly services for her elderly neighbors, many of them too infirm or just uninspired to go to a local shul. Still later, she moved to a retirement community not far from my parents' house rightly called The Palace, a luxurious place with a nice mix of well-off Jewish and Hispanic seniors (and some Hispanic Jews, I imagine). She remained a danger to any woman with a boyfriend and to any man or woman who said a bad word about Israel.

Bar Mitzvah Boy, Temple Israel: 137 NE 19th St, Miami, FL

Figure 4. My bar mitzvah, 1983, Gumenick Chapel, Temple Israel

I wasn't yet friends with the editor of this volume, so none of the Jewish kids I knew went to our synagogue, Temple Israel. They went instead to big Reform shuls in Kendall: Beth Am or Bet Breira, which my parents wanted no part of because of their flashiness and *big macher* syndrome. Although Temple Israel had a featureless Kendall branch that we often attended, the main synagogue was in Miami proper, in a hard-bitten area boxed in to the east and west by I-95 and Biscayne Bay and to the north and south by the two arteries to the beaches, the Julia Tuttle and MacArthur Causeways. Temple Israel was on the northern edge of Overtown, one of the sites of the Miami Riots of 1980 that erupted upon the acquittal of the policemen who beat Arthur McDuffie to death after stopping him for speeding and driving with a suspended license. Jeff Rice ties his memories of the riots to the bigotry facing both African Americans and Jews in Miami. My experience of it rhymes with his: I dimly recall a haze of images on the local and national news of rocks being thrown through windows and cars being overturned and set ablaze and angry masses of black folks. Although the riots were close to our shul, although my friends whispered and joked about it, and although my parents were outraged at the cops' acquittal, it seemed like it was happening in a very different Miami, but one my parents wanted to make sure that we knew existed. Our drives to Temple Israel exposed me to the first time to the homeless, huddling under overpasses, and although the neighborhood now boasts an emerging art district, it still has its share of thrift stores, missions, and homeless shelters.

Along with its lack of pretension, Temple Israel's keen political consciousness attracted my parents. The rabbi was Joseph Narot, nationally known for his outspoken stands for Civil Rights and against the Vietnam War. As for ritual, he was committed to the purest form of Reform. Kipot and tallit smacked of superstition and were rarely seen in Temple Israel. I'm sad to say that I can't remember a thing about Rabbi Narot beyond a vague memory of him up on the bema at the Miami Beach Convention Center, which is where we had to have High Holy Day Services because Temple Israel's 1800 families, the most in any synagogue south of New York, could not fit into the downtown worship spaces. More vivid was Cantor Jacob Bornstein, a short man with a face as round as a grape and a booming bass that could split wood; he was quick with a smile and a hug. What also lingers is the sound of the choir in the balcony and the organ belting out tunes that I now know had as much in common with the Protestant Church than the indigenous music of European Jewry. I sat at Yom Kippur services in my uncomfortable tie, buoyed by my ability to follow along in Hebrew in *The Gates of Repentance* even as the service droned on, my restlessness exacerbated by a day of fasting, which I was also proud to suffer. To pass the time, my brother and I would spot silly hats or go up to the balcony where there were an increasing number of empty seats on Yom Kippur between the Torah reading and Yizkor, or I would push down the various tabs marking donations to Israel Bonds on the envelope stuck into our *siddurim*.

We weren't involved in the life of the synagogue; my parents have never been joiners and would much rather spend their time with each other, their kids, and a few select friends. But my brother and I did, of course, go to Hebrew School, and we did, of course, get bar mitzvahed. My bar mitzvah service was in the Gumenick Chapel, a flowing, irregular shape of liquid concrete sprayed onto a steel skeleton, its exterior is marked by bulging "sculptural windows," as the architect called them, made of epoxy and cast glass, which turns the bright light of Miami into blue, red, and purple in the interior. The bema had an enormous copper menorah and its ark was carved out of the root of a lignum vitae tree, topped by two flame-like wisps of copper that reach toward the roof. In a history of Temple Israel published just a couple years later, the author struggles to find language for this radical structure, which moved those less impressed to label it "a big stone igloo with holes chopped in it" and "Joe's Cave": "The chapel certainly personifies the experiment in Reform Judaism which the congregation is sometimes called" (Tebeau 78–79). Of course, I didn't know anything about this even as an intellectually precocious thirteen-year-old, but I do remember feeling proud that my synagogue was more interesting than the safe, gilded spaces where my friends went. I stood at the bema in my navy blue suit, paisley tie, and perfectly feathered hair chanting my Torah and Haftorah portions and trying to avoid eye contact with my brother, who was trying to make me laugh as I did to him five years earlier. The Torah portion told of Korach, who dared to challenge Moses' leadership; for his trouble he was swallowed up by the earth along with all his family and 250 of his sympathizers were consumed by fire. Lines, the Torah reminds us again and again, must be drawn.

Dueling Receptions: 350 Ocean Drive, Key Biscayne vs. 10333 SW 120th Street

My reception re-drew those lines. Although I still detested many of the Jews south of 124th, I now had a fair number of friends who lived there, too. They typically had their receptions at the Sonesta Beach Resort across the Rickenbacker Causeway on ritzy Key Biscayne, where Nixon had his Florida White House and where his good friend Bebe Rebozo lived. Themes for *b'nai mitzvah* sprang up just as I was heading toward mine. Eric's was Apple computers; his father had bought him one of the earliest Apple II's, and we spent many hours revenging ourselves on the Nazis by shooting them in *Castle Wolfenstein*. Scott Fiedler's theme was rockets. Sam Moskowitz's was preppies; *The Official Preppy Handbook* had come out in 1980, and like many other Jewish teens he seemed to miss the mockery in it. Although the themes varied, the basic shape did not. Guests were greeted with a life-size cut-out of the bar mitzvah boy or bat mitzvah girl, which we covered with signatures and witty remarks like "Stay cool!" or "You really screwed up the Haftorah!" Then hors d'oeuvres and an open bar, where we always hoped for a lax bartender but were usually reduced to drinking what was left of others' beer and wine. Awaiting us in the main room was a DJ or a live band cranking out dance music and lots of cheesy patter. Many of the boys, including me, were awkward and also shorter than most of the girls, so we stayed on the sidelines and made fun of the boys who did dance to Kool and the Gang's "Celebration," Air Supply's "The One That You Love," and The J. Geils Band's "Centerfold," which in retrospect doesn't seem all that appropriate even for a Miami Bar Mitzvah. But we did all join in "Shout," which was popular thanks to *Animal House*; all you really had to do was jump around and then wriggle on the floor—a big Jewish mosh pit. At some time later in the reception, the mother and father would come up to the background music of "Sunrise Sunset"—*Fiddler on the Roof* marked the limits of our knowledge about the *shtetl*—and lay on the schmaltz. This was our cue to head to the dessert bar, where we would fill our mouths with whip cream straight from the can. Then, hopped up on sugar, we would play various obnoxious games in the reception hall or out in the lobby until a member of the staff would come down on us.

My reception was different. It was on our patio. A string trio played classical and folk music. The food was provided by my mom, Grandma, and Aunt Sally, who spent the thirty-six hours prior preparing 120 Chicken Kievs and other dishes. There was dessert—my mom did give in and order a cake—but no cans of whipped cream to suck down.

Figure 5: My Bar Mitzvah reception

Most of my friends were cool with it, but some grumbled, and there was one South-of-124ther, Scott Waranch, who got pretty snarky. When someone told me what he said—I forget what exactly—I managed to rough him up a bit until some friends pulled me off him. After everyone left, my close friend Greg, who lived at the end of 120th street and who was not Jewish, said, "Well, Steve, you're a man now. I guess we should get drunk." I agreed and went to my brother and asked him what sort of alcohol didn't taste bad. Vodka, he said. So I snuck the bottle away from the still-open bar on the patio, and Greg and I downed very large glasses of it, managing not to wretch. The next thing I remember is staggering down the sidewalk of 120th street with Greg, helping him to get back to his house at the end of the block and suddenly lying down sidewise in the parking strip between the Blatstein's house and the road, watching the houses spin. I managed to make it back home where I was very, very sick—another rite of passage. I can remember my Uncle Arthur laughing at me from the sofa and the grim look on my Mom's face. She forgave me once I fessed up. Afterwards, I complained to my brother that the vodka tasted awful; turns out he thought I was asking about what alcohol wouldn't give you away by stinking up your breath.

The Road to Excess and Hypothetical Grids: Kennedy Park, 2400 S. Bayshore Drive

A few weeks later, my brother and his friend Dave gave me a late Bar Mitzvah gift by getting me stoned on a brilliant April day under a sea-grape tree in Coconut Grove. I took a few hits, which were followed by fits of coughing, followed by the best iced lemonade I will ever have, followed by a ludic bike ride that had me giggling crazily during the wobbly twelve miles home through the fringes of Matheson Hammock, mesmerized by the aerial roots of the banyan trees on Old Cutler Road dangling like frozen ropes and by the grand old homes and McMansions of Coral Gables and Pinecrest, but also quaking at the suddenly-much-louder cars passing by and at the possibility that my parents would spot my blood-shot eyes and pot breath, as Keith and Dave told me they surely would. They didn't, thank G-d.

The ride home pointed toward where I was headed post-Bar Mitzvah. No more Hebrew School, and while I continued observing Shabbat in my family's way and going to High Holy Day services, that was the extent of my organized Jewish life. Many of my nights were spent drinking lots of cheap beer after Scott Waranch—we were cool again after he admitted he had been a dick at my bar mitzvah—found a twenty-two-year-old's driver's license, which was enough for the indifferent clerk at the closest convenience store. Miami was literally awash in pot then, and I partook with the stoners I started hanging out with in eighth grade; an acquaintance of mine named Jim used to make trips out to the mangroves south of the city to recover "square groupers," stray bits of bales dumped by dealers being pursued by the Coast Guard. Coke was also around, though it was too expensive for me and most of my set and anyway the high and the long-term effects scared me; a girl named Bridgette seemed to bleach away month by month as she went from powder to crack.

Richmond Heights, Grand Avenue, South Beach, Haulover Beach

If I had continued on this path, my Miami grid might have differed. It might have charted the streets around Richmond Heights, a lower middle-class largely African-American area to our south and west founded by Capt. Frank C. Martin, a white pilot who had come to admire the African-American flyers he served with in WWII. I had some friends there, but I have to admit that my white friends and I saw it as a place to cop weed. Or I might have made more frequent visits to the ghetto along Grand Avenue that dated back to the Bahamian laborers who came at the start of the 1900s; this was the old Coconut Grove, right next to the rapidly gentrifying Grove that lost much of its hippie character that came with the Miami Vice-ing of the city in general. There, I heard you could buy a speedball or anything else you wanted if you were willing to take the risk of getting ripped off or worse. A farther drive would take you to the junkie beaches like Haulover or South Beach before the Art Deco Renaissance.

I didn't go to those places, but I did stupid things like jumping off a Florida Turnpike bridge forty feet into a canal with god-knows-what chemicals in it—an unofficial use for one of the waterways Bradley Dilger discusses—and joyriding at fourteen with Greg after he stole his mom's car late one night, the streets of Kendall emptying under the orange sodium lights as the night turned to gray morning. I got bored, though, with the stoners who cut class and made fun of nerds who read books (like me), and I was worried about getting into fights. I started learning to put my dad's lesson in my back pocket once I realized that plenty of kids at Arvida Jr. High and then Killian Sr. High would think nothing of gathering a group of friends to jump you and carried knives or even guns. When in tenth grade I tried to talk to sense to a pudgy eleventh grade dealer named Raul who was harassing my friend Suzanne, hoping my weight-lifter's bulk would encourage him to ease off, he beckoned me over and opened the trunk of his Mustang to show me what I think was a MAC-10. I held up my hands and backed away. I'm sure my dad would've wanted me to. Better Alive Jew than Tough Dead Jew.

Graceland (SW 138 St. and 109th Ave) and Crossing SW 124th Street

As I learned to find less-dangerous ways to be a man in Miami, I fell in more with my friends in my Honors and AP classes. Why I did so isn't clear; there were plenty of Jewish waste cases—Scott Waranch became one of them—so it wasn't that. Probably a combination of dumb luck, my desire not to disappoint my parents, and the fact that these kids were smart and fun and kind to each other. I can't remember the specifics, but I think that's how the editor of this volume also fell into this group. We smoked and drank our share, but there was no pressure, and in general nobody did anything too stupid. With rap in the ascendant, we mockingly called ourselves the Get Fresh Crew, a winking appropriation of African-American culture by a bunch of white kids—about ten of us, guys and girls, Jews, Christians, atheists—though we never dated each other out of awkwardness or concern it would cause friction. We had a spot we called Graceland, in honor of the Paul Simon album, a rubbish heap near a stalled development a couple miles south and west, where we drank beer and wine coolers and occasionally sparked up. We spent an inordinate amount of time at Eric's house, swimming, watching movies, and eating his dad's Dole Fruit Juice Bar pops. It pained me to hear that he lost the house as a knock-on effect of the realestate bubble that popped nowhere more intensely than in South Florida. As I grew up, I realized that underneath his hyper-competitiveness and behind the screen of his compulsive puns, Stan was actually a shy person who had his own shtick. Like we all have.

The Get Fresh Crew all went away to college and turned out pretty well given how many ways there were to lose yourself in Miami in the 1980s. None of us lives in South Florida anymore. To my surprise, Eric married an observant Jewish woman; I was blown away when I went to his son's bar mitzvah a few years ago and Eric himself led part of the service. The reception in the synagogue's social hall had no theme and no DJ. It is a blessing that Eric was smart enough to run away from me thirty years ago.

If Eric scrambled my map from one direction, my parents did from the other. After I left for college, they sold our house and moved south of 124th Street, their finances having improved significantly with my mom's becoming a CPA. But despite their posh new address they continue to be the same sensible, loving, and liberal Jews who raised me. I go back now with my wife and two kids when we can, and it all comes back to me as we drive around Kendall and sit around that same Shabbos table under the same chandelier, and I share the stories it's safe to share with my eight-year-old daughter and four-year-old son.

Of course, their Jewish identities will differ from mine, not only because of the differences between 1975 and 2015 but also the differences between Judaism in suburban Miami and our corner of Philadelphia, a *haymishe*, progressive (if somewhat self-congratulatory) neighborhood called Mt. Airy. Having gone to the local synagogue for pre-school, they already know more about the Jewish holidays than I knew at my bar mitzvah. But if there is a rootedness to Judaism here and less of the status chasing I saw in Miami, it's also true that they'll never know the pleasures of listening to the alter kockers, as they called themselves, schmoozing at my Grandma's parties about the old days or the stern glories of a Reform service for thousands, complete with choir and organ, or exiting the Yom Kippur service into the mild air of a late-September night in Miami. In any case, they'll be charting their own grids.

Works Cited

Cohen, Rich. *Tough Jews: Fathers, Sons, and Gangster Dreams*. New York: Vintage, 1999. Print.

de Certeau, Michel. *The Practice of Everyday Life*. Trans. Steven F. Rendall. Berkeley: U of California P, 2004. Print.

de Certeau, Michel, Luce Giard, and Pierre Mayol. *The Practice of Everyday Life, Vol. 2: Living and Cooking*. Rev. ed. Trans. Timothy J. Tomasik. Minneapolis: U of Minnesota P, 1998. Print.

More, Deobrah Dash. *To the Golden Cities: Pursuing the American Jewish Dream in Miami and L. A.* New York: Free Press, 1994. Print.

Prell, Riv-Ellen. *Fighting to Become American: Assimilation and the Trouble Between Jewish Women and Jewish Men*. Boston: Beacon Press, 1999. Print.

Taylor, Jean. *The Villages of South Dade*. St. Petersburg: Byron Kennedy, 1985. Print.

Tebeau. *Synagogue in the Central City: Temple Israel of Greater Miami, 1922–72*. Coral Gables: U of Miami P, 1972. Print.

Whitfield, Steven J. "Blood and Sand: The Jewish Community of South Florida" *American Jewish History*, 82.1–4 (1994/1995): 73–96. Print.

Florida Studies

9 West Palm

Bradley Dilger

As a boy, I lived in Stuart, Florida on the St. Lucie River, an estuary praised for its snook fishing and proximity to the Gulfstream via the St. Lucie Inlet. I spent hours playing on a small beach a few houses south of ours. I fished, snorkeled, dug for clams, and water-skied with friends in the river. Down the street, I built a tree fort over a small inlet and dammed its outlet to make it deeper after rain. When I visited my grandparents, I played in their backyard, near the seventeenth hole of the Lake Worth municipal golf course, not far from the Lake Worth Lagoon itself. In both places, I listened to osprey hunt, watched boats zip or sail by, and dodged the afternoon thunderstorms that filled the streets with rainfall and thickened the summertime air with moisture. I lived with the droughts which browned our lawn and brought salt water upstream far enough for porpoises to swim by our house, and the rainy periods which made our yard squishy and blackened the river with runoff. Hurricanes, too, were a part of life, as they were for Jeff Rice and others in this collection: helping my father board up the house, then heading to the shelter for a few days. To me, playing in the river, or on the edge of the golf course, came naturally, and the water I lived in was natural like me. The droughts, rainy seasons, and hurricanes were part of normal cycles. As I grew up, I learned that the rivers, lagoons, and marshes that were "natural Florida," to me were far from natural. I learned that artificiality was the real normal in Florida—especially where water is concerned.

The most important networks in Florida are water works: the aquifers of clean fresh water that flow from north to south far under the ground; the rivers and lakes all over the peninsula, and the swamps, marshes, and wetlands that connect them and of course the oceans surrounding Florida, bringing it the warm climate and sunny beaches that are the stuff of postcards. Natural bodies of water like these are joined by thousands of artificial ones humans have created: canals, levees, spillways, and other structures which move water from one place to another, or prevent its movement. When I was young, I knew the river behind my house was different from the canals that emptied into it. I knew times of hard rain meant releases from Lake Okeechobee into the St. Lucie—pushing the porpoises back toward the sea and making my older neighbors complain bitterly about the poor fishing. I did not realize the extent to which that river had been transformed. As David Grant demonstrates for suburban spaces in Florida, I did not know its wildness had been domesticated, nor did I know that West Palm was the center of it all—the place where the cultural, political, and legal networks of Florida's water came together.

Figure 1. St. Lucie lock release

All water in South Florida, from the top of the Kissimmee River watershed near Orlando, through West Palm to the Everglades, and past Miami down to Key West, is regulated by the South Florida Water Management District (SFWMD), the largest and most powerful of five similar bodies in Florida. From its headquarters in West Palm, near a bend in the West Palm Beach Canal, the District engages diverse activities related to water: flood control, water supply, wastewater treatment, emergency management, transportation, recreation, environmental monitoring, and Everglades restoration. Under SFWMD's direction, water networks are literally and figuratively portrayed as standardized, regular systems drawn in near hub-and-spoke arrays. The irregular, wandering contours and fuzzy, fluid boundaries of natural water systems—rivers, wetlands, lakes, and aquifers—are replaced with rectilinear or circular shapes with stable, clearly defined boundaries. Like all networks, the water works of Florida are not well represented by two dimensional diagrams that imply distinct agents, clear flows of power and influence, and tight correspondences between intents and realized purposes. The London Underground diagram designed by Harry Beck is famous for sacrificing geographic accuracy for design functionality (Garland 2); similarly, maps of Florida water networks give up hydrological integrity; erase legal and political struggles; and show neither the dynamic, unpredictable nature of Florida water, nor many of the agents and actors impacting the long term health of the ecosystems SFWMD literally controls through its power over water flow and use.

In this chapter, I will use West Palm, and my childhood in and around its water works, to focus a case study of networks which illuminates many of the issues faced by network theorists as they attempt to represent networks in their richness and complexity. I will focus on canals, particularly those closest to the places of my childhood, given their importance in Florida's water networks. Beginning from West Palm, I will show three evolving purposes for canals, discussing both seen and unseen elements of these artificial waterways, and recovering elements of complexity lost in the oversimplified model of networks which dominate Florida water. I conclude with a sketch of future work which could carry this thinking forward for the St. Lucie, with an eye to changing thinking about water networks in West Palm.

Florida Is Canal Crazy: Canals as Improvement

I was born in West Palm Beach, at Good Samaritan Hospital, less than ten miles north of my grandparents' home just off Lake Worth. About five miles inland are the headquarters for the SFWMD, near a bend in the West Palm Beach Canal. This "C-51" canal, one of the oldest and most important in the extensive system of canals supervised by the District, meets the Lake Worth Lagoon just north of my grandparents' home. It's not a happy meeting, as a Florida Department of Environmental Protection report makes clear. Discharge from the canal has deposited heavy metals and other pollutants in the lagoon. Because the canal flows irregularly, with "releases" of fresh water from the canal coming when rainfall raises water levels above a certain point, fluctuations in salinity in the Lagoon result, disrupting the long-term establishment of marine life. As the DEP notes, "the combined effects of discharge from the West Palm Beach canal have had a significant adverse impact on the Lake Worth Lagoon" with a "severely impaired zone" surrounding the canal's point of discharge (Graves 1, 2).

On the one hand, it's significant that SFWMD headquarters are near this important canal. On the other hand, it's hard to be far from a canal in Palm Beach County. The county is covered with a grid of canals, excepting several large wildlife refuges also used for water management, which are surrounded by them. Some canals are as large and deep as C-51, and some even deeper, but most are little more than drainage ditches. The Lake Worth Drainage District, which covers a huge chunk of the developed area in southeastern Palm Beach County, measures 500 miles of canals under its authority, most in Palm Beach County. SFWD manages "more than 1,600 miles of canals" and numerous other "water control structures" (SFWMD, "Managing"). Although canals were once vital transportation networks, today they serve only recreational boat traffic. Today, their central intended function is moving water for irrigation, drainage, or flood control. Florida is, and has been, canal crazy.

> At the turn of the century, the United States, flush with the success of building the Panama canal, was canal-crazy. The construction of the lock-laden interoceanic Panama Canal was a crowning achievement of American know-how and persistence. After draining the great malarial swamps in the mountainous jungles of Panama, Florida looked easy, since it was flat—perhaps the flattest area in the world. The land under [Florida] swamp was extraordinarily fertile, crying out to be drained. (Mykle 17)

Hamilton Disston made the first concerted efforts to use canals to drain or "improve" large areas of Florida in the 1880s, purchasing huge tracts of land as part of Florida's "Internal Improvement Initiative." Engineers working for Disston dynamited the waterfall that separated the Caloosahatchee River from Lake Okeechobee, establishing a path for drainage to the west. Disston's crews began cutting canals in the Kissimmee River basin, but the work proved more difficult than first imagined, and efforts produced mixed results (Hanna & Hanna 95, 101-3). Not long afterward, Henry Flagler extended his railroad down the east coast of Florida, planning to stop at

West Palm. But freezes in 1894 and 1895 ravaged the citrus industry, pushing Flagler to continue further south to Miami and eventually to Key West (Grunwald 105). At the turn of the century, with the Spanish-American war and the Panama Canal excavation underway, empire was in the air, and an emperor came to West Palm: Napoleon Bonaparte Broward, a politician who took up the charge for developing the Everglades. A Duval County politician, steamboat captain, and sheriff who made his name running guns to Cubans revolting against Spanish rule in the 1890s, Broward was elected governor of Florida in November 1904, largely on his promise to reclaim the Everglades as state property, undoing the privatization coordinated by Disston and others. At campaign stops, Broward had repeated over and over, "Water will run down hill!" (Hanna & Hanna 124).

> A newly elected Broward toured Okeechobee in February 1905, promising development and "improvement" by an equation with canals at the center: immediate dredging of a canal from Lake Okeechobee to the St. Lucie River, a distance of twenty-two miles, to be followed by another canal, eight or ten miles long, making connection with the St. Johns River. This new waterway, some thirty miles in all, coupled with the Caloosahatchee opening already dug [by Disston] and needing only improvement, would give a transstate passage. [. . .] By 740 miles of inland waterway some 6,000,000 acres would be opened for improved cultivation and transportation. Broward expected this prospective operation to prevent Lake Okeechobee from spilling over its shores and to turn "overflowed" lands into "lowlands;" it could be done in eighteen months by four dredges at a cost of $250,000. (Hanna & Hanna 124–5)

Flood control, transportation, drainage, and economic development in one fell swoop of "improvement," delivering immense and quantifiable benefits at little cost. Thirty miles of canals would yield untold riches (never mind the vast difference between this number and the immensity of Florida's waterways Sid Dobrin with which opens "An American Beach"). Such is the promise of canals. Broward was the first to propose a drainage district "empowered to make assessments of benefits and damages"—the Everglades Drainage District, the forerunner earliest predecessor of SFWMD (SFWMD). Though as for Disston, establishing a network of canals across Florida proved more difficult than Broward envisioned, taking far longer than eighteen months. But eventually, canal development came to pass, following Broward's "down hill" plan rather than heading northeast from Lake Okeechobee to the St. Johns. The West Palm Beach Canal was started in 1906 and completed around 1917 (Gould), providing an eastern outlet for draining the great lake. Here is how it was described not long afterward, back when the number of canals around West Palm could be counted on one hand:

> The Palm Beach Canal, the only transportation link between West Palm Beach and Lake Okeechobee, cut a straight line through wetlands, water sloughs, and sawgrass prairies. Running daily from the turning basin near the railroad tracks in Palm Beach, the mail boat took four hours to reach Canal Point on Lake Okeechobee. In 1921, there was little in the way of developed land in between. For the first part of the trip, jungle leaned over the banks of the canal. There were majestic stands of cypress trees that soared to the sky, pines alongside an occasional live oak. Once past Loxahatchee the jungle ended and the cypress trees disappeared. The forest gave way to a prairie of sawgrass that stretched to the horizon. No one said a word as they gawked at the seemingly endless expanse of sawgrass. It was a new world—a wondrous watery world so foreign that the passengers stared in anxious silence. (Mykle 46)

Not long after the West Palm Beach Canal was dug, the second connection Broward called for was realized, when the St. Lucie Canal was completed. There were now multiple ways to move water away from the center of Florida and tame the vast and powerful Lake Okeechobee. Investment came immediately, and the glitter of progress was finally at West Palm's door, with the family of Carnegie investment partner Henry Phipps "plotting Port Mayaca, a city-to-be which glittered with gemstone names: Topaz Lake, Sapphire Inlet, Crystal Lake" (Hanna & Hanna 230). Similarly, West Palm businessmen sought their pieces of the Florida land boom, pushing projects such as W. J. "Fingy" Conners's highway from West Palm to Tampa via Okeechobee (Grunwald 182). Around this time, the Lake Worth municipal golf course opened behind what would become my grandparents' home, built on landfill from dredging the lagoon. West Palm, like the rest of Florida, was booming, and permanent greatness seemed imminent.

After Hurricanes, a New Mission: Canals as Control

But success proved elusive for West Palm. The real estate boom began to fizzle as the scams of real estate con artists became apparent to out of state prospects, and the bust accelerated when a hurricane smashed into south Florida in 1926, devastating Miami, killing almost 400 people around Lake Okeechobee and inflicting damage in Palm Beach County as well (Historical Society of Palm Beach County). A second hurricane in 1928 was far more disastrous for West Palm, when the hastily constructed dike around Lake Okeechobee failed. As Zora Neale Hurston wrote in *Their Eyes Were Watching God*, the conditions were gruesome. Rains from the hurricane caused local flooding, made much worse when the dike failure sent a wall of water through towns filled with African-Americans who worked the farms near the lake. Thousands of people were killed by debris or swept into the lake and drowned, and the exact death toll is not known to this day. Many of the victims, as black Bahamian migrant farmworkers, were not well-documented; floodwaters swept many bodies away, and others were hastily cremated or buried in mass graves (Pfost 1370). Many lakeside communities were devastated, all but destroyed by the storm and the floodwaters from the failed dike. As Hurston and others wrote, residents of Belle Glade, Canal Point, and other communities pummeled by the flooding looked to West Palm for help after the storm. In the face of gruesome conditions, doctors coordinating relief efforts directed women and children to walk along the West Palm Canal. Six miles into their march, the refugees were turned back by the news that West Palm had all but vanished:

> There wasn't a building or house that had not been damaged. Windows had been blown out; roofs had collapsed. At the height of the storm, the entire downtown area was under water. Dunes of beach sand covered the main streets. . . . There was no electricity, no transportation, and little unspoiled food left. . . . For all practical purposes, Florida's third largest city had simply vanished. (Mykle 189)

Soon coffins, not refugees, lined the roads along the canal, as bodies washed out into the Everglades were gradually found. Even as recovery efforts continued, and funeral pyres burned, calls to return to the boom years were quickly published. The *Everglades News* complained, "The stacks of coffins on the dock at Canal Point are hurting the real estate market" (qtd. in Mykle 212). As before, the solution imagined was "improvement"—more and better canals, more and better drainage, and a bigger and more powerful government organization to manage it all. The 1928 storm led to the creation of the Okeechobee Flood Control District (Huser 23) which partnered with the US Army Corps of Engineers to build the Herbert Hoover Dike, a massive wall of earth surrounding Lake Okeechobee and turning it into little more than a reservoir (Cavros 8). No longer would water drain gradually from the southern half of the lake into Florida Bay through the Everglades; instead, water would be under human control—released for agricultural needs during drought, or into containment areas and the sea through canal networks when storms or wet seasons came, as directed by "regulation schedules" developed in the 1940s and updated periodically thereafter (Vearil 5).

Not even twenty years later, in 1947, another round of hurricanes brought the new dike to the breaking point, "reflooding just about every wetland that had been drained or paved for agriculture or development—from the pastures of the Kissimmee Valley to the farms of the upper Glades" (Grunwald 218). Though the narrative was by this time familiar—Sean Morey's "A Network of Bones" reminds us that between these Okeechobee disasters, a hurricane had smashed much of the Keys, including Henry Flagler's Overseas Railroad—Florida politicians looked to Washington for help. Everglades Drainage District water managers filled a report with photos of the damage, including a "crying cow" cover illustration, and Florida senator Spessard Holland successfully secured federal funding for multiple responses: extensive strengthening of the Hoover Dike; a plan to "channelize" the Kissimmee River, turning it into a canal, in order to better drain the land above Lake Okeechobee; and deepening and improving canals dug in Broward and Miami-Dade counties. A huge section of the Everglades would be set aside for agriculture, the "Everglades Agricultural Area," and other areas intended for releases of excess water from Okeechobee. The wilderness would be tamed, turned into farms and golf courses, with great levees of muck shaping water works, as with the TPC Sawgrass Stadium Course James Beasley describes in his chapter. And government agencies were renamed again, with the Okeechobee Flood Control District becoming the Central & Southern Florida (C&SF) Flood Control District, forerunner of SFWMD. This new agency, located in West Palm, would manage Senator Holland's $208 million "Central & Southern Flood Control Project," to once and for all solve the south Florida water problem (Grunwald 218–229). As numerous chapters in this collection point out, public reaction to natural disaster was to make Florida more artificial, with an even bigger scope of digging, draining, and deforesting which promised to once and for repel the advances of nature.

New Levels of Control: An Okeechobee Hub with Canal Spokes

On the one hand, a lot had changed: the threat of flooding from the north had been mitigated by the dike and miles of canals which could direct water from the center of the state to the ocean. On the other hand, the image of the water network remained simple: a hub-and-spoke system, centering around Lake Okeechobee drainage, with clear boundaries and clear chains of cause and effects—and canals at the center. Call it the "Okeechobee hub, canal spoke" model—a rectilinearity and regularity reflected in District publications like "Managing Every Drop," which includes a schematic with square lakes, no rivers, and no wetlands. Steve Newman points out repeatedly that "the grid is never merely a grid"—but this message has still not reached the managers of the SFWMD.

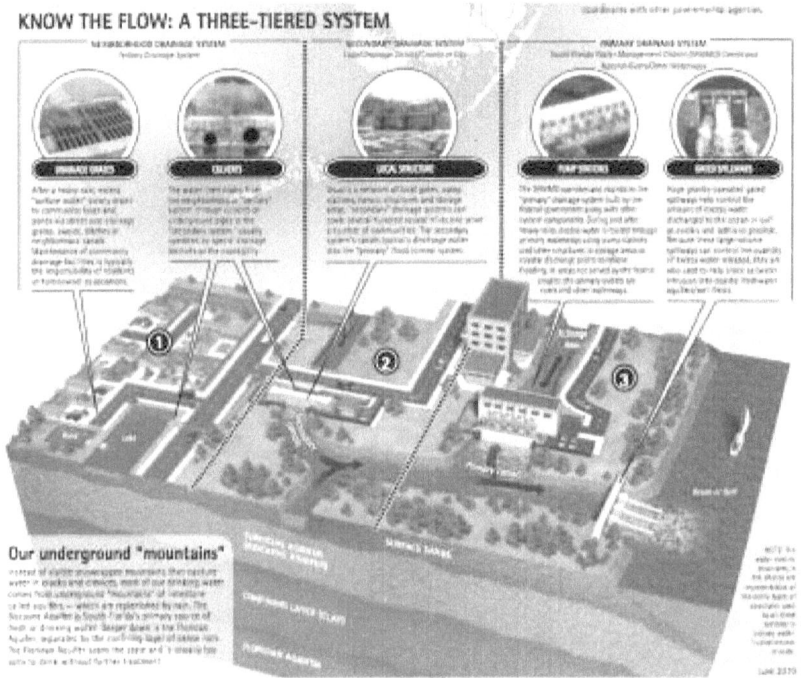

Figure 2. Managing Every Drop

The Kissimmee River basin would be drained into Lake Okeechobee. Irregularities in lake levels from rainfall, hurricanes, or drought would be corrected by releasing water through the canals—St. Lucie, West Palm, and others—as necessary. Under C&SF control, from West Palm, the lake would become an economic engine, delivering water to agriculture while keeping the subdivisions sprouting all over South Florida dry. It was Broward's vision, slightly modified, illustrated by the "wealth of riches" around Lake Okeechobee, as portrayed by Florida road engineers for Hanna and Hanna's *Lake Okeechobee*. Once called "improvement" and "reclamation," this transformation was now called "flood control," perhaps an admission that though Florida was very flat, it was also persistently very wet. From this perspective, the water network corrected this natural deficiency by eliminating the complexities inherent in the natural system.

Figure 3. Hanna Lake riches

But elements of complexity have remained persistent. In the narrative of canals, whether we imagine them as "improvement" or "control," changing water networks always turns out to be more complex than originally promised. Napoleon Bonaparte Broward's vision of draining Florida in eighteen months, with $250,000, via thiry-odd miles of canals, was not realized in fifty years, though millions of dollars were spent, thousands of lives were lost, and more than three thousand miles of canals dug. Perhaps most importantly, the image of canal networks focused on the benefits of "flood control," not the environmental changes canals produce. Negative impacts had first become a part of the narrative around this time, with the 1947 publication of Marjory Stoneman Douglas's *The Everglades: River of Grass*. The simplistic vision of water networks was also strongly questioned by Florida residents who witnessed the complexities it elided. As *Stuart News* publisher Edwin Menninger complained in a letter to Holland, "The engineers think only in terms of ditches" (qtd. on Grunwald 228). After the 1947 hurricane resulted in huge releases of muddy fresh water from Lake Okeechobee into the St. Lucie River estuary, Menninger wrote:

> Our St. Lucie River, around which the entire tourist and commercial picture revolved, has been turned into mud soup. The finest fishing grounds on the east coast of Florida is now a mud hole which no respectable fish would inhabit . . . feeling is extremely bitter here. (quoted on Grunwald 219)

But though Menninger, Douglas and similar critics of the simple "improvement," "drainage," or "flood control" models would have to live with environmental damage for years to come, development continued despite this collateral damage, as if the canal solution would achieve "control" once it was scaled properly. It didn't help that many who championed the Everglades did not yet understand the danger the "improved" and "controlled" Okeechobee model represented—for example, though Douglas rejected the "reclamation" of the Everglades later in life, at the time *River of Grass* was first published, she supported the C&SF project, too. Throughout the 1950s and 1960s, engineers directed the expansion and development of the canal networks of South Florida, again in partnership with the US Army Corps of Engineers. Massive projects conceptualized in order to bring the "Okeechobee hub, canal spoke" model to fruition, such as the channelization of the Kissimmee River, were engaged—and massive complexities arose to meet them. The transformation of the Kissimmee from a river which meandered for 103 miles through wetlands to a fifty-six mile water highway known as the C-38 Canal also turned it into a fast track for nutrient runoff from farmland, pasture, and homeowners' non-native lawns. Even before the project had been completed, the harmful impacts on Lake Okeechobee were apparent. Elevated levels of nitrogen and phosphorus from runoff which coursed directly into the great lake rather than being filtered out by wetlands and the meandering Kissimmee caused algae blooms, rapid declines in water quality, and silting of channels. Discussions about reversing the "improvement" of the Kissimmee began in 1972, while the project was not even complete

(Purdum 8). Today restoration is underway, with more than ten years of work completed at a cost of over $908 million, to acquire land, "backfill" dredged canals, restore the original river channel, re-establish marshes and wetlands, and modify water management and control systems (Bousquin 1–2). Here, the readily admitted complexity is that undoing the rectilinear, hubandspoke structures of canals costs a lot more than establishing them. Even though restoration is not complete, "the river and its floodplain have improved in remarkable ways, surpassing at times the anticipated environmental response," with water quality improving, native plants returning, and fish counts improving (Jinks & Colangelo 1). But researchers cannot say if the Kissimmee River restoration will repair the damage done to the great lake. Given that Lake Okeechobee's water quality is not yet improving, and some argue it will take years for the "backlog" of nutrients and sediments in the lake to dissipate, the true extent of the damages of Kissimmee River channelization are still unknown.

The narrative of canals shifted again in the early 1970s, when the 1972 Water Resources Act was passed in Florida, establishing the South Florida Water Management District and four other water management districts, and enacting changes in Florida water law which made SFWMD the managers of permitting processes for water use (Purdum 10–11). It was the year of the first Earth Day, and this change in perspective reflected the environmental awakening taking place all over the United States at the time. Water would no longer be considered private property—it would now be a public resource, with impact of use on public interests the prime consideration.

> Permits would be issued or denied on the basis of "reasonable-beneficial use," which includes "water in such quantity as is necessary for economic and efficient utilization, for a purpose and in a manner which is both reasonable and consistent with the public interest," according to the 1972 Water Resources Act on which the rule revisions were based. (Huser 94)

The establishment of the District, especially the change of its name from "control" to "management," reflected the realization that the simple vision of water networks which had so long dominated Florida was inadequate. Tom Huser's history catalogs the huge number of changes which took place in West Palm soon afterward: the name "South Florida Water Management District" explicitly made flood control one purpose of many, and the agency's offices were expanded, as more employees were needed to complete their expanded mission. The long period of canal craziness had come to an end— but the role of West Palm in Florida water would become more important than, ever now that it was clear canal craziness had neither improved nor controlled Lake Okeechobee, as promised.

From West Palm to the River Today: "Mucking Up the St. Lucie"

Living on the St. Lucie in my childhood, I remember releases of muddy water similar to the 1947 releases Menninger lamented: periods when water managers would lower the spillways and release dark, cloudy water from Lake Okeechobee through the St. Lucie Canal into the south fork of the St. Lucie, pushing salt water back to the ocean. Since I left the river in 1989, releases have continued, and the damage Menninger and other *Stuart News* writers like Ernest Lyons lamented has intensified. Many times since 1997, the St. Lucie River has suffered from algae blooms and high levels of bacteria which have resulted in multiple closures to swimming and fishing (Cavros 4). Bjorn Turnberg, a marine ecologist studying sediments deposited in the river from canal discharges, was hospitalized as a result of a serious bacterial illness contracted from the contaminated waters of the St. Lucie (Margasak). Ecological damage to the St. Lucie has been detailed in reports from the Rivers Coalition, a grass-roots organization in Martin County, and by the "Florida Slime Crime Tracker," a Google Map produced by the Central Florida Sierra Club. Reports published by these organizations, citing substantial amounts of scientific evidence, emphasize that canal networks move far more than water—they transport nutrients such as phosphorus and nitrogen, silt, and sediment, all byproducts of agriculture and development. The movement of water through canals, especially water laden with nutrients, results in environmental impacts which are certainly neither improvement nor merely "flood control." The story of the St. Lucie shows that water is far more than an agent of flood and its agency far more complex than the "Water flows downhill, and prosperity follows" framework advanced by Broward a century ago. Time and time again, the two-dimensional, hub-and-spoke vision of water networks has failed to account for the real-world complexities of water in Florida. The Hoover Dike around Lake Okeechobee leaks, diminishing the amount of water that can be stored in the lake in times of rainfall, and making more frequent releases into rivers necessary (Treadway). The length and frequency of droughts or rainy periods remains impossible to predict and far exceeds the "one hundred year" extremes of models used SFWMD. Managers often fail to recognize differences between multiple and very differing human uses of water such as drinking, agricultural irrigation, or residential irrigation. Slow-flowing canals become choked with exotic weeds and trash. The list of difficulties goes on and on.

In the simplistic Okeechobee hub, canal spoke model of water networks, the canals of Florida are easily managed lines: efficient, endless flows of water from the hub lake to the sea, or from subdivisions to other canals, or from the lake to agricultural areas. They have one dimension: a velocity of water. But in reality, again turning to Newman, a grid is never merely a grid. No matter what the purpose, canal flow is multi-dimensional, a mix of water and other things. Speed of flow in canals is minimal, allowing the buildup of silts and sediment, and must be actively managed through a system of locks, pumps, and other "control structures," to use District parlance. Water will flow down hill, but there are few hills in Florida—and even if water flow was up to speed, fresh water releases in salt water estuaries would still disrupt salinity, almost certainly result in flocculation of sediments, and deliver nutrients and other pollutants with potentially devastating impacts.

We can look at the St. Lucie in depth to find one of those impacts—a complexity of Florida water networks the Okeechobee hub, canal spoke model does not account for. As I have noted above, in the artificial water networks of Florida, with filtering wetlands vastly reduced by projects such as the channelization of the Kissimmee River, the formerly meandering courses of rivers and streams straightened, and development increasing the amount of storm water runoff, nutrient and sediment levels in water rise, and the water darkens, as is clearly visible in aerial photos of Lake Okeechobee water mixing with ocean water in the St. Lucie. Dissolved oxygen is forced downward by the introduction of organic matter. In the poor quality water, the death rates of fish and other animals increase. Nutrients like phosphorus and nitrogen can make algae blooms occur, adding more organic matter to the system. Sediments which are suspended in fresh water settle out in the presence of salts from the ocean. The result is a layer of sediment and organic matter settling out, in both canals and natural water bodies—a slippery, sticky mud many people call "muck."

Robert L. P. Voisinet, who collected samples of the muck accumulating in the St. Lucie estuary in 2007, described it this way:

> a very sticky consistency, representative of clay. It is as black as India ink and stains your hands, boat, and clothing. It also has a shiny sheen. The muck appeared to gel or form a pudding-like consistency, similar to black mayonnaise. When mixed with water, the muck globs formed a black suspension in the water which did not settle out easily. (Voisinet 13)

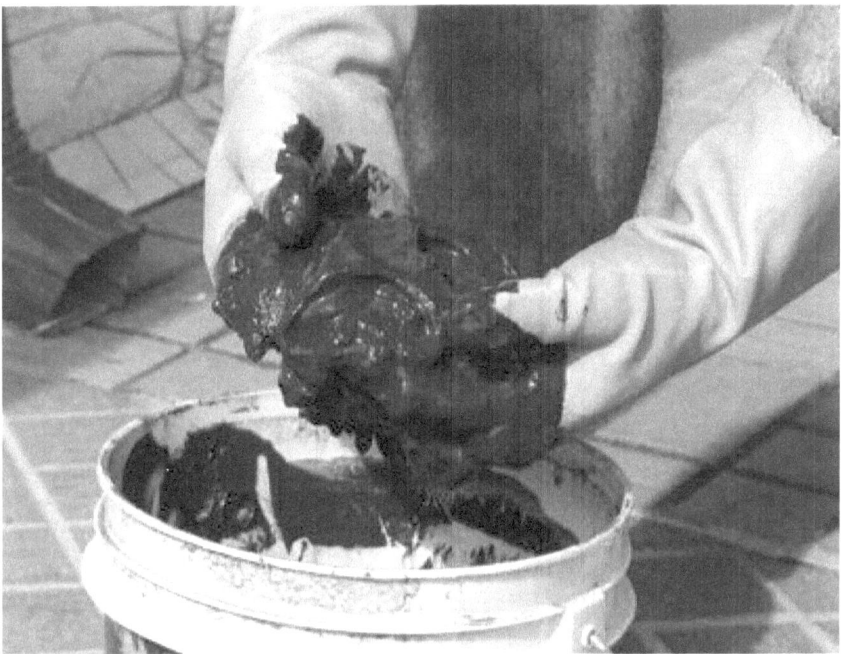

Figure 4. Voisinet muck St. Lucie

Settlement of muck in the St. Lucie and other rivers has been a tremendous problem. Voisinet's research was prompted by his awareness that muck deposits had long been a problem—recall Menninger's complaints about the St. Lucie becoming a "mud hole no fish would inhabit" after releases from Lake Okeechobee. Voisinet did not measure the depth of muck, but pointed to studies which showed depths of 2 to 6 feet were common and deposits of up to 15 feet had been recorded (Voisinet 14). A 2009 study found the average depth of muck deposits was 20 inches in the West Palm Beach canal, with depths of nearly five feet in some places. In the Lake Worth Lagoon, where the canal's releases of fresh water emerge before flushing to the Atlantic Ocean, muck depth averaged two feet (Trefry *et al.* 3). Multiple scientific sources document tremendous impacts of muck deposits on all kinds of marine life, from sea grasses to fish, with cascading effects resulting from the death of animals such as oysters which, under normal conditions, improve water quality and help maintain estuarine health. The result is a "biological desert," to quote a source Voisinet summarized.

> The accumulation of muck on available substrate or nearby areas makes the substrate unsuitable for oyster larval settlement and thus recruitment and growth of larval oysters (RECOVER 2007a). In ad-

> dition, accumulation of muck may also impact the dissolved oxygen content making the area/substrate unsuitable for larval settlement and growth (RECOVER 2007a). . . . By blanketing the substrate, the sediments inhibit colonization by desirable flora and fauna in the lagoon (PBCERM 2003b). The unconsolidated sediments are prone to re-suspension through wave or tidal action, reducing light penetration and blocking the growth of submerged aquatic vegetation (Crigger et al. 2005), further inhibiting the growth of sea grasses and other natural vegetation. (Palm Beach County 18, 38)

Scientific documentation has been joined by public outcry, with activists in the St. Lucie arguing "De-ooze it or lose it," the Martin County Board of County Commissioners starting a "Save the St. Lucie" media campaign, and a Fort Myers newspaper printing "Stop the Muck" signs for a public meeting (Pittman). Voisinet's reports are featured on the Rivers Coalition website, and water managers recognize, at least to an extent, that muck is a problem. For example, a 2009 project coordinated by Palm Beach County, SFWMD, and the City of West Palm Beach removed muck from the West Palm Beach Canal and added a trap near a bend in the canal to collect and remove sediment before it could enter the Lake Worth Lagoon. The federally funded Everglades restoration project includes several studies of "muck remediation" that seek to discover the best ways to remove muck deposits (for example, Sime *et al*). The Lake Worth Lagoon study includes eight recommendations for addressing muck problems, from re-engineering spillways to keep muck out of the lagoon, to asking the public to keep organic matter such as lawn clippings out of waterways (vi).

But the releases of fresh water, and the muck that comes with them, have continued. In August 2012, Tropical Storm Isaac dumped up to eighteen inches of water on South Florida. To prevent flooding, water managers at SFWMD supervised massive releases of fresh water into the Lake Worth Lagoon, with flow from the West Palm Beach Canal reaching "its highest recorded rate of 10,300 cubic feet per second, as water control gates remained open and pump stations operated at maximum safe capacity" (Smith & Margasak). Runoff also flooded the St. Lucie Estuary, and impacts were easy to see, with aerial photos clearly showing dark, sediment-laden fresh water mixing with ocean water at the St. Lucie Inlet, and USGS measuring stations in the estuary showing a precipitous drop in salinity which put marine life at risk.

Figure 5. Owens aerial water mixing

On September 19, with Lake Okeechobee levels still high, the US Army Corps of Engineers began the release of billions of gallons of water into the St. Lucie River. The impact on the St. Lucie was immediate. Salinities which had begun to recover plummeted. Two weeks later, on October 9, the Martin County Health Department issued a water advisory for the St. Lucie, advising people "avoid contact with the water near the Roosevelt Bridge after testing revealed higher than normal levels of enteric bacteria," and noting the risk of "upset stomach, diarrhea, eye irritation and skin rashes." As Menninger had in 1947, *Stuart News* writer Ed Killer reacted angrily, pointing out the history of damage to the St. Lucie—fish kills in 1998, algal blooms in 2005, and five years of destruction of oyster beds since 2001. In a *Miami Herald* editorial, novelist Carl Hiaasen highlighted the muck problem, writing, "The lake is silted with fertilizers, nitrogen and other agricultural spillage that stirs whenever the gates are opened. Enough polluted muck to fill 12 dump trucks is entering the St. Lucie Estuary every day." The releases stopped on November 6. But as in years past, the damage had already been done.

Ironically, much of the purpose of canals like the St. Lucie Canal is *preservation* of muck—the rich muck soils of the Everglades Agricultural Area and other Florida swamplands drained for sugar plantations, vegetable farms, and cattle ranching. Napoleon Bonaparte Broward used to speak of the "wealth of the fabulous muck" (Grunwald 136) as he stumped across Florida to gain support for his empire of Everglades drainage. As Robert Mykle writes, it was the stuff of farmers' dreams: "what caught Henry's eye was the soil—the unfathomably rich soil, that incredibly rich dirt that shamed the tan-colored sandy loam of Frostproof... Like the first sweet taste of a narcotic, the idea of owning a piece of that black soil planted itself and smoldered in Henry Martin's brain" (37). The farmers and migrant workers who worked the Everglades in the time of Zora Neale Hurston's *Their Eyes* were often called "muck rats."

Though the creation of muck in canals is seemingly automatic, the preservation of muck soils is not. Muck soils must stay wet, or they can catch fire during natural cycles of drought and fire in Florida—and keeping muck wet to maintain its agricultural value is a large reason for imagining Lake Okeechobee as a reservoir under human control. Florida muck fires still make headlines, with a one thousand acre fire burning near Dundee, Florida in May 2012 (Adams). These fires create irritating smoke with high concentrations of carbon monoxide and are "notoriously difficult to control." Firefighters battling muck fires must use specialized equipment, and sometimes drill wells to get the massive amounts of water to extinguish them—"the equivalent of more than three inches of rainfall" (Watts & Kobziar). Muck fires leave behind "biological deserts" much like those created when muck deposits coat river bottoms:

> A muck fire is exceptionally grievous. After a fire, a forest will eventually grow back, if a city block burns it can be rebuilt, but once muck is burned, like oil or coal, it is gone forever. A muck fire leaves a sterile ash where nothing will grow. Once muck ashes moisten, they form a cement-like substance. Hundreds of acres of land burned down two or three feet, leaves a bare limestone scar on the surface. (Mykle 60, 61)

Even massive public works projects like the Kissimmee River Restoration can't replace land consumed by muck fires—the land is simply lost, unfit for farmland, forest, or swamp. As with other dimensions of Florida's water networks, the part muck plays in the Okeechobee-centric model of water is too small, and far more simple than it should be.

Keep Mucking Up

The complexities of muck offer several powerful illustrations of the real character of water networks. Muck is a nebulous, sticky, hard to measure substance—not at all like the clean lines of canals and control structures portrayed in District maps. Muck is created when the balances of nature are disrupted and nutrients move in the system, causing effects which in turn cause effects—feedback loops not well accounted for in a model of networks as one-way flows of simple, discrete entities. Todd Taylor's "Tampa at the Sunset of Western Civilization" shows the pristine beauty of freshly dug canals is elusive, quickly giving way to muck and stagnation. And preserving muck valuable in one context—the forests and farmlands of Florida—may give rise to muck harmful in different places in the network. The cost, diversity, and number of solutions proposed for muck problems in the St. Lucie and other Florida rivers offer another indicator that a more complex model of water networks is needed, and also show that water managers themselves almost certainly realize the inertial model isn't adequate. Indeed, current Everglades restoration efforts are considering long-neglected plans to alter the system to release less water through the St. Lucie and more through the Everglades—a possibility which suggests that West Palm is listening, if only a little, to the story the St. Lucie's muck has to tell.

Citizen groups like the River Coalition who want to respond to the negative impacts of water management, who want to see the releases of contaminated lake water stop and the muck removed, would do well to keep mucking up—to focus on muck as a powerful representative of the complexity inherent in Florida water systems, but nearly completely absent from the canal-focused model. If I were still living in Florida, I would seek the opportunity to consider what a focus on muck might offer research into the representation of networks. For me, given the complexities I have traced in this chapter, an in-depth study of communicating about muck and water networks using action research methods would combine these two possibilities. One model is the "Harbor" project Stuart Blythe, Jeff Grabill, and Kirk Riley describe in "Action Research and Wicked Environmental Problems." Blythe, Grabill, and Riley describe a three-year outreach during which they worked with members of a Great Lakes community nicknamed "Harbor" where the US Army Corps of Engineers (USACE) planned to dredge several canals to remove sediments—even though extensive issues with contamination raised questions about health risks for residents of nearby neighborhoods. Like all academic researchers, Blythe, Grabill, and Riley fully planned to return new knowledge to their home discipline of professional and technical communication, but this goal was second to producing knowledge that benefited the "nonscholarly communities" they engaged—the citizens of "Harbor" themselves (282). As such, their "critical action research" project was concerned not only with the collection and analysis of public documents, not only with understanding how those documents circulated and were understood by the citizens of "Harbor," but with facilitating effective citizen understanding and response through research collaboratively developed with the participants themselves.

Many strong parallels can be drawn between the situation in the community nicknamed "Harbor" and the St. Lucie River community: the large role of canals; the dangers and benefits of actively cleaning up sedimentation in waterways; the involvement of, and tensions between, the USACE, other government agencies, and the public; the interactions of multiple citizen groups; and the many "citizen-scientists" involved in both projects. While Florida water networks, considered from West Palm to Orlando to the Everglades, represent a system with a much larger scope and perhaps greater complexities than "Harbor," considering only the St. Lucie offers a slice of the problem which includes sufficient but not overwhelming complexity. With their participants, Blythe, Grabill, and Riley developed research questions focusing on the ways community members were able to communicate with representatives of government organizations involved. In the same way their research, over time, illuminated ways different conceptions of "public meetings" and mapped the networks of communities in "Harbor," I imagine an action-research approach focused on mucking up the discourse of water networks in Florida. To that end, as preliminary research questions, I imagine, "Why don't our models of water networks better explain the movement, production, and impacts of muck?" and perhaps less generally "Why don't we call it the South Florida Muck Management District?" As I've already noted, several public campaigns have focused on the muck and slime produced by water pollution. Action research would ask how they have and have not effectively shown the connections between muck in the St. Lucie and hydrological models in West Palm (SFWMD) or Jacksonville (USACE). "Keep mucking up" would seek to raise the profile of muck and the practices which create muck (mucking) as agents in water networks.

Engagement with community organizations like the Rivers Coalition and its citizen-researchers like Bob Voisinet would offer researchers an opportunity to "Speak up for the St. Lucie," while learning much about how networks are represented and how non-human entities like muck gain agency and are represented as well. This is not to disavow traditional research; it has had notable positive impacts, and recent studies like Lapointe, Herren & Bedford's 2012 analysis of releases into the St. Lucie raise questions about the Okeechobee model of water which should be hard for the South Florida Water Management District to ignore. But experience suggests simply highlighting the problem of muck, creating awareness, is not enough. Rather, both those on the St. Lucie and those in West Palm must better understand the networks which create muck: hydrological, political, social, and communicative; natural, artificial, transient, and permanent. From the muck of the St. Lucie or the Lake Worth Lagoon, those looking to speak to West Palm need fuller representations of the networks which connect them: the nutrient-stuffed waters of Lake Okeechobee; lobbyists whispering in Tallahassee; the ebbs and flows of the Atlantic; resonances of local politics in Washington; the thousands of miles of canals, levees, and water works waiting their turn for maintenance and upkeep; and whatever storms shall take names and visit Florida come summer and fall.

Acknowledgments

I want to thank Jacqui Thurlow-Lippsich, Bob Voisinet, Cris Costello, Gabriella Ferraro, Jerry Reves, and Adam Watts for their help getting access to the photographs used in this chapter.

Works Cited

Adams, Robin Williams. "Dundee Muck Fire Grows to 1,000 Acres." *The Ledger*. TheLedger.com. May 27, 2012. Web. 20 Dec. 2014.

Blythe, Stuart, Jeffrey T. Grabill, and Kirk Riley. "Action Research and Wicked Environmental Problems: Exploring Appropriate Roles for Researchers in Professional Communication." *Journal of Business and Technical Communication* 22.3 (July 2008): 272–98. Print.

Bousquin, Stephen G. "Kissimmee River Restoration Project Fact And Tour Sheet." *South Florida Water Management District*. n.p., n.d. Web. 20 Dec. 2014

Cavros, George. "The Plan Six Concept." *Rivers Coalition*. Rivers Coalition, LLC, n.d. Web. 20 Dec. 2014.

Garland, Ken. *Mr. Beck's Underground Map: A History*. Capitol Transport Publishing, 1994. Print.

Gould, A. G. "West Palm Beach Canal." *American Canal Society Index*. The American Canal Society, n.d. Web. 20 Dec. 2014

Graves, Greg. "Ecosummary: West Palm Beach Canal." *Florida Department of Environmental Protection*. Florida Department of Environmental Protection, n.d. Web. 20 Dec. 2014.

Grunwald, Michael. *The Swamp: The Everglades, Florida, and the Politics of Paradise*. New York: Simon & Schuster, 2006. Print.

Hanna, Alfred Jackson and Kathryn Abbey Hanna. *Lake Okeechobee: Wellspring of the Everglades*. Bobbs-Merrill, 1948. Print.

Hiassen, Carl. "Slime torrent polluting state's coast." *Miami Herald*. MiamiHerald.com. October 6, 2012. Web. 20 Dec. 2014

"The Bust." *Historical Society of Palm Beach County*. Historical Society of Palm Beach County, n.d. Web. 20 Dec. 2014.

Huser, Tom. *Into the Fifth Decade: The First Forty Years of the South Florida Water Management*. Web.

Jinks, Tiphanie, and David Colangelo. "Kissimmee River Restoration Project Facts and Information." *Headquarters*. US Army Corps of Engineers, July 2012.Web. .20 Dec. 2014.

Killer, Ed. "Discharges from Lake Okeechobee killing St. Lucie Estuary slowly, surely." TCPalm. E W Scripps LLC, 4 Nov. 2012. Web. 20 Dec. 2014

"Our Future Water Supply: Regional C-51 Reservoir Plan." *Lake Worth Drainage District*. Lake Worth Drainage District, n.d. Web. 20 Dec. 2014.

Margasak, Gabriel. "Research in 2008 could direct tens of millions of dollars toward cleaner waterways, better environment on Treasure Coast." *TCPalm*. E W Scripps, LLC, 19 December 2007. Print.

Martin County Board of County Commissioners. "Speak Up for the St. Lucie." *Martin County, Florida*. Martin County, FL, n.d. Web. 20 Dec. 2014.

Mykle, Robert. *Killer 'Cane: The Deadly Hurricane of 1928*. New York: Cooper Square P, 2002. Print.

Palm Beach County Department of Environmental Resources Management. "Lake Worth Lagoon Management Plan Revision, March 2008." Web.20 Dec. 2014.

Pfost, Russell L. "Reassessing the Impact of Two Historical Florida Hurricanes." *Bulletin of the American Meteorological Society* 84.10 (October 2003): 1367–72. Print.

Phlips, E., et al. "Climatic Influences on Autochtonous and Allochthonous Phytoplankton Blooms in a Subtropical Estuary, St. Lucie Estuary, Florida, USA." *Estuaries and Coasts*, 35 (2012): 335–52. Print.

Pittman, Craig. "Liquid Poison." *Tampa Bay Times*, 27 Feb. 2006: . Print.

Purdum, Elizabeth D. *Florida Waters: A Water Resources Manual from Florida's Water Management Districts. Southwest Florida Water Management District*. Southwest Florida Water Management District Headquarters, 2002. Print.

Rouse, Renay. "Water Advisory Bacteria Levels Elevated at Roosevelt Bridge." *Florida Department of Health*. Florida Department of Health,7 October 2012. Web.

Sierra Club of Florida. "Florida Slime Crimes." *Sierra Club*. Sierra Club, n.d.Web.. 12 Dec. 2014.

Sime, P. L.; Goodman, P.; Roderick, G. N.; Stoffella, P. J. "Remediation and beneficial reuse of contaminated sediments." *Proceedings of the First International Conference on Remediation of Contaminated Sediments*. 10–12 October 2001, Venice, Italy: Batelle Press, 2005. Print.

Smith, Randy and Gabe Margasak. "A Storm for the Record Books' in Palm Beach County." Web. 12 Dec. 2014. PDF file.

South Florida Water Management District. "Managing and Protecting Water." *South Florida Water Management District*. SFWMD Headquarters, n.d. Web. 12 Dec. 2014.

"The State Steps In." *South Florida Water Management District*. SFWMD Headquarters, n.d. Web. 12 Dec. 2014.

Torrent, Danielle. "UF-led study: Invasive amphibians, reptiles in Florida outnumber world." *UF News*. U of Florida: 15 September 2011. Web.

Treadway, Tyler. "Harbor Branch study conclusively ties St. Lucie Estuary damage to Lake O releases." *TCPalm*. E W Scrips, LLC: 4 January 2013. Web. 12 Dec. 2014.

Trefry, John H., Robert P. Trocine, and Hester Bennett. "Sediment Sourcing Study of Lake Worth Lagoon and C-51 Basin, Palm Beach County." Florida Institute of Technology, November 2009. Print.

Vearil, James. "History of Lake Okeechobee Operating Criteria." Greater Everglades Ecosystem Restoration Conference. Naples, FL: 2008. Web. 12 Dec. 2014.

Voisinet, Robert L.P. "Mucking Up the St. Lucie." *Florida Master Naturalist Program Final Report*.n.p., 14 December 2007. Print.

Watts, Adam C., and Leda N. Kobziar. "Smoldering Combustion in Organic Soils: Peat and Muck Fires in the Southeastern U.S." Southern Fire Exchange, n.d. PDF.

10 The Spectator, the Spectacle, and the Spectral at the Stadium Course at the Tournament Players Club, Ponte Vedra Beach

James P. Beasley

Introduction

The Players Championship at the TPC Sawgrass Stadium Course in Ponte Vedra Beach, Florida is the most watched golf tournament on the PGA Tour not only in the numbers who attend the four-day tournament every May, but the television audiences who are also the largest of any tournament in the world. In 2011, over 160,000 spectators attended the four-day event and its television audience averaged over six hundred million viewers. This chapter examines the reasons why The Players is the most watched tournament in golf and those reasons are first of all found in the history of the tournament itself, designed to facilitate the gaze of the sports spectator. The second reason is in the stadium design of the course, which while facilitating the gaze of the sports spectator, transforms that gaze into its own spectacle. And then third, how the design of the course is complicit within the state of Florida's gaze industry and in the spectrality of the course itself, for more than any other course, TPC Stadium is the course which watches. While the design of the TPC Stadium course allows the course itself to gaze at the players and spectators, in as much as the players and spectators are inhabitants of a specifically Floridian space of tourist consumption, the TPC Stadium course watches Florida itself. While "all eyes are on Florida" has recently been made more conscious due to hanging chads and long voting lines, the Players Tournament was designed with this very purpose in mind from its inception.

For this study, I have examined historical accounts of the origins of the PGA Tour and the Players Championship. Second, as a Jacksonville resident and golfer, I have utilized design principles of golf course architecture and personal photographs to examine gazing as an inherent presence of the Stadium Course. Third, I utilized the concept of the tourist gaze and histories of Florida tourism to examine the Stadium Course at TPC as Florida tourist consumption. This cycle of watching and consumption builds throughout the course, from the spectacle of the clubhouse to the spectrality of seventeenth "island green," the most photographed and most imitated golf hole in the world.

The Tournament Players Championship and the Origins of Golf Spectatorship

In 1971, then PGA Tour Commissioner Deane Beman conceived of a tournament that the players would consider their "home course." The time was ripe for such a bold move since golf was coming into a newer, younger, more invigorated field starring Jack Nicklaus and a "home course" tournament would capitalize on this invigorated base of golf viewers worldwide. While the idea to create a "fifth major"-in addition to the storied Masters, the US Open, The British Open and the PGA Championship-was initiated to broaden the golfing fan base, it would have the added benefit of increasing the coffers of the PGA itself.

The first years of the tournament were played in 1974 to 1981, and Jack Nicklaus was the winner in 1974, 1976, and 1978. In 1974 it was played at the Atlanta Country Club, in 1975 it was played at the Memorial Country Club in Fort Worth, TX, the third year it was played at the Inverry Country Club in Fort Lauderdale, and from 1977–1981 at the Ponte Vedra Country Club in Ponte Vedra Beach, FL. It was during this period that professional golf was being torn apart. The USGA, or United States Golfer's Association, and the "PGA Tour" are distinct and separate entities. The USGA is the governing body for the rules of golf, founded in 1894. The PGA Tour, on the other hand, has a distinct and more market-influenced history. Before Beman became the commissioner, the PGA Tour simply was responsible for scheduling of tournaments, but under Beman's leadership, he expanded the responsibilities to include the negotiation of television rights, marketing, and most importantly the design and management of its own golf courses. While Beman believed that he could best watch out for the players by watching out for the Tour, many players did not see it that way at the time. These moves created direct competition for players who had their own golfing corporations, such as Jack Nicklaus's "Golden Bear" enterprises. The players revolted. They ran letters off to the PGA Tour's board of directors, demanding that Beman be stopped. Jack Nicklaus, who won the TPC three out of its first four years, writes, "Deane worked as hard as he could to have a socialist state" (Schupak 11). In May of 1980, chairman of the Tour board of directors, E.M de Windt, invited several top professionals to hear their concerns about Beman. As CEO of the Eaton Corporation, a major sporting goods manufacturer, de Windt could have also been seen as having conflicting interests with Tour players such as Nicklaus. After several top professionals spoke, de Windt rejected their concerns, most forcefully because the most controversial of Beman's innovations had not yet been tested. The Tour's board of directors had bought Beman some time, but the clock was ticking. Beman's innovations had a short shelf life, and the upcoming Tournament Player's Championship at the newly designed and Tour-owned Stadium Course at TPC Sawgrass would be the determining factor in whether or not he would survive.

The first round of the Tournament Players Championship at the Stadium course began on March, 18, 1982. Beman had given the professionals the choice to return to the Sawgrass Country Club, on the eastern side of A1A, but they declined. This first round did not go well. Scores were high and the players made no attempt to hide their frustration. Jack Nicklaus commented, "This course plays all around my game and never touches it. I've never been very good at stopping a five-iron on the hood of a car" (Passov). Fuzzy Zoeller remarked, "Where are the windmills and the animals?" (Passov) Not to be outdone by Zoeller, one unidentified professional commented, "The seventeenth is a ridiculous piece of shit, reminiscent of some putt-putt carnival course" (Dye 136). In designer Pete Dye's account of the first tournament held at the Stadium Course, he writes, "Looking back, I realize that the radical design of the Stadium Course wasn't something the Tour professionals were ready for. They had never seen anything like it, and they were displeased when a wayward bounce or unexpected roll of a green ruined what they felt was a perfectly hit shot" (138). Based on the historical context, however, it is no wonder the initial assessments of the tournament were extremely negative, i.e., the players utilized the frustration with the course design and the concept of stadium golf as push-back against Beman. While the players did not want the Tour administrating the business of golf, the comparisons to putt-putt golf after the first round illustrate some deeper points about the direction that professional golfers believed Beman was headed. It was not just a business, but a tourist business, and tourist business attracted a baser, more frivolous participant and spectator.

If after the first round, the players were embarrassed by the carnival nature of the course, they must have winced a bit more when after winning the tournament, Jerry Pate threw both Pete Dye and Dean Beman into the lake off of the eighteenth[h] hole before jumping in the lake himself, behavior not even allowed on putt-putt courses. In his on-air announcement, Vin Scully remarked, "If this isn't right out of . . . *Animal House*. With that, there's no other way to go to Brent Musburger in New York" (Schupak, 112). As these images were broadcast around the country, the sport of golf and the public's relationship to it monumentally shifted. Jerry Pate's golf game was no longer the spectacle; the influence of spectator golf prompted Pate to continue making a spectacle of himself, Dye, and Beman. Pate's spectacle demonstrated Beman's strategy: television rights were the key to growing the Tour. "When Beman took the reins as a commissioner on March 1, 1974, the Tournament Player's Division existed on one-year TV agreements. ABC televised the bulk of the tour's coverage, including most of the early-season events. At the time, the network also held the rights to three of the four majors, none of which the TPD operated or received a rights fee for its player's participation" (Schupak 68). The fans could not literally see the events due to a lack of broadcasting. As one of the last professional sports to pay attention to the revenues that television coverage could bring, professional golf would have been considered by theorists like McLuhan as a "hot" medium, relying on reporters to bring spectators the action in journalistic print. In Beman's tenure, he first began negotiating a multi-year deal with ABC, but in 1977, Beman negotiated a twenty million dollar television deal with CBS. Then with NBC, "He enabled television to provide extended coverage of golf compared to what it was in the mid 1970's the former CBS sports president said, 'We have Thursday-Friday golf, prime time golf, golf on multiple channels, and there's Golf Channel itself.' All of these in one way or another, Deane was responsible for and helped bring to fruition" (Schupak 68). Beman did this through corporate sponsorship, convincing the networks that if the tournament had a corporate sponsor in the title, they themselves would buy enough advertising to make its broadcast profitable. The plans worked. Just three years after E.M. de Windt squashed the players revolt against Beman, de Windt's writes in his annual report:

The new strategy and programs appear to have had a positive impact. For example: television ratings and sales substantially increased, resulting in new multi-year contracts at significantly higher rights fees; both total prize money and charitable contributions by tour sponsors increased to record highs; the first Players Championship at a stadium golf facility produced considerable public interest and new income for the tour; and the first two $1,000,000 tour events were announced" (24–25).

While the shared ownership of television rights and tour courses was merely controversial, it was the concept of stadium golf that was radical. Through Beman's negotiations, he had made golf, "cool," meaning he had changed golf spectatorship from high-information media to a low-information, high-participation media. McLuhan writes, "Any hot medium allows of participation than a cool one, as a lecture makes for less participation than a seminar, and a book for less than dialogue" (162). Beman had succeeded in creating the avenues through which the golfing public would be able to watch the sport of golf like never before, but now there had to be something to watch.

STADIUM GOLF AND THE GAZE OF THE SPORTS SPECTATOR

The TPC Stadium Course in Ponte Vedra, Florida was designed in 1980 from 415 acres of marsh and swamp. In a December 2000 interview with *Golf Club Atlas*, TPC designer Pete Dye was asked, "How is your design influenced when you build a course knowing that it will host tournaments like the TPC Stadium Course at Sawgrass?" Dye replied, "Gallery, Gallery, Gallery" (*Golf Club Atlas*). In wanting to establish a home for the professional golfer, Beman knew who he wanted to design the course. By 1977, golf course architect Pete Dye had already designed some of the most interesting golf courses in the United States, the most notable being the Harbor Town Golf Links at Hilton Head, South Carolina in 1969. For many of his courses, Dye's design philosophy was to negate as many conceptions of golf course design as possible. Of his design at Harbor Town, Pete Dye writes the following:

> In an ironic way, my design concepts at Harbor Town were influenced by the architecture of Robert Trent Jones, in that I took Mr. Jones's ideas and headed in the opposite direction. Instead of long tees, flowing fairways, and elevated large greens, I deliberately chose to design multiple tee position, small to medium size 'shot demanding' greens, undulating fairways, long waste areas, and abrupt, steep pot bunkers. (94)

For Dye, Robert Trent Jones represented "classical" golf course design, and classical meant disembodied, a course which had the grotesque, and its subsequent life-giving forces, cut out of it. Virgina Wright Wexman writes, "The new bodily canon, in all its historic variations and different genres, presents an entirely finished, completed strictly limited body, which is show from the outside as something individual. That which protrudes, bulges, sprouts, or branches off is eliminated, hidden or moderated. (25). For Dye, these protrusions and bulges would become Dye's signature design element, and the mounds themselves would facilitate the initial spectator gaze in a newly created network of tourism, gazing, and consumption.

By now, the famous meeting between Dye and Beman at a Jacksonville diner to draw up the course design on a napkin is legendary. Dye gives credit to Beman's vision, "Deane Beman's stadium-golf principle was not a new one, but no one had ever taken the innovation as far as Deane envisioned. In effect, he wanted to create several hubs of activity where spectators could watch the competitors on as many holes as possible" (130). The TPC sells forty thousand tickets per day to the tournament, and in this way it is more like a true sports stadium. The spectator mounds are measured to know how many people they can hold. At first, Dye began creating grass "bleachers," rows of grass that were elevated every three feet, but the effect was too artificial. The spectator design was too obvious, spectators needed to be able to watch the action, but not in such a way that would resemble other sporting events such as basketball bleachers. Dye describes how the stadium design organically developed, "During the months of constructing the course, the huge mounds simply evolved. The more muck I dug up, the higher the mounds became, but to our pleasant surprise they looked great. We planned on ten-to twelve-foot-high mounds, but they soon approached thirty to forty feet and provided an amphitheater effect that really embellished the course" (132).

On the par-three third hole, the spectator areas are around twenty feet above the tee area. This particular vantage point is directly on the path of the parade of flags, one of the busiest hubs of activity on the course.[1] What is unique about the par-three third hole is that this vantage point is approximately seventy-five yards on the left hand side of the fairway, too far to see a right-handed player's face. However, this vantage point, where several thousand spectators will pass in their daily tournament pass, has the position of seeing directly across the short water hazard at the spectator mounds on the right hand side of the tee. In other words, Dye not only created spectator mounds to view the golfing action, but created spectator mounds for spectators to view other spectators viewing the golfing action.

Figure 1. Parade of Flags

Dye not only wanted spectators to view the shots, but more importantly was the ability to view the golfer's reactions to those shots. "These spectator mounds were positioned on the right side of the hole so the gallery would be looking into the golfers' faces, and they were built on the northwest side to block out the prevailing wind. This also permitted the walking gallery plenty of room to move about the course" (133). As one can see in this photo of the sixteenth hole, this vantage point is 25–30 feet well above the action on the right side of the hole, giving the spectator an unprecedented view of a player's *reaction* to a shot over the water into the green.

By creating a natural amphitheater around tee boxes and greens, Dye increases the voyeurism of the experience not only through spectators being able to see the players' reactions, but to hear them as well. Dye writes, "But while the professionals rebelled, the fans loved the course. The spectator mounds were packed all day long, especially at seventeen and eighteen, as the fans cheered the successful shots and groaned with those players who found the water" (138). The grotesque movements of the spectators contribute to the carnivalesque experience, again differentiating his course from the classical disembodied courses of Robert Trent Jones.

Figure 2. The Sixteenth hole

Bakhtin writes, "The entire logic of the grotesque movements of the body ... is of a topographical nature. The system of these movements is oriented in relation to the upper and lower stratum: it is a system of flights and descents into the lower depths (353). This subversion of the upper and lower stratum literally refers to the process of moving the muck on top and switching it with the sand on the bottom. Dye writes "At TPC we wanted a sandy-soil base to grow the Bermuda grass. We therefore dug out all of the muck that was on top, removed the sand below it, and then flip-flopped the two" (132). Quite literally, the soil itself was a 'system of flights and descents into the lower depths,' but when seen through Dye's description of how it was the spectators who loved the course and the professionals which hated it, the grotesque subversion of the body through the development of the spectator mounds and the elimination of classical elements combine to illustrate the true carnivalesque nature of the TPC. The seventeenth and eighteenth holes were the penultimate spectator experience.

At 137 yards, the seventeenth, "island green" is the shortest hole on the course, but when one considers that the landing area is a miniscule 26 yards deep (PGA Tour), the consequences of playing poorly on this hole are intensified. Dye writes, "The island green at the seventeenth made me realize that I had created a hole that was planted in the player's mind from the very first tee. Knowing they ultimately have to confront the do-or-die seventeenth, competitors subconsciously realize that no lead is secure until their ball is safely on that green" (135). Dye's realization of the island green's image is essential in the Stadium course's ability to facilitate the gazing inherent in sports spectatorship. As one can see in this photo of the seventeenth island green, spectator mounds surround the entire hole. The spectator mound is around 25 feet above the island green, and the spectator mounds are up to 40 feet above the tee box.

Figure 3. The Seventeenth Island

What Beman gave golf spectators to watch would not be golf, but the watching itself. Dye comments, "Though the seventeenth was an immediate success with the fans and the media, many of the professionals hated the hole because there was no bail-out area. But the audience—at the course and watching television at home—loved seeing their favorite players struggle to hit the green. Even when the players were successful, their animated sighs of relief brought huge roars from the fans" (138). Such an effect had never been more orchestrated in the history of the sport. Watching the seventeenth island green at TPC Sawgrass is a tourist industry all its own. Not only is the most photographed golf hole in the world, but "getting on" the island green is the main reason why the course is the most played during the year of any course to be used for a PGA Tour-sponsored tournament.[2]

The spectator experience at the seventeenth island green builds to the finishing eighteenth hole. Again, spectator mounds line the entire right side of the fairway, allowing spectators to view the faces of the players in the tee box.

Figure 4. Spectator Mounds

This hole has the added design feature of the finishing amphitheater green. In their book, the *Architects of Golf,* Geoffery Cornish and Ronald Whitten write, "The finishing hole was meant to be one giant amphitheater, capable of holding fifty thousand people, the entire audience of a typical tournament's final round, so that every paying customer could witness the climactic final putts" (148).[3] Beman knew that in order to broaden golf's fan base beyond those who were golfers, he would have to broaden the viewing access to golf via greater television broadcasts. He also had to give golf spectators something to witness, and the more people that could witness, the more they could participate in golf tournaments not as the achievement of one golfer over others, but they could participate as part of the spectacle of the scene itself. Gary Crawford writes, "The presentation and the spectacle within the sport venue should not be viewed as a one way process of production and consumption, in which the audience constitutes passive consumers of the spectacle—as the audience themselves often constitute an important role in the creation of spectacle and atmosphere within the venue" (85). Golf spectators had become golf consumers, and the more they could gaze, the more they could consume. The demand for the consumption of the seventeenth island green itself became so great, that by playing any island green on any course, a golfer could by proxy play the seventeenth at TPC Sawgrass. Cornish and Whitten write, "Perhaps the players' protests solidified the general public's admiration for [seventeen]. Whatever the reason, island greens began popping up with regularity on courses in the 1980's. Architects claimed course owners demanded them. Island greens certainly became the star attractions at many new courses and focal points for countless photographs and advertisements"(151). Because the "island green" at TPC Sawgrass is designed to court disaster, the watching of players expressing fear and frustration is part of the design. Of this hole, Dye explains, "Golfers love to be punished" (Stine 8), and because of the appearance of island greens in many other course designs, especially more PGA Tour designed and own courses, more golfers could participate in Dye's punishment. Schupak writes, "As one of golf's most influential temples, TPC Sawgrass inspired a generation of target golf courses and started a trend of 'heroic holes'—with disaster waiting at every turn. Elements of Dye's demonic design became *de riguer*: nightmare-inducing carries of water, steeply banked greens, and severe putting surfaces" (161–162). Dye's prediction that "golfers want to be punished" is further illustrated in the fact that the revenue from PGA Tour owned courses, most of them utilizing the "island green" feature, has eclipsed the revenue from its television rights. "A decade after TPC Sawgrass opened, revenue from operations, royalties and licensing fees, management fees, and membership sales totaled $63.5 million—eclipsing revenue from television" (Schupack 162). While Dye and Beman increased television access and developed stadium golf to enhance spectatorship, PGA Tour owned courses are now watching more expressions of punishment than ever before.

In the next section, I will discuss how this need for gaze and its corresponding consumption has its roots in Florida tourism and how both the TPC Sawgrass course is both a product and perpetuator of this environment.

The Tourist Gaze, Florida Tourism, and Spectral Impact

In his book, *The Tourist Gaze,* John Urry writes, "Because of the universalization of the tourist gaze, all sorts of places (indeed almost everywhere) have come to construct themselves as objects of the tourist's gaze; in other words, not as centers of production or symbols of power, but as sites of pleasure" (125). While the TPC Stadium course may facilitate pleasure in watching the pain of others, the clubhouse devotes itself to more overt pleasurable gazes of the tourist. The current TPC clubhouse was built in the thirteen months between the 2005 tournament in March, and the 2006 Tournament in May 2006. As one can see in this photo, it is not only worth looking at, but the clubhouse becomes a site/sight worth looking *from,* especially when one considers that the old clubhouse that served the club from 1980–2006 was a low profile building whose roofing tiles were eaten by neighboring goats that could easily climb onto the low-lying tiles.

Figure 5. The Old Clubhouse

The new clubhouse is not low-lying. At 77,000 square feet, it commands the views surrounding the neighboring first, third, and eighteenth holes. Inside the clubhouse the spectatorship does not end, for portraits of significant moments of the Players tournament line the mammoth walls such as Hal Sutton's pleading "Be the right club today" cry from the eighteenth fairway in his 2000 win over Tiger Woods, and going back to Jerry Pate's dunking of Deane Beman and Pete Dye in 1982.

Figure 6. Jerry Pate's dunking of Deane Beman and Pete Dye in 1982

Upstairs in the clubhouse, more portraits line the walls. A local artist captured winning moments of all the tournaments, and the one constant in all of them is the presence of spectators under whose eyes the champions prevailed. Not guides but "Storytellers" provide commentary on the clubhouse portraits and scenes. When I inquired after the many number of portraits available for viewing, a guide ssured me that I was not the only one watching. "The artist painted the faces of her husband, her hairdresser, and her neighbor in every gallery of each portrait. They are watching you look at the winner."

The TOUR Shop concludes the tour, where tourists can purchase TPC Sawgrass merchandise. Television screens are everywhere in the clubhouse. Some screens are tuned into live Golf Channel coverage, while some are video replays of the Players' greatest moments.[4]

On the relationship between the television and the sports spectator, Guttman writes,

> The psychological mechanism of identification completes the process. Through the mechanism of identification, the spectators in the stands and before the flickering TV sets join vicariously in the violent release achieved by the players on the field. Drained of all hostil-

ity by the spectacle of aggression, the fans are devoid of any interest in political action. They are apathetic, infantilized, cretinized; in a word, dehumanized. (Guttman 150).

In many ways, before Beman's tenure as tour commissioner, golf spectators were too human, those who attended the tournaments were golfers, and because of golf course design of designers such as Robert Trent Jones, galleries had to follow around and strain to see the shots and victorious moments of the champions. By bringing golf tournaments into America's living rooms, by creating tournaments for the non-golfing spectator, and by creating the TPC Stadium course in Ponte Vedra Beach, Beman and the tour gave golfing spectators the right to be just as dehumanized as soccer fans in Europe or football fans here in the United States. This dehumanization takes on a more overt character while on the course itself. While driving along the sixteenth fairway, my guide, known as a "storyteller" at the TPC clubhouse, remarked on the presence of a member of each foursome in all white. "The men in white are forecaddies, and they are required by every group that goes out on the course. This is really pretty land, as you can see, and they don't want a bunch of drunks out here ruining the course. They help the players, tell them what club to use, and things like that, but their main reason is to make sure that no one misbehaves." Riding further, he sees a young couple with Starbucks coffees leisurely walking up ahead. "Hello, folks," he calls out. "Guided tours are available from the clubhouse; why don't you hop in the cart so I can get you out of harm's way here." A smiling young couple announce, "We're from Madison, Wisconsin," offering their tourist status without solicitation. After he safely drops them off back at the clubhouse, he remarks that "We have more people visit from foreign countries than we do Florida residents. Most people that live around here don't know all this is back here." While over half of the attendees of the Player's Tournament are not from the Jacksonville area, most of the players who play the course year-round are also not from the Jacksonville area. This is not to say that the PGA Tour's influence is not felt in the Jacksonville community, however.

The effect of the Player's Championship on the city of Jacksonville, Florida and the greater Northeast Florida economy was also manipulated by Beman to afford greater participation. According to Adam Schupack, "The Greater Jacksonville Open was considered the stepchild of what pros dubbed the 'Winter Tour.' It didn't have a popular course like Doral or Harbour Town. The Jacksonville event skipped from Selva Marina to Hidden Hills to Deerwood, where it was being played at the time. It didn't have the celebrity appeal of Jackie Gleason, who hosted the south Florida stop at Inverrary Country Club" (117). Comedian Jackie Gleason made Florida golf tourism a second calling. Thanks to television and his television appeal, Gleason's celebrity golf tournaments around South Florida introduced Florida golf to much larger national audiences, and his connection to South Florida golf was a major source of contention with north Florida tourism and with the PGA Tour in particular. While south Florida golf could rely on Jackie Gleason to promote its courses and lifestyle via his large television audiences, the combination of unproven stadium golf and difficult negotiations with television executives would have to work for North Florida. In other words, while North Florida golf had to work to manufacture its audiences, all Jackie Gleason had to do was wave his hand, and with a jaunty "And away we go!" millions of viewers were easily transported to Fouth Florida and its tourism dollars. Writing on the appeal of Jackie Gleason, Virginia Wright Wexman comments, "TV characters strike us a being just like the actors who play them, who, in turn, seem like the audiences who watch them and fantasize about them" (20). While the winner of the first Tournament Player's Championships, Jack Nicklaus, was a widely known television star, he was not a widely known television *character*. If the TPC was going to lure tourists to North Florida, it would have to create characters. Jerry Pate's dunking of Deane Beman after the first tournament became part of this role. Wexman writes of the role that Bahktinian theory plays in Jackie Gleason's celebrity and it bears examination in connection with celebrity creation in north Florida and the TPC. She writes, "Bakhtin associates such uses of the body not with the activities of everyday life but with performative events such as carnivals and artistic representations. Further, Bakhtin is specifically concerned with the role played by the exaggerated forms associated with comedy in the articulation of these meanings" (21).The creation of the Stadium course as exaggeration, i.e., "Where are the clowns and the windmills?" and Jerry Pate's jumping in the lake next to the eighteenth green, was the TPC Stadium course's response to Jackie Gleason in South Florida, as comedy spectacle in larger than life Technicolor.

Golf in Jacksonville before the Players and the tour had been anything but Technicolor. The Greater Jacksonville Open was the only tournament on the Tour's schedule, and while it had bounced around local clubs unequipped for national television coverage or spectators, "Beman admired the commitment of the volunteers and the way the tournament had become an integral part of the Jacksonville community" (Schupack 117). Beman convinced the tournament to give up its identity in order to partner with the charities it sponsored. Under Beman's chairmanship, all PGA Tournaments had to register as 501-c3 organizations, and The Players would be the first with its partnership with the Jacksonville business community in its charitable entrepreneurship and subsequent tax benefits. According to Ken Wilson, vice president of GL National, Inc., the real-estate division of Gate Petroleum, "It wasn't the only factor, but the tournament helped coax Merrill Lynch & Co. to move some of its operations to Jacksonville in the early 1990s" (Szakonyi). Again, the luring of the business community into Jacksonville has in part the promise of being watched, at least during TPC weekend. The golfing tourism industry of Ponte Vedra Beach prior to the Players tournament had emphasized Ponte Vedra's solitary golfing community, as seen in this postcard of the Ponte Vedra Golf Club from around 1965.[5]

Here in this postcard, the gaze of the viewer sees a pastoral scene of golfers playing on a flat, "classical" design. There is no rupture of the physical environment or the social environment as evidenced in the architecture and purpose of the Stadium course built for the tournament in 1982. The players themselves have their backs to the gaze of the viewer, unaware that they are being watched, in contrast to the overt knowledge of the players at the Stadium course being watched on every shot. TPC Stadium course represented a radical shift in Ponte Vedra Beach tourism, from a place of idyllic solitude to overt participation in the cycle of consumption. In a postcard from around 1970 indicates, Ponte Vedra is "romantic," where couples could pass hours of time in solitude with no one watching their tourist behaviors.[6] In both of these postcards before the development of the TPC Stadium course, the Ponte Vedra Golf club serves as a backdrop for unwatched tourist behavior. This change from being a romantic vacation spot to a space of perpetual spectatorship and consumption was difficult for many residents to understand. Jacksonville resident and PGA Tour professional Mark McCumber writes the following:

> I love everything about my hometown, but it is South Georgia-North Florida. We don't have palm trees everywhere. We have a bit of winter. It's a blue-collar town. It's not Miami Beach. It's not on a bay. You're going to build in an area that at the time you wouldn't want to drive through at night without an extra canister of gas in your car? And now it's going to be the home of a high-end resort and community and host the best golfers every spring? (Schupak 158)

The most important factor in this turnaround is the increase in the spectators that could attend the tournament and that could watch the tournament on television. Perhaps the most important aspect of the tournament is that its gaze can be expanded to one of the largest television audiences in sports. In an interview with the *Florida Times-Union,* Jacksonville chamber of commerce's Jerry Mallot says, "The coverage on TV paints the most appealing picture of Northeast Florida that you could ask for. An estimated 120 million US viewers and 600 million internationally will see some of those pictures during the course of the week" (Ezell). Even as these pictures are broadcasted to increasingly international audiences, a type of cultural exchange has taken place, since according to the *Florida Times-Union*, Mallot believes the tournament is underappreciated here in Jacksonville (Ezell). His view is supported by recent research on the Players tournament.

The Institute of Food and Agricultural Sciences at the University of Florida has investigated the economic impact of the Players Championship on the Northeast Florida Region in 2005 and then two years later in 2007. The major differences in the tournament between 2005 and 2007 are the moving of the tournament from March to May and the demolition of the old clubhouse and the building of the new 77,000 square foot clubhouse with its new features to enhance the tourist gaze. According to Stevens, Hodges, and Mulkey, "Designed not only to make the course more challenging and consistent across varied weather conditions, these renovations also expanded the course's spectator capacity" (1). For example, while there was an overall fourteen percent increase in attendance from 2005 to 2007, there was a three percent decline in "Local (north-east Florida residents)" attendance, but a 12.3% increase in "Non-local" attendance (16). Those who stayed overnight in commercial lodging represented an increase of seventy-seven percent from 2005 to 2007 (16). These additional tourist gazes correlate to increased consumption. According to Stevens, Hodges, and Mulkey, "Average on-site spending per day increased from $83.23 (in 2007 dollars) per attendee at the 2005 event to $123.07 at the 2007 tournament. In real terms, this represents a forty-seven percent increase. On site spending by non-locals at the 2007 event increased by 114 percent over 2005 levels, while on-site spending by local attendees grew by forty-three percent" (17). The total expenditures in 2005 for all attendees was $57,261,932 compared to $88,027,191 in 2007, a 53.7% increase in total expenditures from 2005 to 2007 (19). This increase in consumption is commensurate with the renovations of the clubhouse to enhance tourist gazing. Urry writes the following:

> Given the emphasis on tourist consumption as visual, and the significance of buildings as objects upon which the gaze is directed, it is essential to consider changing patterns and forms that those buildings might take. Moreover, it is of course impossible to consider postmodernism without consideration of the built environment, surely the sphere which many would say best demonstrates such cultural paradigm (120).

The forty-seven percent increase in expenditures from 2005 to 2007 certainly suggests that the increasing spectrality of the Players is commensurate with an increase in consumption. In fact, the Stadium course at TPC Sawgrass has always had such a connection, dating back to the creation of the course itself. Dye writes, "When we emptied out space for a lake or pond, the resulting muck was piled up in the areas along the fairways and roughs and alongside the greens. Using this excess muck, we began to build the large spectator mounds that would provide perfect viewing areas for the golf fans" (132). In order to create the course, Dye and his crew had to eviscerate hundreds of acres of wetlands. In other words, TPC Sawgrass is an ongoing process of spectacle and consumption. By consuming the wetland areas surrounding the course, the spectator mounds were created; but by increasing spectral spaces, the greater the consumption. The confluence between spectator and consumer is complete; in the evolution from spectator to spectacle and back again, TPC Sawgrass has become a spectral site/sight. As Italian philosopher Giorgio Agamben has written, "Spectrality is a form of life, a posthumous or complimentary life that begins only when everything is finished" (39). However, the cycle of spectator and consumption has been completed in only some respects, in others, it is an ongoing completeness, and this is a different kind of spectrality altogether, "But there is also another type of spectrality that we may call larval, which is born from not accepting its own condition, from forgetting it so as to pretend at all costs that it still has bodily weight and flesh" (40). This is type of spectrality that exists at TPC Sawgrass. The rebuilt 77,000 square foot clubhouse, with its appearance of age and permanence, both conceal and reveal its dependence on the elimination of its previous residence. The cement cartpaths and stone course markers both conceal and reveal its dependence on the elimination of four hundred acres of wetlands.

This cycle of spectral consumption makes the Stadium course at TPC a truly postmodern space, and in doing so, makes a uniquely postmodern tourist space. Urry writes of the importance of the postmodern in the creation and maintenance of the tourist gaze in the process of consumption:

> I shall argue that there are a number of postmodern architectures; second, that the impact of these different architectures depends upon whether we are considering private or public buildings; third, that architects and architectural practices are of major importance in shaping the contemporary tourist gaze; fourth that tourist practices have to be taken much more seriously by commentators on building design; and fifth, that tourists are socially differentiated and hence gaze selectively upon these different architectural styles. (120)

While Urry is specifically talking about postmodern buildings rather than golf course architecture, it is easy to see how architectural alterations in the history of the TPC Stadium course and its clubhouse have evolved to increase the tourist gaze and its subsequent spectral consumption. The relationship between the TPC and the environment has become the most obvious consumption alteration. While the very construction of the Stadium course began through wetland consumption, Dye writes, "Based on the current environmental rules, it would be impossible to build the Stadium course at TPC today. Reclaiming usable land from swamps and marshes by draining the water into lagoons was allowable then, but would not be permitted today" (132). Dye uses "draining" a little loosely in this description. The water could not be "drained," since drainage technically utilizes gravity to direct the flow of water downward, and since the TPC was basically at sea level, the water had to be pumped into the lagoons, the Guana Preserve to the east of TPC and the Intracoastal waterway to the west of TPC. Pumping water into the Guana Preserve and in the Intracoastal could not be done before environmental impact to the wildlife and ecosystems of both these areas. Dye is correct that this could not be completed today, since the ecosystems to the east and west of TPC are now protected from having water pumped into them.[7]

The construction of the Stadium course, especially as it relates to the creation of spectral consumption, is central to both the health of the Florida tourist industry, both economically and ethically. Ironically, tourism both unites and divides Floridians simultaneously. Revels writes, "Florida cannot be content to become a disposable state. Floridians already suffer from a lack of common identity, and few issues unite them. A stronger stance on tourism, especially an insistence on more careful planning and management of it, might be a good start on building a cultural bridge" (152). With all the beautiful the Bermuda grass, the great moments in the history of the Players in the clubhouse, and sparkling merchandise at the gift shop on the way out, it would be easy to believe in the fantasy of this cultural bridge. It is difficult to imagine so spectral a space with so little *terra firma*. The tourist that leaves TPC Sawgrass may believe more firmly in the permanence of spectator golf, but the course itself can have no such illusion. In the sense that the course "remains behind" after its spectral consumers have abandoned it, the course is the true "resident." Revels writes, "There is a certain pride in being a Florida resident, in living in the fantasy land that so many Americans eagerly pay to see, for only two weeks or less, because they expect it to be better than the 'real world' they left behind" (151). This is why many Floridians struggle with a shared cultural identity: while some take residing in someone else's fantasy land as a source of pride, others do not. While much has been written on TPC Sawgrass's ability to torture the golfers who play the course, Agamben demonstrates how residing in that fantasy's land plays a role in that torture, "While the first type of spectrality is perfect, since it no longer has anything to add to what it has said or done, the larval specters must pretend to have a future in order to clear a space for some torment from their own past, for their own incapacity to comprehend that they have, indeed, reached completion" (40). Perhaps this is why the Stadium course at TPC is so sinister on its players, for, because of its design to facilitate gazing, it can witness the faces of those tormented, disposable consumers, the Tour-ists, staring back.

Notes

1. All figures in this chapter were photographed by the author.

2. While I was taking this picture at the seventeenth island green, a foursome spilled out of their golf cart also taking pictures. Thumbs up all around were exchanged before they teed off. The first player hit three shots in the water before landing one on, and the second player hit three shots in the water before landing one on. The third player landed his first shot on in the middle of the green, then hit another shot on a bit further from the hole. The fourth player put one in the water before hitting his second shot on the green. He turned around and said, "When you go back home, and you tell people you played Sawgrass, that's all anybody will ask you, what did you do on 17?"

3. Some "paying customers" pay more than others. In 2011, premium tickets at the "Benefactor" level were sold for fifteen thousand dollars for a package of thirty tickets, and packages in the Dye Pavilion, which overlooks the eighteenth green, were sold at fifty thousand dollars for forty tickets.

4. In the massive Tour Gift Shop, the television sets on the walls were all tuned to Fox News. Commenting on the live feed from Fox, one of the sales clerks remarked, "Now Obama's gonna spend more of my money to kill babies. I talked to one of my friends who voted for Obama and told him what he was really about, and he's pissed. He wants his vote back. There's so many people that didn't know him. They just don't live in the real world."

5. Postcard and image courtesy of University of North Florida Library, Special Collections. Used by permission.

6. Postcard and image courtesy of University of North Florida Library, Special Collections. Used by permission.

7. In an interview with Florida golf course engineer Al Hammock, on January 15, 2013, Hammock says, "Yes, it's true that couldn't have been done now, but golf course design has become so integrated with environmentalism that most environmental groups actually want golf course designers to build in order to create habitats for indigenous species

Works Cited

Agamben, Giorgio. *Nudities*. Trans. David Kishik and Stefan Pedatella. Stanford, CA: Stanford UP, 2011. Print.

Cornish, Geoffery and Whitten, Ronald. *The Architects of Golf.* New York: Harper-Collins Publishers, 2003. Print.

Crawford, Garry. *Consuming Sport: Fans, Sport, and Culture.* London: Routledge, 2004. Print.

Dye, Pete and Shaw, Mark. *Bury Me in a Pot Bunker: Golf Through the Eyes of the Game's Most Challenging Course Designer.* Lincolnwood, IL: Contemporary Books, 1999. Print.

Ezell, Wayne. "The Players Championship: Director Has Big Aspirations for Expanding Scope of Tournament." *The Florida Times-Union.* Jacksonville.com. 30 April 2011. Web.

"Interview with Pete Dye." *Golf Club Atlas.* GCA, December 2000. Web. 15 May 2014.

Guttman, Allen. *Sports Spectators.* New York: Columbia UP, 1986. Print.

McLuhan, Marshall. "Media Hot and Cold." *Essential McLuhan.* Ed. Eric McLuhan and Frank Zingrone. New York: Basic Books, 1995: 161–68. Print.

Passov. Joe. "The Best TPC Golf Courses You Can Play." *Golf.* Golf Magazine, 15 Dec. 2006. Web. 30 Nov. 2012.

PGA Tour. *The Players Stadium Course Yardage Guide.* Mesa, AZ: Best Approach Publications, 2012. Print.

Revels, Tracy J. *Sunshine Paradise: A History of Florida Tourism.* Gainesville: U of Florida P, 2011. Print.

Schupak, Adam. *Deane Beman: Golf's Driving Force.* Orlando: East Cottage Press, 2011. Print.

Stine, Joseph. "When Pete Dye Talks, People Listen." *Florida Golf Magazine.* Winter, 2009: (8–12). Print.

Szakonyi, Mark. "Recession Expected to Cut Economic Impact of Player's Championship." *Jacksonville Business Journal.* American City Business Journals, 11 May 2009. Web.

Wexman, Virginia Wright. "Returning from the Moon: Jackie Gleason, the Carnivalesque, and Television Comedy." *Journal of Film and Video.* 42:4 Winter 1990 (20–32). Print.

Urry, John. *The Tourist Gaze: Leisure and Travel in Contemporary Societies.* London: SAGE Publications, 1990. Print.

11 Shell Games: A Eulogy Against Suburbia

David M. Grant

Sprawling on the fringes of the city
In geometric order
An insulated border
In between the bright lights
And the far unlit unknown.—Rush, "Subdivisions."
In the morning everything will be the same
Open up your world (watch the children play)
In the sun or rain
Thinking of the town and the country
—America, "Town and Country."

What is useless can nevertheless be a power—a power in the rightful sense.
—Martin Heidegger, *Introduction to Metaphysics.*

It is in the manner of immense parentheses that non-places daily receive increasing numbers of individuals

—Marc Augé, *Non-Places: Introduction to an Anthropology of Supermodernity.*

I.

Town 'n' Country, Florida is a census-designated place (CDP) situated between the city limits of Tampa and the Hillsborough—Pinellas county line. These political borders form its eastern and western flanks. At its southern and northern edges lie the mangrove shallows of Old Tampa Bay and the sinkhole lakes of Citrus Park. Political boundaries define one dimension, topography another. Even the name forms parallel borders that promise two antithetical geographies: town *and* country. But it's not just any combination of the two; the doubly abbreviated "and" forces the speaker to repeat or lengthen the phoneme, /n/, so it is pronounced more like "townin country." From there it's not a far step to add a little twang, making it sound as "tannin country" though the cypress stands that make a tea of Florida's waters are few and far between. Still, Town 'n' Country is a strangely appropriate place to mediate on certain surrealisms—how two seemingly separate things come to form something new. There are *choric* layers to trace, folds to follow, avenues that turn into waterways strewn with shipwrecks and old bones.

On the surface, Town 'n' Country is typical of suburban areas built up out of citrus groves and grazing land during the 1960s and 1970s. It's not too different from nearby Lutz, where Tim Burton filmed exterior scenes for his movie, *Edward Scissorhands*. The name reflects an idyllic, imagined geographical mix that sells the dream of affordable suburban living. The comfortable confines of town co-exist with just a bit of pastoral country, though the nature of this co-existence remains a question. Is it bifurcated along the middle somewhere, or, perhaps, checked and alternating like a chessboard? Even further still, is it dotted like dumpling batter simmering in chicken broth? What is on the other side of the country if not more town?

There is no reference to any historical figure or event. No predominant landmark lends its features. There are simply the generic terms "town" and "country" barely connected by the doubly-shortened conjunction. The terms are juxtaposed, almost casually tossed together. It thus retains a certain ambiguity necessary for broad, generic appeal by allowing others to fill in the missing connections. The name is an empty placeholder, a folding together of disparate monads, each casting forth their own set of relations.

In *The Fold*, philosopher Gilles Deleuze revises Leibniz's concepts so that "each perceived set of relations is made up of monads, which are the self-sufficient substances prior to all relations. Each monad perceives the whole of the world from its own point of view, creating its own perceived relations" (Colebrook xxv). Monads are not atoms or quarks or anything "out there," but a certain intensity which has coalesced into being—a blade of grass, a weathered brick, Interstate 75. For Deleuze the true task of thinking lies partly in the task of affirming all these points of view, "for each perception affirms this eternal whole differently (and also, through perception, contributes to the change and creation of the whole)" (Colebrook 175). As a certain intensity, Town 'n' Country offers a relative absence of privileged planes of perception about it. There are no master narratives as there are about places like Gettysburg, Boston, or Dallas, no lens through which we tend to view it as commonplace. Its relative absence of history, emptiness, and generic appeal mark it as a kind of contemporary space popping up all across the globe, what Marc Augé calls a "non-place."

II.

CNN reports that nearly half of the United States lives in a suburb (2006). Sam Roberts at *The New York Times* talks about the increasing racial diversity of suburban demographics and that "in the nation's 100 largest metropolitan areas, black, Hispanic and Asian residents constitute a majority of residents younger than 18—presaging a benchmark that the nation as a whole is projected to reach in just over a decade." As Andres Duany and Elizabeth Plater-Zyberk have argued, America is suburb nation.

Like other Sunbelt states, Florida is often representative of urban sprawl and suburban blight. There may be some truth in this as many of its residents live in the residential areas created during the housing boom in the middle and late parts of the twentieth century. But "suburb" is a confusing term. Like an urban area, suburbs are marked by a dense cluster of man-made structures: houses, strip malls, roads, water towers, churches, power lines, parks. Such structures and land use may be more highly segregated in suburbs compared to urban areas, but as Laura Vaughn, et al. (2009) point out, there is an "epistemological fragility of the term" that precludes any neat division between suburban and urban (1). Instead, we are left with a "fog of competing representations" which tend "to obstruct the possibility of meaningful generalization" (1). Some aspects of suburbs are more like town, others more like country.

Perhaps this is why suburbs are so despised. They confound our sense of order. James Kunstler's *Geography of Nowhere* comes to mind as an oft-repeated trope about suburbs: built for automobiles and not people, suburbs kill civic life, degrading just about everything from the environment to aesthetic sensibilities. Suburbs are empty, hollow, abject and symptomatic of all that is wrong with America and late capitalism. As non-places, they do not hold enough significance to be meaningful. They are to be passed through rather than actually inhabited. We arrive to a "home" in the suburbs only to continue our travels into virtual terrains—to Skyrim, Mario World, and Fox News. There is no final destination.

Yet stating this is to argue a privileged perspective. It is a convenient trope that casts our own perceptions onto a plane where we can readily deal with such spaces, hide the complexities, and dismiss them. There is no monad for each suburban place, only the monad for all suburbia everywhere. We need to recover something here, something that has disappeared into watery depths.

III.

As with suburbs, we often think of shells as hollow. When I lived In Arizona, I took home some shells from a trip to Puerto Peñasco, Mexico, a tourist town on the Gulf of California. Even though I was careful to inspect them, a hermit crab had escaped my sight until it reappeared from its shell on my dining room table. It's like Freud's story of the fort—da game: now you see it, now you don't. From one angle, something is apparent. Shift the angle of perception and it isn't. We aren't talking about camouflage or obstruction when it comes to the perceptions of monads and the relations between them. Rather, it is a matter of functioning or prehension—how we grasp things with and through our senses. Deleuze shows us this through the fold. Monads are enfolded within others but ever-shifting so that they appear and disappear kaleidoscopically. We can use the analogy of the trick with the dollar bill where it is folded one way and then unfolded differently so everything comes out upside down, or backwards. Possibilities branch out with each finger touching paper.

As Deleuze reads Heidegger, it is *Zweifalt,* where "differentiation does not refer to a pre-given undifferentiated, but to Difference that endlessly unfolds the one only while refolding the other" (30). In other words, the bill becomes deterritorialized and then reterritorialized as its inverse. It is a calculus. A different/ial equation. It is non-linear, complex, and emphasizes paratactic connections, ecologies of jokes, puns, and Jabberwocky. It is a re-creation, just as Moon Watcher re-creates a jawbone as a weapon in Arthur C. Clarke's *2001: A Space Odyssey.* As in any ecology, nothing is either created or destroyed here; only reality recycled, refolded, re-created as part of some new territory within an always productive movement of desire.

So, what are the modes of production in suburban spaces? How might we prehend suburbia differently and re-think these places? If a bone can escape along a line of flight to the moons of Jupiter, where might suburban spaces take us?

IV.

Suburban space is often horizontal in its design, something of a counter-point to the verticality of urban space. This is largely true of Town 'n' Country as well. Horizontal suburbia is a place to move through and to always be on one's way to work, the store, or the soccer game. One exception is the library at my old school, Morgan Woods Elementary. It rises from the center of the almost flat, off-white pods used for classrooms and resembles a ziggurat with a steep, wooden-shingled roof capped by a short, vertical column. Steel beams anchor the structure from each corner to four smaller pyramids of rough concrete resting on, and probably in, the ground. That's the school's library, or it was. It is now the media center.

Figure 1. Morgan Woods Elementary (Courtesy Google)

The architecture resonates with cultural metaphors about learning. We talk of branches of knowledge growing like a tree. Education *lifts* students' minds from ignorance. We progress *up* through complexities of knowledge and levels of learning. Smarter people have *higher* IQs. This extends onto our cultural associations of light (above) and dark (below). It is the literal center of the school and so acts as a repository for what is dispensed around it in six (K-5) grades.

Ironically, the Morgan Woods media center is not actually multi-storied. There is no hierarchy of knowledge, no place to be lifted to inside its vaulted roof. The horizontal design of the school extends right through this structure, never actually breaking its plane, for the roof of the library is nothing more than a shell rising above the single layer of low, child-sized shelving for books, some reading spaces, offices and a circulation desk. It is simultaneously empty and full.

Think of this: the shell of the library contains shell-ves of books, and each book (or video) is another shell, another fold, another monad that can be juxtaposed with something else, like another book, and made into something new. Deleuze might see school students doing the work of the fold: writing papers, taking words of one shell and folding them into words of their own or into words from another shell in a ceaseless creation of difference. School authorities might disagree, and certainly it is part of their desire to fold with uniformity, consistency, and specific metrics; theirs is but one way to grasp a school's beating heart.

v.

Brion Gysin and William Burroughs are well known for popularizing the cut-up method, now an important method of invention in new media composition (Wardrip-Fruin and Montfort 2003). Gysin cut up newspapers and rearranged them to create interesting juxtapositions between image and text. Burroughs would similarly "fold in" pages of text by cutting and recombining them vertically. Such methods of invention span artists from Tristan Tzara to T. S. Eliot to Thom Yorke. According to its practitioners, new connections become apparent in new placements and unforeseen truths are revealed. In collaboration with Gysin, Burroughs wrote, "When you cut into the present the future leaks out."

Town 'n' Country is a place of the cut-up method: town and country, cut and pasted; local and national definitions; a suburb with its epistemological fragility. Even the attempts to fix and regiment it as a CDP are fraught with complications. According to the US Census Bureau, Census Designated Places (CDPs) are the "statistical counterpart of incorporated places and are delineated to provide data for settled concentrations of population that are identifiable by name but are not legally incorporated under the laws of the state in which they are located" (*Census of the Population,* 1980). While the names and boundaries for CDPs are "are defined in cooperation with local or tribal officials," the areas have no legal status and do not elect officials to manage the municipal functions within their borders.

CDPs can also change over time. Census records indicate that in 1970, Town 'n' Country it wasn't yet a CDP, but much of it was listed under the designation "Sweetwater Creek." This CDP had a population of 19,453 (*Census of the Population,* 1970). By 1980, the CDPs were reorganized and Sweetwater Creek was no more, but some of the same area was now "Town 'n' Country," which had a population of 37,834 (*Census of the Population,* 1980).

These census documents show the rapid growth in population and imply the negotiation between local organization and broader systems of national control and regulation. While the US Census Bureau might classify one home in Town 'n' Country and another in Carollwood, the residents themselves may classify their residence differently. Where one lives may also change over time even as residents cling to older terms out of a sense of belonging or just habit. This isn't necessarily a fluidity of meanings across scale—what locals think versus what the Census Bureau thinks—it is something that requires a juxtaposition between different things.

Such juxtapositions are a condition of non-places and supermodernity. Augé argues that supermodernity is characterized by excesses in time, space, and the individual. With telecommunications the difference between meaningless and memorable events cannot be discerned. We have an overabundance of spaces to inhabit, such that we do not know where to turn and so we withdraw into non-places, familiar in their ubiquity, be they in Wichita, Kyoto, or Kuala Lumpur. As Augé writes, "The temptation to narcissism is all the more seductive here in that it seems to express a common law: do as others do to be yourself" (106). We are told we aren't anywhere unless we have global chain stores, global networks, and all that come with them. With such excess, what difference is there really between two non-places? One is equally alone in each of them.

VI.

Natural sinkholes and depressions, such as Lake Carroll, north of Town 'n' Country, or Tarpon Lake to its west, retain water and are often bordered with cypress and marshes. Before settlement, many of these wetlands seeped out across the flat terrain north of Tampa Bay, eventually forming small creeks that were part of the saline/ freshwater cycle of the estuarine environment and gave rise to oyster beds and mangrove swamps. With suburbs comes a need for dry land, or at least land dryer than the dairy grazing lands that existed before Town 'n' Country's rapid development in the 1960s, 70s, and 80s. Canals helped drain these lands and now act as floodwater protection from both fresh and salt sources. The earth dug up from the canals—earth from cuts up to thirty feet—channel heavy rainfall flowing out through the canals as well as storm surge flowing in from a potential tropical storm or hurricane. Canal G drains the eastern part of Town 'n' Country and feeds into Rocky Creek just above a small spillway that acts as a salinity barrier.

As a kid, between about six and fourteen, I would regularly disappear into this green space, home to soft-shelled turtles, frogs, water hyacinth, water beetles, wild taro, and a host of other plants and animals. One day, my elementary school friends claimed to have seen an alligator resting below the Hanley Road Bridge, though that was disputed as being simply a log. At that time, the banks of the canal were weedy and unimproved except for a dusty pair of ruts made by the trucks of local fishermen. It offered a great place to let my dog off her leash so she could run furiously in great circles and with even greater abandon. The ruts have now been claimed as a bike path and the raised berms seeded with grass, trees, and park benches.

In such green spaces, "country" becomes problematic because of the wildness within suburbia. Even in dense urban areas, wildness will find its way through cracks and other untended areas. In suburban spaces like Town 'n' Country, there may be more acceptance of "nature," but wildness is to be contained. Fire ants, palmetto bugs, and mole crickets are treated with poison. The trees are planted, mulched, and trimmed at proper distances from buildings. And in Town 'n' Country there is a ubiquity to underground sprinkler systems that I haven't seen matched in the Midwest.

William Cronon argued, "there is nothing natural about the concept of wilderness. It is entirely a creation of the culture that holds it dear, a product of the very history it seeks to deny. Indeed, one of the most striking proofs of the cultural invention of wilderness is its thoroughgoing erasure of the history from which it sprang" (79). This is a necessary move if suburbs convert space into non-place. The past and its inhabitants must be hidden within various shells so that certain relationships are made more difficult and less productive than others. This is a familiar move, applicable to much of human expansion and Florida's history.

This is also an example of how solitude becomes individualized. The green spaces along Canal G in Town 'n' Country were sites of withdrawal for me. Yet, despite the allure of some "tawny grammar," they were unlike a grove of California redwoods or the exposed bluffs of the driftless region in the upper Midwest. In my youth, along Canal G were waste spaces—buffer zones requiring little to no management. In the weeds along the ruts lay the suburban debris of Styrofoam cups, old tires, fast food wrappers, and broken beer bottles. Much of that, I am sure, has been swept away in the storm of redevelopment. But I am also sure that the tempest has actually changed very little of the green space itself. Debris still falls from bikes, out of the pockets of middle-aged ladies out for a stroll, and from the hands of children. The trees planted there catch plastic shopping bags adrift on breezes off the bay. The reclamation has only inscribed Town 'n' Country further as non-space. The bike trail is a route of transit not unlike a highway or airport. Just about anyone, even if they do not know the language, can find their way.

VII.

Edward Scissorhands makes an animated appearance in the Season 11 episode of *Family Guy,* "Lois Comes Out of Her Shell." The reference to shell is the change in Lois' persona from mother and wife to outgoing party girl, a change spurred on by her birthday. Lois' children comment on her odd behavior and the dangers of "pretending to be like something you're not." In an immediately following cutaway scene, Edward is hired as a "night nurse" and makes a flowery promise to provide the most excellent care so the parents can rest and wake refreshed to their child in the morning. He leaves the scene with the baby only to quickly return with the news that it is dead.

On the surface, it's just a gag. We see the irony of how Edward wants to care for the child the way others do though he is incapable. Like Lois, he pretends to be something he is not and with disastrous results. This is a remediation of the original movie. The original film participates in a dialectic of claims to authenticity, both self and place. It shows suburban life as inauthentic, shallow, and unwelcoming of difference. The film offers neither overt critique nor remedy since, as Robert Markley explains, its suburban life world "has no history and engenders no analytic; its mythology finds its expression in the remediated, televisual terms of subcultural identification" (282). *Family Guy* takes that remediation one step further, folding it into this episode about identity.

Bolter and Grusin characterize remediation as "a . . . complex kind of borrowing in which one medium is itself incorporated or represented in another medium" and a defining characteristic of new media (45). *Family Guy* borrows extensively from the medium of film, incorporating allusions and outtakes into its own animated comedy. In this sense, too, remediated works are supermodern. Far from being something new, remediation exists within the aesthetic tension between immediacy and hyperreality. Bolter and Grusin cite Richard Lanham's distinction between these two aesthetics as the difference "between looking *at* and looking *through.*" Rather than destination, we have only travel.

VIII.

Town 'n' Country exists because of a complex play of forces: local and global politics, natural and social forces, individual and common desires. Such forces remediate each others' desires in order to produce Town 'n Country. As Bolter and Grusin make clear, "media technologies constitute networks or hybrids that can be expressed in physical, social, aesthetic, and economic terms. Introducing a new media technology does not mean simply inventing new hardware and software, but rather fashioning (or refashioning) such a network. The World Wide Web is not merely a software protocol and text and data files. It is also the sum of the uses to which this protocol is now being put" (19). Town 'n' Country is a production of protocol. In aesthetic terms, it is a cut-up place in the sense of Grison and Burroughs—invented and composed through a breaking up and reordering typical of new media.

Yet, there is a distinction here between this kind of understanding of place and what Varnellis and Friedberg call a networked place. For them, Augé's "non-places" are "an artifact of the past" because of computational technologies such as new media, GIS, and RFID chips. I certainly agree that these technologies are changing our relationship to place, but I question their definition of "alone." They assert that "The proliferation of mobile phones and the widespread adoption of always-on broadband Internet connections in homes and offices in the developed world means that we are not necessarily alone even if we are not interacting with those in close physical proximity to us" (3). This misses Augé's point that non-places exist precisely because of the ever-present, supermodern abundance of both real and virtual space. Augé notes that "in the world of supermodernity people are always, and never, at home" (109). Is one's home a structure, a community, a landform, a virtual page, or is it the movement through these things? If space, both real and virtual, is now superabundant, what sort of room is left to move in?

I used to cross Hanley Road from my family's townhome complex, Morganwoods Greentree Phase IV, to the Magic Mart that anchored one end of the strip mall across the street. The black asphalt baking in the sun gave off a rubbery smell, strongest just after resurfacing but fading with time. Inside the Magic Mart I played arcade games like *Pac Man* and *Robotron 2084*, inspected taboo publications like *Heavy Metal*, and more often than not purchased the latest issue of a superhero comic like *Fantastic Four* or *The Avengers*. As an only child, I often went on these excursions alone. While the stories and thrills they provided might not pass as solitary—they were a mediated form of communicating with others through art, narrative, and play—I was often lonely with them.

The Morganwoods Greentree Phase IV complex where I lived was designed with no through streets. The drives within the townhome complex were lined with carports and parking spaces and the entryways to the townhomes were always referred to as "the back door." Front doors let out onto a patio, which then let out onto sidewalks, which snaked between the townhomes and connected them by walk ways bordered with azalea, bottlebrush, sand pine, and eucalyptus. Hardly anyone ever used the sidewalks, though. Trees sometimes hung over the roofs of the single-story units and I would climb them with new comics in hand to read in the shade. Sometimes, I would cache objects on these roofs for short periods of time if I decided to wander off and stir up a nest of fire ants or try to catch the anole lizards that teemed within the slat fences and underbrush. Perhaps this has to do with my being an only child, but animals, trees, and comics were common companions. And they were no substitute for knocking on a friend's door and finding someone present.

Figure 2. Eucalyptus (Courtesy Google)

IX.

My step-father moved us to Florida when I was four. My step-dad had a job as a realtor with the Jim Walter Corporation and when the opportunity to transfer from St. Paul to Tampa came, he took it. At first we lived in Carrollwood, renting a second-floor apartment between Carrollwood Lane and Latania Drive, but soon my parents bought a new townhome in the Greentree subdivision of Town 'n' Country. Jim Walter and his company made their fortune building shell houses. As the history of Walter Energy, a division diversified from the original Jim Walter Corporation, tells it, "In 1946 James W. Walter borrowed $400 from his father, a citrus grower, and purchased a 'shell,' or unfinished home, for $895 from Tampa, Florida, builder, O.L. Davenport. When just three days later, the 23-year-old, newly married Walter sold the home to a passerby for a profit, he saw a way out of his $50-a-week truck-driving job and $50-a-month apartment." Walter successfully repeated that formula, selling unfinished homes as affordable, alternative housing. The wood homes were built on concrete foundations or wood pilings. Each home was completely finished on the outside with an unfinished interior. Buyers installed plumbing, electrical systems, insulation, walls, and doors themselves. Homes were sold directly to owners prior to construction, through a Jim Walter Homes Division sales office. This is what my step-father sold: empty shells. Walter's model allowed for affordability "by leveraging buyers' sweat equity; people bought a lot, the company put up the shell of a home, and the buyers finished the home out" (Yaussi 2009). Walter Industries is now mainly an energy company and is based in Alabama, though Jim Walter Boulevard still greets visitors and business travellers just outside Tampa International Airport.

Like many stories of Florida, then, Town 'n' Country has its stories of real estate and the American dream. David Nolan's *Fifty Feet in Paradise* traces these land schemes, successes, and stories and details how they coalesce as a series of booms and busts, often fueled by an exuberant idealism. General Lafayette, Harriet Beecher Stowe, and Walt Disney planned utopian communities. From the fountain of youth to mulberries to phosphate to cheap housing in a warm climate, something has always lured people to Florida's land. But the temptations have rarely been sustainable. The stories repeat predictably. The real estate is always unimproved. As the old saw goes, "I've got some swampland in Florida to sell you." Speculation fuels cycles of boom and bust. Cycles, rather than weather, poor soil, or illness play a strong role in churning the population. So, shells are offered to clamoring investors who may profit for a time, but eventually, they come up empty. It's a shell game.

x.

The townhome where I grew up in Town 'n' Country was foreclosed on after the housing collapse. I found the listing on Trulia.com while researching this project. The website claims it "sold for $54,000 on Mar 8, 2013." Previously, it sold for eighty-nine thousand in 2004. Before that, in 1999, it sold for fifty-eight thousand. Not bad for 1256 square feet. It's a good starter place or rental. Somewhere in these records, though, are people who moved on. The evidence only gives us room to speculate. Perhaps the people who bought it in 1999 and sold it in 2004 moved on to something more suited to them and their desires. Perhaps the people who bought it in 2004 weren't so fortunate. Either way, such speculations coalesce and accrete around the material of a stable-enough location. The townhome remains a shell, filled with the hopes and dreams of its migratory inhabitants.

Figure 3. Author's home (Courtesy Google)

One record not so easily noticed is that my step-dad adopted me in that home. Even while living in Carrollwood, I remember asking my mom "When will my name change?" and, while still in Carrollwood, I was given the option to call my mom's new husband "Dad" or keep calling him by his first name. But it was in Town 'n' Country where the adoption became legal. Such things are not easily indexed by the home itself, but events like this were folded into it. It is a significant one for me since it concerns one of the most important shells we have—our identity.

XI.

My father, Tom, had a half-brother, Artie, literally a bastard child. As Artie relates it, their dad was "still married to Tom's mother until the day of my fourth birthday" when Tom's mother, Mabel, died. I think that was 1962. Their dad was a Teamster working for what was then the Public Service Coordinated Transit in Maple Shade Township, New Jersey just outside Camden. As a widower, he married Artie's mother, Eva, had more children with her, and moved to Ocala. In 1973 he and his brother disappeared off the Gulf Coast near Yankeetown. No wreckage or fuel spill was ever found. Apparently a storm had rolled through that day and F-4 Phantom jets were dispatched out of Orlando in the search, but all efforts turned up nothing. Strangely, too, Artie related to me that "this was our second boat, and it was double-hulled, and even if it developed a hole, it would float. And it had two big outboard motors. But nothing was ever found." A little more than a year after this, I moved to Town 'n' Country with my mom and Tom.

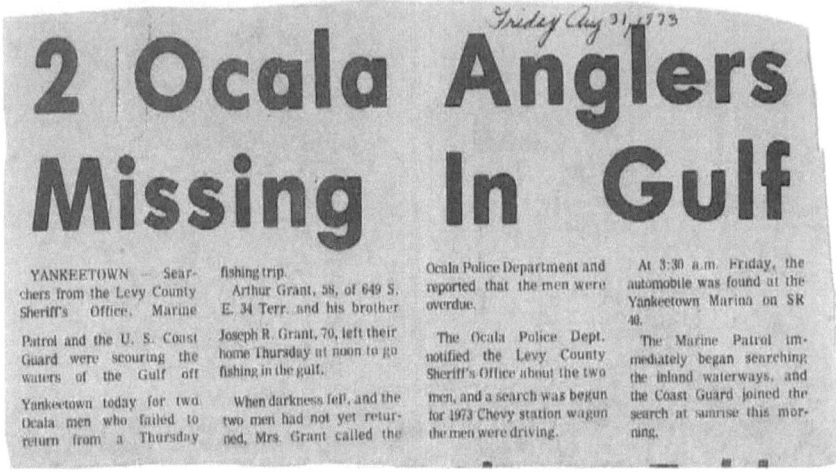

Figure 4. Newspaper heading of father's father and his brother's disappearance (Courtesy Art Grant)

From these juxtapositions of fragments—Teamster, an illegitimate birth, two tragic deaths, no wreckage, the double hull offering a level of "unsinkability"—fabulations arise. To hear Artie joke about it, my grandfather spent his last days lounging on a Mexican beach with Jimmy Hoffa. Perhaps that humor hides the resentments he has towards Tom's side of the family taking the insurance money and much of the value of the estate before Artie came of age. In our conversation, it deflected questions I had about the odd coincidence of my paternal grandmother's death and my half-uncle's fourth birthday. The only answer I have is the dense hole of speculation.

In writing about the detective novel in Deleuze's development of literature, Russell Ford notes how Deleuze focuses on "hard-boiled" detective fiction rather than the type of fiction organized around reason and truth (59). Deleuze refers to French pulp fiction, especially *La Série Noir*, rather than English detectives like Agatha Christie or Sherlock Holmes. Accordingly, the structures of these detective stories differ so the "English" types "exhibit a structure that closely follows the methodology proper to the tradition of platonism, where questioning is governed by a prioritization of the method of search and discovery" (60). By contrast, hard-boiled detective fiction like *La Série Noir* "the problem is not posed in terms of truth. Rather, it is a question of a surprising compensation of errors" (61). In such cases, there is always the "dick," a transient figure, "The hack, the salesman" (60). There is also no proper bringing to justice before the law. Rather, "the crime is never resolved or explained, but it is paid for" in another series of events (61). Ford gives the examples of Al Capone never serving justice for murder, but for tax evasion and of "Lou Ford, the protagonist of Jim Thompson's classic *The Killer Inside Me,* [who] is never brought to justice but is killed in the explosive confrontation with one of his victims—an encounter orchestrated by the police" (61).

In 2000 Tom, still a real estate salesman though living in Minnesota, drove to Florida by way of New Mexico after stealing money from an estate for which he had been named executor. He did a little financial consulting on the side, shuffling money here and there. The money from the estate was never found. My father claimed he had to pay people off, hinted it was the Russian mob. He deflected questions I had about his crime just as Artie deflected serious questions about their father's disappearance. While Tom was in prison, the joke was that he buried the money somewhere along his route to Florida and he would someday dig it up and retire on a beach somewhere. He died of colon cancer ten years later, never telling the woman he had moved to North Carolina with about his unpaid debt. So, his crime was paid for. He was a dick, sure. But he was also my father.

XII.

This short excursus serves to think again about the political dimension of how we think about Town 'n' Country as a suburban space or as one of many supermodern non-places. Ford follows Klossowski's discussion of "fable" and "fate" as related terms and Bergson's argument that the power of fables lies in their ability "to produce images that 'are defensive reactions of nature against the representation, by the intelligence, of a depressing margin of the unexpected between the initiative taken and the effect desired'" (Ford 67). How does one bridge that margin? Ford argues we should link fabulations with the political order. Such tales can "use language to develop styles of thinking that resist entrenched value systems through the inventive exploration of new values" (67). Fables, with their own margins to be bridged, are the sound of the ocean contained in seashells. Fables are not hope, but imbued with hope and the potential for hope, even when one's intelligence balks at the difference between needed effort and desired effect. What will it take to promote greater civility in the suburbs? How can we reduce CO_2 emissions in our economy? Can we ensure a good education for our children? How can we love those who have wronged us? To work on any of these, even in small part, is to engage in something fabulous.

In this sense, Town 'n' Country-as-non-place holds potential precisely because it is generic, named in the language of marketing, and presented as commodity ready for remediation. Relying on the term "suburb" or on grand appeals to "suburbia" as endlessly generic conceals so many associations and these concealments all too often pass unnoticed. In our unnoticing, we miss what else we might fabricate. Instead of the routinized and predictable patterns of binary oppositions or comparisons between idyllic past and fallen present, we might look to the empty shells of suburbia in order to move past hackneyed stereotypes and address the millions of real and particular human beings whose lives make contributions in the world. Perhaps to bridge that margin between what we want our places to be and the way they actually are is the hard work of mourning. We can grieve for these places and closely examine how the global is interpellated through the local to amplify the ghosts still evident in the palimpsest of place. Through radical juxtapositions and new media methods, we might turn the flattened and the useless into the fabulous.

Works Cited

Augé, Marc. *Non-Places: Introduction to an Anthropology of Supermodernity.* Trans. John Howe. London: Verso, 1995. Print.

Bolter, Jay David and Richard Grusin. *Remediation: Understanding New Media.* Cambridge, MA: MIT Press, 2000. Print.

Burroughs, William S. and Brion Gysin. *The Third Mind.* New York: Viking, 1978. Print.

"U.S. Population Now 300 Million and Growing." *CNN.com.* Cable News Network and Turner Broadcasting Corporation, 17 Oct. 2006. Web 8 March 2013.

Colebrook, Claire. *Understanding Deleuze.* Sydney, NSW: Allen and Unwin, 2003. Print.

Cronon, William. "The Trouble with Wilderness or, Getting Back to the Wrong Nature." *Uncommon Ground: Rethinking the Human Place in Nature.* Ed. William Cronon. New York: W. W. Norton, 1995. Print.

Deleuze, Gilles. *The Fold: Leibniz and the Baroque.* Trans. Tom Conley. Minneapolis, MN: U of Minnesota P, 1992. Print.

Duany, Andres and Elizabeth Plater-Zyberk. *Suburb Nation: The Rise of Sprawl and the Decline of the American Dream.* New York: North Point Press, 2000. Print.

Ford, Russell. "Deleuze's Dick." *Philosophy and Rhetoric* 38.1 (2005): 41–71. Print.

Kunstler, James. *Geography of Nowhere: The Rise and Decline of America's Man-Made Landscape.* New York: Simon and Schuster, 1994. Print.

Markley, Robert. "Geek/ Goth: Remediation and Nostalgia in Tim Burton's *Edward Scissorhands.*" *Goth: Undead Subculture.* Ed. Lauren Goodlad and Michael Bibby. Durham, NC: Duke UP, 2007. Print.

Nolan, David. *Fifty Feet in Paradise: The Booming of Florida.* New York: Harcourt, Brace, Jovanovich, 1984. Print.

Roberts, Sam. "Population Study Finds Change in the Suburbs." *New York Times.* NYtimes.com. 9 May 2010. Web. 15 March 2013.

United States Bureau of the Census. *Census of the Population: 1970, Vol. 1, Characteristics of the Population, Part 11, Florida.* Washington, D.C.: GPOffice. April 1973. Print.

United States Bureau of the Census. *Census of the Population: 1980, Vol. 1, Characteristics of the Population, Chapter A Number of Inhabitants, Part 11, Florida.* Washington, D.C.: GPO. February 1982. Print.

Varnellis, Kazys and Anne Friedberg. "Place: Networked Place." *Networked Publics.* Ed. Kazys Varnelis. Cambridge, MA: MIT Press, 2008. Print.

Vaughn, Laura, et al. "Do The Suburbs Exist? Discovering Complexity and Specificity in Suburban Built Form." *Transactions of the Institute of British Geographers* 34.4, (October 2009): 475–88. Print.

Wardrip-Fruin, Noah and Nick Montfort (Eds.). *The New Media Reader.* Cambridge, MA: MIT Press, 2003. Print.

Yaussi, Sarah. "Jim Walter Homes Closes Shop." *Builder.* Hanley Wood Media Inc, 6 Jan. 2009. Web. 20 March, 2013.

12 An American Beach

Sidney I. Dobrin

With 1,197 statute miles of coastline; 2,276 statute miles of tidal shoreline; 663 miles of beaches; more than eleven thousand miles of rivers, streams and waterways; more than 4,500 islands greater than ten acres (in the US, only Alaska has more); and more than 7,700 lakes larger than ten acres, Florida is delineated by its water, or more specifically, it is delineated by its contact with water. Florida may be known as The Sunshine State, but it is Florida's water that determines a good deal of its identity. In particular, Florida's beaches stand as paramount in Florida's identity construction, for locals, residents, tourists, and even those who only ever visit Florida through word or image. For most of the state's history, Florida's beaches have been publically owned; however, for a hundred years following the abolition of slavery in the United States, African Americans were denied access to nearly all of those beaches. This is a chapter about beaches, exclusion, and transition. It is about learning to read beaches and knowing the historical contexts of beaches in Florida's history.

Turning to John Fiske's semiotic theory of the beach through which he distinguishes among cultural myths of difference between land and sea, this chapter theorizes the space of Florida as defined not by the solidity of its land but by the uncontrolled rawness of its waters. Fiske's beach embodies the space of contact between land and sea, as a space between the solidity of land, which is manipulated and controlled by a human population, and the chaos of sea which is aligned with nature and wildness (though recent debates regarding the privatization of water access and use has disrupted this alignment). The beach signifies the clash of nature and culture. The beach is liminal space; the beach is the fringe. The beach is natural and cultural; it is space "that has too much meaning, an excess of meaning potential, that derives from its status as anomalous" (Fiske 120). The beach is not Florida; the beach is the end of Florida, the edge of Florida. The beach is the edge of chaos. And, the beach seeps; fluid and flow move wild water from swamps to the north underground, releasing streams and rivers from the northern part of the state to the River of Grass in the south, emptying into gulf and ocean, creating beach under the ground, on the surface, along thousands of miles of rivers and streams, saturating the land in its wildness. Florida's history is rich with wildness and its taming. This chapter seeks to re-see that history as one of water, of fluid and flow, of nature and culture that converge on the beach, and see Florida not as a solid, controlled place, but as a saturated place, where beach emerges endlessly.

Reading Beaches

To name is to impose meaning. To name something *beach* is to distinguish it not just from land or water, but to distinguish it from coast, shore, oceanfront, waterfront, bank,[1] or any of the other signs we use to indicate the geographical point of convergence of land and sea.[2] Thus, the beach itself is written in the shade of the idea of the beach. If written, the beach can be read, is read, and will be read not just as geographical function, but as cultural function. In Florida, the cultural function of "the beach" is imbricated in the very idea of Florida. To say "Florida" is to say "beach" (imagine Florida's tourism industry producing a commercial without mention of Florida's beaches), and certain beaches in Florida maintain almost mythic reputations, pushing them to serve as iconic not only for Florida, but for the very idea of beach: South Beach, Miami Beach, Daytona Beach, Jacksonville Beach, or Clearwater Beach.

Media scholar John Fiske has proposed that we can read beaches in the same ways that we can read any other text, and his essay "Reading the Beach" is one of the very few attempts to do so. Fiske provides an interesting start to understanding *beach*, but his idea of reading only initiates any serious reading. Likewise, Fiske reads Australia's beaches, which by his own definitions are not the same beaches as Florida's beaches and, thus, should not be read the same way. Fiske is unclear as to whether he means this to suggest that the text necessarily determines the reading, which is problematic, or if differences in texts are but one contributing factor in differences in reading. In the second part of this chapter, I begin to read what is likely to be one of Florida's lesser known, but more historically significant beaches: American Beach. In order to initiate such a reading, though, let's first consider how to read a beach.

When I say "let's first consider how to read a beach," of course, I am talking about a particular way of reading, a way of reading that suits my objectives in this chapter. We all read differently, and we all read/write meaning differently. In fact, we all read beaches differently: an angler reads a beach differently than does a surfer, a beachcomber, a sailor, a sunbather, an ecologist, a Midwesterner, and so on. Even someone accustomed to reading another beach, say, a Californian beach or a Tahitian beach, reads all other beaches differently, thus a Tahitian beach reader reading a Florida beach reads differently than do native Florida-beach readers. How one reads a beach is, in part, attributed to how that reader identifies use value in the beach; how would I use this space? For fishing, beachcombing, surfing, sunbathing, treasure hunting, or whatever the hell Midwesterners do. This "space," of course, is an anomalous space, a space between spaces. It is a transitional space. As Fiske puts it, the beach is an "anomalous category between land and sea that is neither one nor the other but has characteristics of both" (43). For Fiske, the geographical opposition between land and sea has no meaning until we impose a particular ideological meaning upon it, most often in the form of an opposition between nature and culture. This distinction, he explains, emerges when we recognize nature as "pre-cultural reality," which he distinguishes from what is natural, which is what "culture makes of nature" (44). Thus, the geographical/physical structure of land/sea is overwritten and mediated as culture/nature. Land, the space of people and culture; sea, the space of nature. The beach is the transition between the two.

Yet, even as transition, we tend to understand the beach as being closer to Nature than culture. The beach is where we go to escape culture—as much as that might be possible. Humans, of course, cannot escape culture. Even ventures into the sea, into nature are limited by cultural apparatus. Boats, rafts, swim trunks, masks, and so on protect the human/culture body from the potential threat of nature, much as a seawall or bulkhead protects land/culture from the sea during storms. Culture works to hold back nature. Nature threatens culture with erosion and intrusion. As Fiske puts it, "swimming is the furthest man [sic] can penetrate into nature" (46). Yet even such penetrations do not free the human from culture as the human totes human and posthuman baggage no matter whether wearing the material trappings of culture or not. That is, to be human (and post-human) is to always already be culture. Culture is not something the human wears as cover, but is co-constitutive.

Fiske notes that for many who visit the beach, their skins serve as a sign that they have ventured to the edge of nature. Tanned skin, he contends, "is a sign to be read by others, particularly others in the city" (46). This signifying function is to display that the wearer has been "in nature" and is returning from nature with "both the physical health of the animal and the mental health that contact with nature brings to the artificiality of city life" (46). The tan, by Fiske's definition, is natural, not Nature, and was likely attained through the material barrier/screen of culture (i.e. sunscreen and aesthetic). Fiske, however, does not address the simulacra of the natural attained within the city through mechanisms like tanning booths and spray tans, cultural technologies employed to mimic the natural, to present a visual cue suggesting an escape to the beach. Likewise, as Fiske notes, wearing a tanned skin signifies a class dimension. What's interesting in this acknowledgement, though, is that Fiske's reading of the sunbather is, without acknowledgment, a reading of the Caucasian body. The tan, while hinting at a venture into nature or even a temporary "going native" is not only not-permanent, but is never cast in the cultural lexicon as authentic; it is nothing more than a souvenir. As I begin to examine American Beach—a traditionally African American beach—I want to be clear that tanned skin also marks a transitional space much akin to the beach itself.

The beach, then, represents (granted, somewhat reductively) not only a transition between land and sea, but between culture and nature; the beach mediates between the safety of land and culture and the red-in-tooth-and-claw of sea and nature. The tan represents the embodiment of human venture to the edge of culture. For Fiske, the tan is an "anomalous category between *skin* (human, culture) and *fur* (animal/nature)" (46). The tan of a sunbather signifying class status, the ability to relax in the sun as a distinctly different from the tanned skin of the outdoor laborer, from the "farmer's tan," which marks class in its partial coverage of the body as opposed to the sunbather who seeks an even tan. The tan distinguishes between those able to work indoors, protected from the elements of nature and those of lower class distinction whose relegation to the outdoors is read as imbuing wildness, a step below the human, and often as a threat to the colonial Caucasian body, which is protected by culture. The soft white underbelly of the Caucasian body is always at risk of exposure. The elements threaten it. The Caucasian cultural body often fails in its recognition that culture contributes to this threat by its inability to understand the transitional spaces between nature and culture. Depleted ozone levels, a result of cultural action, stand as exemplary of the natural threat to the body, particularly when the body ventures to the transitional beach space, which is not a space of reconciliation, but one of transition in which the human, cultural, Caucasian body is simultaneously privileged and at risk.

The tanned Caucasian body, the body proclaiming visually its survival at the edge of Nature, in Florida is to be read also as opposed to dark skin, despite that the Caucasian body tans naturally through a biological/chemical reaction of melanin to the sun. Dark skin in Florida is historically read as a marker of permanent ties to the wildness of nature, the not-fully cultured. Dark skin pigments lack the transient properties of the tan; dark skin cannot be washed away as one might wash off with fresh water (non-seawater) the sand and salt, residues of the beach. Dark skin clashes with the Caucasian body's Eurocentric ideologies about bodies and beaches. Dark bodies in Florida historically lived beyond the beach, across the seas, in lands not of culture but of wilderness beyond wilderness, in lands the Caucasian body deemed in need of cultural infusion by way of colonization. The dark body—in all of its manifestations and variants—cast as the inferior body. But this unremarked reading, this uninformed reading, of dark bodies and beaches is geographically unaware, unable to accept the idea of the beach as being present in Africa or on the coasts of other continents.

Thus, the transitional space of the beach can be read as providing the Caucasian body a safety zone, a space of protection. This space, of course, is regulated by the Caucasian body to ensure safety from the wildness of the sea and Nature. Florida's beaches, for example, are regulated to maintain as much of a cultural atmosphere as possible in the transition. Dogs are often prohibited from beach access because something as natural as dog poop on a beach is read as vile, as something beachgoers should not have to see, and as a potential health risk to the human bodies that venture to the beach. Dog poop is too natural, too risky for even the fringes of cultural intrusion. It can be regulated because the "dog" is not Nature; it is culture. Bred and domesticated, brought to the beach tethered to human culture genetically and literally. The same regulations can't be applied to seagulls, though some beach-adjacent businesses and communities may enact don't-feed-the-sea-gulls rules in order to discourage seagulls from frequenting areas where seagull poop violates the cultural standard.

Nude sunbathing, likewise, is prohibited on nearly all of Florida's beaches. There are fewer than a dozen designated clothing optional beaches in Florida. Nudity represents the removal of most visible signs of culture (haircuts, sunglasses, and other trappings often remain); nudity is seen as a return to nature. The tan also marks our understanding of (so-called) class sophistication in the confirmation and permissibility of nudity or near-nudity in relation to the space of beach. This is seen in the certainty of subjectivity of the well-tanned Caucasian body that is not made vulnerable by her own nakedness on the beach, but rather is, to some degree, empowered by it while simultaneously gendered by it. The regulation of nude sunbathing is prohibition against nature. The cultural control of the transitional space of the beach works to conceal. Consider, for example, Italo Calvino's chapter "The Naked Bosom," which appears in his 1983 novel *Mr. Palomar*. In "The Naked Bosom," Mr. Palomar walks along a beach and notices a woman sunbathing topless. Mr. Palomar discreetly turns toward the ocean, away from the woman, acknowledging to himself how uncomfortable it must make a woman when a man, such as himself, looks at her body while she sunbathes. Mr. Palomar then questions his own actions, asking as to what he should and should not see on the beach. He worries about dehumanizing the body by pretending to see the woman as only part of the landscape and worries about refusing to let himself see as complicit in making the sight of a topless woman something illicit and perhaps inappropriate. What makes Mr. Palomar's inquiry dynamic is the location of the scene on the beach. The topless woman, if situated in another space, requires an entirely different set of questions. But because the beach is transitional space, the barriers between culture and nature can be let down a bit; sunbathers wear clothes, but bare more skin than if in another place. Exposure is tolerated a bit more, but culturally coming to terms with the naked body—particularly when men (like Mr. Palomar) talk about women's exposed bodies within a culture that maintains stringent institutional centers that remain tied to systems that allow for such distinctions as culpability of women's clothing choices in rape cases-makes coming to terms with that exposure uncomfortable. The risk of exposure is tolerated-particularly by the male within patriarchal culture-at the edge of nature, but the grasp of culture still works to retain control of the space and of the un-tanned (female) body. The un-tanned body may reveal more skin, but the cultural line places restrictions on the visibility of the naughty bits, for such exposure would be uncivilized and immoral. Thus, Fiske's nominal reading of the beach and the sunbather, as well as Calvino's *Mr. Palomar*, anaesthetize the sunbathing (female) body by failing to address sex, gender, and violence as they pertain to the culture that extends from land to beach. Consider, for example, that we even name swimming without the barrier of clothing *skinny dipping* to distinguish it from swimming, which is an entirely appropriate action because one has not completely gone wild. Swimming that is, is acceptable because culture can venture into nature, but shedding all vestiges of culture puts the human at risk from nature.

It is with these distinctions in mind between culture and nature, between land and sea, that I turn to consider American Beach, a beach of transition.

American Beach was and is a traditional "Black beach," a beach developed by and visited primarily by African Americans.

Black Bodies and North Florida Beaches

Geologically speaking, the Florida landmass is a plateau of Karst limestone, a kind of soluble rock rendered porous through ages of contact with acidic rainwater. Karstified limestone is characterized by its caves, sinkholes, and endless systems of dissolved fissures, pockets, and tunnels. Florida's Karstified limestone sits atop the Florida Platform, a base of bedrock formed during the Eocene (56–34 million years ago) and the Oligocene (34–23 million years ago) epochs. What we now call Florida is the portion of the plateau that emerged from the waters. Over millions of years, sands from these ancient transforming beached amassed along with silt and clay to form the Florida landmass. Florida emerged as a beach.

Twenty years after the US Civil War, the Emancipation Proclamation, and the ratification of the Thirteenth Amendment to the United State Constitution, there were six public beaches just east of Jacksonville, Florida. Local laws denied African-Americans access to these beaches. In 1884, Pablo Beach (later renamed Jacksonville Beach) permitted Black visitors only one day a week. It wasn't until the early 1900s when Henry Flagler's Florida East Coast Railway sold some of its beachfront property to a group of railroad laborers that Black beach goers had regular access to Florida's beaches. Flagler had made similar sales to railroad works all along Florida's east coast as a method for establishing railroad villages, communities, and station stops. Flagler built the line from Pablo Beach to Manhattan Beach (now part of Kathryn Abbey Hannah Park) in 1899 on the east side of Mayport, a small fishing community on the southern shore of the mouth of the St. John's River, later to be subsumed as a US military base. Manhattan Beach had been part of the 1790 DeWees Land Grant which entrusted Andrew DeWees, with 2,290 acres by Charles IV King of Spain. On May 4, 1804, the military Governor of the Spanish province of Florida, Enrique White, granted Andrew DeWees' heirs rights to 2300 acres granted by the Spanish King. John Quincy Adams signed the Florida Purchase Treaty in 1819, ceding Spanish Florida to the United States. In 1822, DeWees' remaining heirs filed a petition to retain ownership of the land grant, initially asking for rights to 2,633 acres, but later amending the request to 2,290 acres. On September 26, 1825, the United States General Land Office issued a degree of confirmation which was confirmed by Congress on February 8, 1827. In 1833 the Surveyor General of Florida approved the first boundary survey of the land claims attributed to DeWees' heirs; the survey was conducted again and confirmed in 1850 and

1857. In 1882 legal disputes over the land boundaries were filed, but were dismissed in 1886 (Interior 546–48).

Of course, prior to ownership and legal claims like these, the areas of North Florida's beaches, like Pablo Beach, were occupied by Timucua peoples, one of the largest groups of indigenous populations in what is now the Southeastern United States, specifically within Florida and Georgia. Like most North American indigenous populations, our only knowledge of them comes by way of European colonization. Though the Saturiwa—one of the 35 Timucua chiefdoms—referred to all speakers of Timucua dialects generically as Timucua, the Spanish adopted the term to identify all indigenous people in southern Georgia and Northern Florida. Thus, Spanish and Early US record keeping homogenizes all written record of the Timucua as identifying only one population (Milanch xviii); this colonial linguistic legacy remains.[3]

When African-Americans did have access to public beaches—like Pablo Beach—their excursions to the beach were large social and religious happenings. As noted in the June 2, 1888 *Pablo Beach Breeze*, "The colored excursion last Monday was a jumbo affair; there being between six and seven hundred of Jacksonville's colored population on the beach during the day" (qtd in Phelts 1). But, these visits were limited as Marsh Dean Phelts has explained, often, when granted to perform ocean baptisms on Sundays, Black church congregations were required to immediately leave the beaches and return to their churches to complete their services (3).

It wasn't until the railroad workers acquired what would become Manhattan Beach that Jacksonville's Black population would have consistent access to the beach. Manhattan Beach developers built Manhattan Beach to suggest the sophistication of New York, the beach's main attraction a resort called Little Cony Island. Other attractions included Mack Wilson's Pavilion, which offered dining, lodging, entertainment, and bathing facilities day and night (Phelts 4). Manhattan Beach remained the only consistently available beach for Black beachgoers until 1932 when the Mayport/Manhattan Beach rail line closed for economic reasons attributed to the Great Depression. The closure of the railroad reduced access to the beaches to those who could make the journey by automobile or bus (like church busses) (Phelts 9). Coupled with severe beach erosion, decreased transportation to the beach resulted in fewer Black citizens visiting the beach areas. In 1938 a fire destroyed Mack Wilson's Pavilion, its cause never attributed, though assumed to have been intentionally set to discourage Blacks from coming to the beach as white beach communities expanded. The fire, and its assumed message, all but blocked Black beach activity in northeast Florida. In December, 1942, a year after the bombing at Pearl Harbor, the United States military commissioned Naval Station Mayport, subsuming a large part of Manhattan Beach. Despite the attribution, however, that the base was built because of the United States' entrance into the war, the base had actually been in the works since the mid-1930s. In 1939, Duval County citizens voted to approve a $1.1 million bond issue to buy land for the base's development (*History of NS Mayport*). But, no matter the reason for the base's development, its construction shut off Florida's northeastern beaches to African Americans at the time.[4]

Figure 1. Mack Wilson Pavillion (Eartha White Colleciton, University of North Florida)

Looking for other possibilities for beach access, two groups of Black investors sought beachfront property as Manhattan Beach became less accessible; however, white property owners refused to sell to Black buyers. However, in 1926, Edgar Pomar, who had homesteaded seventy-eight acres of beach and river front property on Anastasia Island between the Atlantic and the Matanzas River sold the property to a group of Black investors (Phelts 9). Pomar's property had been devastated by two hurricanes, the same year as the Great Miami Hurricane that is attributed to killing the Florida land boom of the 1920s and pushing Florida into Depression ahead of the rest of the country. Pomar's wife had died that year, as well, leaving him less than enthused to develop the property. Real estate broker Frank B. Butler formed a corporation, purchased Pomar's property, and developed it as an African-American beach resort. In 1958 Butler sold the majority of the property to the state for use as a state park; some of this property is now subsumed in Butler County Park and Butler Beach just south of St. Augustine Beach.

Figure 2. American Beach Advertisement

For African American's living north of St. Augustine in the Jacksonville and Duvall County areas, though, Butler Beach was a long trip, and many sought beach access options closer to home. In 1901, in partnership with seven Jacksonville business associates, Abraham Lincoln Lewis founded the Afro-American Insurance Association. On May 3, 1901, the Associations' headquarter office building was destroyed in the Great Fire of 1901, the largest suburban fire in the Southeastern US. The fire started in a candle factory when a boiler exploded. The fire spread to a nearby mattress factory, but was not reported to authorities before it had spread out of control. The fire destroyed 146 city blocks and more than 2,368 buildings, including the Afro-American Insurance Association office, forcing Lewis and his associates to relocate the office to Lewis' home.

Lewis would become President of Afro-American Life in 1919 and Florida's first African-American millionaire. Lewis was dedicated to improving educational opportunities for African Americans and contributed substantial money to Edward Waters College in Jacksonville and Bethune-Cookman College in Daytona Beach. His great granddaughter Johnetta B. Cole was the first woman to serve as President of Spelman College and served as President of Bennett College, both historically Black institutions.

Lewis recognized the need for the development of recreational areas specifically for north Florida's Black population, what he identified as a need for "recreation and relaxation without humiliation." In 1926 he founded the Lincoln Golf and Country Club, Jacksonville's only all Black golf club. In 1935 Lewis formed the African-American Pension Bureau and purchased land on Amelia Island. As Frank Parker Stockbridge and John Holliday Perry note in their 1938 book *So This is Florida,* Amelia Island is the only location in the US over which flags of eight different nations have flown: the French, the Spanish, the English, the Patriots, the Green Cross of Florida, Mexico, the Confederacy, and the United States (50). Lewis' plan was to develop the area as a location where employees of Afro-American Insurance and African-American Pensions Bureau could take vacations and afford reasonably-priced homes. American Beach became not only the primary beach access for African Americans, but one of the most significant locations in African-American history.

The Act Prohibiting Importation of Slaves, which Thomas Jefferson Signed into law in 1807 brought an end to the legal slave importation in the US (though, the law was not sufficiently enforced in most places). Upon the passing of the law, many New England-based families who were active in trans-Atlantic slave trade reregistered their ships under the Spanish flag and rerouted their ships to deliver their cargo to Fernandina Beach, the northern most point of Amelia Island in order to avoid compliance with the 1807 act.

Slaves were then delivered to and housed in Fernandina Beach and smuggled across the border into Georgia. Fernandina Beach, approximately eight miles north of where American Beach would be incorporated on Amelia Island, became the headquarters of the illegal slave trade in the New World. Amelia Island was known then as a warehouse for slaves. Given its reputation, both American and British ships often patrolled off of Amelia Island looking for ships carrying slaves to Fernandina. The penalty for smuggling slaves was death. Thus, captains of slave trade vessels pursued by the British or American ships would often throw their cargo overboard rather than risk being caught with a hold filled with contraband slaves. The bodies of the drowned slaves would wash ashore along Amelia Island; the beach at what would become American Beach the site of perhaps the worst display of the horrors of the New World slave trade as was witnessed anywhere, its beaches strewn with the Black bodies not permitted to cross the beach.

In 1935, when the African-American Pension Bureau purchased thirty-three acres of oceanfront property on Amelia Island, the island had already established its place in AfricanAmerican history. Lewis opened the property to use by employees of African-American Pension Bureau and often hosted company outings there. By 1940, Lewis had acquired two more tracts of land adjacent to the original thirty-three, expanding the property to 216 acres. At first, Lewis had the property subdivided with the intent of selling parcels to company executives and shareholders, but in 1940 opted to open sales to the to the general African American community. In 1945 when World War II ended, the United States, in general, experienced a building boom, and American Beach emerged as an entrepreneur's dream. Summer homes, motels, guest houses, restaurants, shops, and night clubs turned American Beach into the preeminent vacation destination for African Americans across the country. Buses from nearby Black communities ran excursion trips to the beach for local residents. American Beach had attained a national reputation as the place for African Americans to vacation; Phelts contends the prestige of American Beach in the 1950s was on par with contemporary reputations of vacation destinations like Walt Disney World. Once again the beach at Amelia Island was covered with Black bodies, only now laughing, shell-gathering, ice-cream-eating bodies.

On July 2, 1964 President Lyndon B. Johnson signed into law the Civil Rights Act of 1964 (Pub.L. 88–352, 78 Stat. 241). Title II and Title III of the Act opened access for African Americans to public spaces.[5] While one might assume that this ground-breaking legislation would open the door to further prosperity for American Beach, the Act actually hurt American Beach financially as vacationers now had many possibilities for vacation destination. As Phelts explains:

> The civil rights legislated in 1964 had opened all public facilities to African Americans. Former American Beach vacationers and day-trippers now frolicked on Miami Beach, raced up and down the wide sands at Daytona, wore out the cobblestones of Savannah, and rode high at St. Simons Island. All along the shores of the East Coast, Blacks explored areas that had once been off limits. The three-day weekends at American Beach shrank to one day; the Sunday visitors and day-trippers no longer stayed overnight. Loaded buses no longer caused a bottleneck at the crossroads. With so little business most of the restaurants and resort establishments closed. (120)

To add to American Beach's financial woes, two months after the Civil Rights Act was signed, essentially erasing American Beach's uniqueness as a vacation destination, Hurricane Dora made landfall approximately six miles north of St. Augustine, less than forty miles south of American Beach.[6] Dora thrashed Florida's Northeast coast with hurricane force winds.

In 1951, Dr. and Mrs. Robert M. Harris of Atlanta built the Blue Palace, a two-story, concrete block mansion that the Harris family had painted baby blue. When Dora struck, the Blue Palace was destroyed, its ocean-facing rooms swept clean of everything in them. Its sea wall crumbled, several of its rooms exposed. The house would never be restored or occupied after Dora (Phelts 78). The ruins would remain on the beach until 1993 when it was sold and demolished, replaced with a new house. The Blue Palace was by no means the only home destroyed by Dora. Several homes were swept away, as was William's Guest Lodge, which had been filled to capacity on September 9, 1964 when the evacuation order was issued in anticipation of the impending storm (Phelts 82). What made Dora such a relevant part of American Beach's history is that unlike other storms that had damaged homes and businesses along American Beach prior, the damage from Dora was left unrepaired for the most part. Prior to Dora residents and business owners would repair damages in time for the next tourist season; after Dora, they did not.

In the half-century since Dora, American Beach has clung to some of its cultural history. Houses have been demolished and rebuilt, but the community has managed to stave off construction of beach-front high rises which can be seen on the beaches to the north and south of American Beach. The beach is still primarily a vacation beach; approximately thirty families live in American Beach year round, and of these only a few are of direct descendants of the first African American families to buy property during the time of Abraham Lincoln Lewis.

On May 30, 1994, Memorial Day, American Beach hosted its Fourth Annual Kuumba Festival, attracting thousands of tourists and vendors from around the country. In her history of American Beach, Phelts explains that the weather was less than cooperative on the morning of the festival, but had subsided enough by mid-day that some festival goers ventured on to the beach, some of the children into the water. Riptides pulled several of the children out into deeper water, their cries for help answered by festival goers. Phelts describes the scene:

> As the riptide pulled them farther out to sea, screams from the shore alerted festival-goers. Several men and women took to the sea; all the would-be rescuers could see were small bobbing heads. A forty-three-year-old wife, mother, and grandmother of five raced in. So did a twenty-three-year-old uncle, a young aunt, and several vendors. More men ran into the sea.
>
> In minutes, as quickly as the riptides had come, they were gone. The sea continued to smash against the shore, soon releasing five bodies—a little boy, the grandmother, another man, a thirty-six-year-old New York vendor, and a Jacksonville woman. Rescuers swam past bodies floating face down while bringing those they saved ashore. (175)

There were no life guards on duty; the county had cut life guards from its budget beginning in 1990 to save approximately $100,000 per year. Black bodies again on the beach.

Preserving American Beach

In 1992 the Florida Legislature named American Beach the first of 141 sites that would make up the Florida Black Heritage Trail, a publication now in its third edition, designed to increase public awareness of the contributions of African Americans to the state. Unfortunately, given the objective of the Heritage Trail series and the numbers of listings included, the discussion of American Beach is reduced to just five sentences, three about land ownership. Fortunately though, the Trail publication does include a longer blurb about MaVynee Betsch, Johnetta B. Cole's sister and Lewis' great-granddaughter. Betsch, who was known fondly as "the Beach Lady" and the unofficial "Mayor of American Beach," was a fixture, character, and activist born in American Beach in 1935, the same year that the African-American Pension Bureau purchased the first 33 acres of American Beach. Raised in luxury provided by her family's wealth, Betch would become the most active preservationist and environmentalist dedicated to protecting American Beach and its heritage. Recognized and remembered by her distinctive seven-foot long dreadlocks which she shaped to resemble the southern part of Africa and the Florida peninsula, her flowing ponchos, the plastic bag on her left hand to hide the foot-long finger nails covered in orange nail polish, the necklaces and anklets of shells, and the numerous political and environmental buttons she wore pinned to the hair net that regulated her hair. The shells on her anklet jingle to remind her of the shackles the slaves of Amelia Island, the orange nail polish to recall the orange rope in the water that marked the "whites only" side of the water in South Carolina (Alliniece). The focus of Russ Rymer's book *American Beach: A Saga of Race and Memory* and Nowhere Productions' documentary *The Beach Lady*, Betsch's activism was internationally renowned, her story featured over the years by CBS, PBS, NPR, *The New York Times*, *National Geographic*, *The Smithsonian*, and others. *Sierra Magazine* honored her and credited her with having kept American Beach from "disappearing."

Figure 3. MaVynee Betsch

The Beach Lady was homeless by choice. Betch gave her fortune to sixty environmental organizations, explaining often that she felt boxed in in buildings and preferred to be outside, sleeping on the beach. With no job, no children, no home, she would explain, she could say what she wanted at public meetings with no fear of repercussion because she had nothing to lose, nothing for others to threaten her through. She gave walking tours to visitors to American Beach. She hung hand-written notes of historical facts on utility poles throughout American Beach. "I'm going to make sure they know this is a Black beach," she said of the notes (Franklin).

The Beach Lady died in September, 2005 at the age of seventy. At her request, her body was cremated. A public memorial was held on the beach. Four years before her death, Betch told reporters that when she died she wished to be cremated and her ashes spread in part in the Atlantic because "The Gulf Stream will take you back to Africa" (Franklin) and the other part atop NaNa, the tallest sand dune on Amelia Island, measuring nearly sixty feet tall, which she had worked to preserve; "NaNa" is Twi for "grandmother" (Alliniece). By 2001, more than one hundred acres of the original American Beach land had been lost to developers of Amelia Island retirement, vacation, and golf communities. She wanted her ashes atop NaNa because, as she explained, "I'm going to haunt these (white developers) even when I'm gone" (Franklin). In April, 2009, American Beach and county leaders unveiled a historical marker as NaNa as a tribute to The Beach Lady. "I'm almost becoming a legend," she once said; "Children tell stories that at night I turn into a moonbeam or a snake. I love it" (Alliniece). The whereabouts of her ashes remain unknown.

History

Most historians, community leaders, and activists agree that the future of American Beach is uncertain, a location of perpetual fluctuation. To preserve a location, of course, is to inscribe a use value, a particular cultural demarcation that establishes what is to be preserved, why, and to what ideological privilege. To preserve is to cherish one condition and renounce others. Preservation is a mediated political event. Preservation is an act of naming: naming something of a particular value and in need of a particular kind of authentication as the real. To preserve is to stake claim in hegemony. What we must not overlook in the case of American Beach is that while the claim of ownership of this place is most visibly evident, the claim is, in fact, a claim of time, not place. At each moment throughout the history of American Beach—and here, I speak intentionally of a specifically demarcated moment in history from the time American Beach was named as American Beach through the present and the traces of history that retroactively authorized that place in time—claims to the location as a sacred space for African Americans is always already more so a claim of historical validation, a claim of "we are here now." This claim is, of course, challenged by other narratives: Timucua narratives, Spanish narratives, ecological narratives, and so on, all but convenient glimpses of a chronology of place. But to say so is not to devalue the African-American claim to that history and place; instead it is an elevation of the other narratives as sharing that place along a chronology.

If Mr. Palomar were to take his walk along American Beach and gaze upon the Black bodies that have resided between the culture behind them and the allegorical wild nature that separates them from bodies on other beaches would he pose the questions of what should be seen to the bodies that labored on the railroad to give culture access to the beach? That allowed the culture and tame the land into a place from which one retreats to the wilds of the beach? Would Mr. Palomar's questions ask not just what should be seen here in this place, but what should be seen in transition, what should be seen as inseparable from the condition that allows each of us to read a beach in a particular way in a particular time, whether angler, beachcomber, surfer, Midwesterner, or slave. If, as I have claimed, Florida is as much an idea of Florida, a simulacra of Florida, and its beaches and waters as much a way to lay claim to that idea of Florida, then any act of reading a beach requires understanding that the very idea of beach is always already a reading of bodies and occupation.[7]

Notes

1. I should note that each of these terms is used differently regionally throughout the US, and each has varying regional as well as technical definitions and are often considered synonymous. For instance, *coast* and *shore* are used interchangeably in many places, while in others are used exclusively. However, technically, *coast* refers to the seaward limit of land and *shore* to the landward limit of the sea.

2. In many instances, as well, *beach* is used synonymously with *ocean*, altering the meaning from a geographical point of transition to the thing into which land transitions.

3. Of course, prior to human habitation, indigenous or colonial, prior to cultural demarcations of tribes and states, occupied lands and wild lands, the Florida (La Florida) land mass had a geological, "natural" history, as well; that "history" falls outside of the scope of this chapter.

4. I am, of course, glossing a good deal of this history for the purpose of this paper. The North Florida region played a much more detailed and significant part of North American exploration history as well as American Civil war history and natural history. However, despite the richness of North Florida's history, I have

opted to reduce my coverage of that history to events directly tied to my discussion of American Beach and African-American beach going.

5. Title II of the Civil Rights Act of 1964: "Outlawed discrimination based on race, color, religion or national origin in hotels, motels, restaurants, theaters, and all other public accommodations engaged in interstate commerce; exempted private clubs without defining the term 'private.'"

Title III II of the Civil Rights Act of 1964: "Prohibited state and municipal governments from denying access to public facilities on grounds of race, color, religion or national origin."

6. American Beach and Florida suffered hits from two other hurricanes during the 1964 storm season, as well. On August 27, Hurricane Cleo, a categorytwo storm, made landfall in Miami. The storm traveled north along the Florida peninsula. On August 28 the storm turned east, heading back offshore, leaving between St. Augustine and Jacksonville and pummeling Florida's Northeast coast. On October 14, Hurricane Isbell made landfall in South Florida. Though the storm then moved offshore, it traveled north, its edges bringing storms to Northeast Florida.

7. I have adopted the title "An American Beach" for this chapter in recognition of the research and publication efforts of others interested in preserving the African American cultural heritage of American Beach and their use of this same title in their work. That is, I acknowledge the work of Alliniece Andino, Kathleen Donagy, and Marhsa Dean Phelts in sharing the history of American Beach and in their use of this title long before I entered into this conversation.

Works Cited

Andino, Alliniece T. "An American Beach Original." *The Florida Times Union*. 13 Feb. 2001. Print.
Calvino, Italo. *Mr. Palomar*. Boston: Mariner Books, 1986. Print.
Florida Historical Markers Program—Marker: Duval. Florida Department of State Division of Historical Records. n.d. Print.
Franklin, Marcus. "History in the Sand." *St. Petersburg Times*. 2 Aug 2004. Print.
Heritage Trails. Florida Department of State Division of Historical Records. n.d. 1 March 13. Print.
History of NS Mayport. Navy League of the United States. n.d. 1 March 13. Print.
Milanich, Jerald T. *The Timucua*. Malden, MA: Blackwell Publishers. 1996. Print.
Phelts, Marsha Dean. *An American Beach for African Americans*. Tallahassee, FL: U P of FL . 1997. Print.
Rymer, Russ. *American Beach: A Saga of Race, Wealth, and Memory*. New York: Harper Collins. 1998.Print.
Stockbridge, Frank Parker and John Holliday Perry. *So This is Florida*. New York, R. M. McBride & Company. 1938. Print.
United States Department of the Interior. *Decisions of the Department of the Interior and General Land Office in Cases Relating to the Public Lands from July, 1885, to June, 1886*. Vol. IV. Washington, DC: Government Printing Office. 1886. Print.

Florida Theory

13 EPCOT: FLORIDA'S DISNEY-PSYCHOSIS DREAMS FORECLOSED

*Craig Saper with Channel Two (Adam Trowbridge &
Jessica Westbrook)*

*For the whole human race, there is time, there is space as we reach for
a new horizon. The future belongs to the dreamers, the dreamer inside
of you. Dreams of the future, all shiny and new.*

—Epcot Center 1978 Preview Video

*... nothing bad ever happens in Disney World. It's the only safe place
in this fucked-up state. . . . The place is like a mortuary. . . . The very
idea of Disney World makes me retch..' . . . Wade was feeling dizzy.
The glare and the crowds were swamping him. I'm in Walt Disney
World. I never thought I'd be here, yet here I am. No newspapers. No
litter. No evidence of the world ...*

—Douglas Coupland , selections from *All Families Are Psychotic*

What is this Disney-psychosis that defines Florida's double-bind schizo-foreclosure? Walt Disney died in 1966, seven months before the "Carousel of Progress" ride was re-launched at Disneyland.

It had formerly been presented at the 1964 World's Fair as "Progressland." The ride brought visitors through a technology and science oriented history via a single American family—father John, mother Sarah, daughter Patricia, son James plus a grandfather, grandmother and cousin. After the show, visitors were lead up to an enormous model of "Progress City," an early version of what had become Walt Disney's focus near the end of his life and the reason that The Walt Disney Company had, beginning in the 1963, secretly purchased twenty-seven thousand acres of land in Florida, south of Orlando. Not content to only build another amusement park, Walt Disney had decided to invent and promote entirely new ways of living, taking cues "from the new ideas and new technologies that are emerging from the forefront of American industry." This new project was called the Experimental Prototype City of Tomorrow, EPCOT. In the film announcing this project, a voiceover begins with a utopian vision, "EPCOT will be a planned environment, demonstrating to the world what American communities can accomplish through proper control of planning and design" and continues into a science fiction dream as a glass dome appears over the city, " . . . but most important, this entire fifty acres of city streets and buildings will be completely enclosed. In this climate-controlled environment, shoppers and theater-goers and people just out for a stroll will enjoy ideal weather conditions, protected day and night from rain, heat and cold and humidity."

> *"EPCOT will be a community of ideas, a public forum for information transfer about emerging new technologies, prototype systems and promising new concepts."*
>
> —EPCOT Center 1978 Preview Video

The geodesic sphere at EPCOT, the most famous monument in central Florida to tourists and outsiders, is not under an enormous glass dome nor are visitors to EPCOT able to enjoy climate-controlled, ideal weather conditions. The geodesic sphere was completed in 1982, long after the Walt Disney Company had abandoned Walt Disney's dream of an experimental prototype city, instead focusing on completing and then expanding the Walt Disney World Resort, a complex of amusement parks and supporting hotels located on the land purchased for EPCOT.

Figure 1. Geodisc Sphere 1

The geodesic sphere is located at the entrance to this new version of EPCOT, now an amusement park that only speaks to fragments of the ideas behind "Progress City." The Castle in the Magic Kingdom has an iconic importance because the silhouette of the Castle is Disney's brand logo, but the castle image is both more general and not specific to the "World" located in central Florida. Other built monuments in central Florida, from Bock Singing Towers to Rocket Ships on the space coast, have less iconic status. The geodesic dome is unique, a large reminder of the utopian vision behind EPCOT.

This monument literalizes and narrativizes an entire world-view of teaching and communication or, more precisely, teaching as an experiment in our future of e-media. "Welcome the Future" is what the video postcard announces with the spectator's face pasted in the animated scene, so that, in the age of an experimental prototype-city of tomorrow, you experience a peculiar pedagogy, system of writing, and world-view. The view may efface more than it reveals in this picture-ready world, but no one can say it isn't a pretty picture or the atmosphere anything but sunny.

The frontier between neurosis and psychosis is drawn here, between repression, *Verdrägung,* and repudiation, *Verwerfung,* a term that Lacan will replace by withdrawal, and finally by "foreclosure" (*forclusion*), the former being related to neurosis, the latter to psychosis. The Disney waking-dream, the peculiar psychosis, began in the Ford Motor pavilion at the 1964 World's Fair in Flushing Meadow-Corona Park, New York City. The Ford pavilion used cars to carry people through the history of world progress. Cars functioned there as both the epitome and vehicle of progress. The pavilion played host to many of the 51.5 million visitors to the fair with a theme of "peace through understanding."

That slogan could double as the emblem of Disney myth: healing contradictions in the name of "it's a small world" understanding in order to keep the fantasy of the waking dream alive. The World's Fair's grounds, built on an old garbage dump and swamp, literally covered over the stench with a world of progress just as Disney world even changed the color of the tannic brown water in the bogs that became the dream-world of progress.

The Disney-built creatures throughout the ride had a pop-art flair. The pop-Disney connection had many links including Claes Oldenburg building his "Ice Bag" in a Disney workshop. This pop-psychotic world is reinforced in the Disney ride, "The Wings of Man," and ends with the little cars actually moving very slowly toward a hole in a large movie screen. At the same time, the film of a landscape rushing by toward the edges of the wall creates a powerful illusory sensation of a fast motion forward and falling.

Freud's discussions of fantasy and sublimation already suggest this uneasy and, often, disjunctive relationship between desire, love, socially sanctioned and accepted fantasy worlds, and dreams of the future. His *Civilization and Its Discontent* copiously analyzes the connections among libidinal development and the civilization's dreams of progress (*Civilization* 102). He explains how a frustrated love leads to these generalized fantasies. A few people can "make themselves independent of their object's acquiescence by displacing what they mainly value from being loved on to loving; they protect themselves against the loss of the object by directing their love, not to single objects but to all men alike; and they avoid the uncertainties and disappointments of genital love by turning away from its sexual aims and transforming the instinct into an impulse with an inhibited aim" (*Civilization* 102). He goes on to explain that an obsessive love has an ambiguous relationship with civilization: it resists the interests of civilization and civilization attempts to restrict its bounds. More importantly, "it is always possible to bind together a considerable number of people in love, so long as there are other people left over to receive the manifestations of their aggressiveness" (*Civilization* 114). Love jams the utopian project of the progress machine even as it sets its fantasy going.

In Freud's famous article "The Moses of Michelangelo,"[1] he argues that sublimation requires series of factors rather than a singular hydraulic action (*The Moses of Michelangelo* 233). Few commentators mention the importance of the "gift" of the law or commandments in Freud's model of sublimation. Whatever happens up there in the clouds also motivates the effort to constrain the passions. Certainly, Freud does not want to adopt a theological model of creativity nor does he want to depend on a completely cynical model in which the God's or Pope's power constrains the artist's passion. He does argue in *Civilization and Its Discontents* that "first comes renunciation of instinct owing to fear of aggression by the external authority" (*Civilization* 128). The artist sublimates this anxiety and anger by expressing a love, which necessarily involves the disjunctive hate, in the form of a gift. The gift, as an expression of *renunciated passions* and sublimated anger, only finds itself exposed in the paranoid and punishing civilization. In any other case, the expression remains unconscious to all involved; no one, not even the imagineers, has a transcendent awareness.

Instead of conceptualizing creativity as a pragmatic strategy or as a fount of innovation, as Disney does, Freud's great achievement is to conceive the threatening aspects of creative achievement, as something which pulls desires and passions in to a form which, then, more powerfully pulls others in to its sexual/renunciative collapse of space: as more people give-in to the Disney draw, more people will fill the limited space of Disney's dream of perfect civilization with increasing numbers of veiled hostile and discontented expressions. Paradoxically, this intense collapse of love, hate, and anxiety continues to seduce those that enter Disney's dream of utopia to give-up pieces of order and control. In short, Freud's model of what Disney calls "Imagineering" more closely resembles a cultural black hole than Disney's personal enlightenment and genius. With most commentators seeking to find a common hermeneutic ground for understanding creativity in terms of sublimation, few have appreciated Freud's political maneuvering against a humanism which sees individuals, like Disney, and civilizations working smoothly together for the common good. Instead, he conceives of sublimation in much the same way as something like a primal scene, taken-in as details, fragments, digressions. Although this is not the sexual primal scene, we invariably (mis) understand it in a similar way (as hostile and fear-provoking) without further interpretation.

Laurence Rickels in *The Case of California*, a text with a large scope investigating the connections between Germany before World War II and its literal extension/critique in the emigrant culture of California after World War II and into the contemporary scene, notes how psychoanalytic and psychological researchers argue for a strong link between media-technical apparatuses, like California's Disneyland, and the psyche (Rickels 10–20, 50–69, 103–117, 277–301 278).[2] Rickels traces the history of investigations linking particular mental processes and media massification—the sharing of the same phantasmagoric dream of utopia. Researchers as different as Munsterburg and Staudenmaier use the cinema as an analogy for these processes. Herbert Marcuse, a German Frankfurt School emigrant to California, uses the cinema as a crucial example for his argument, and he also suggests that the media machine creates the massification of privacy. When the rides starts everyone has the same dream, the same Other, the same Unconscious. What is lost in this massification is the ability to create utopian dreams in your own head; it becomes difficult to turn off the ride's projector and begin projecting your own desires and utopian fantasies. The feel-good culture the rides reinforce, the American sentiments for imagineered creativity (shared by the Nazis as well) looks like the "California" version of Freud's Germanic sublimation. It is not by chance that many commentators have noted Disney's interest in fascism. Creativity, especially during the 1950s, epitomized the continuing collective effort to "feel good about one's self;" its big screen familial version of the European mix of übermensch and sublimation made heroes out of happy-go-lucky technicians who followed the rules for the ultimate in individuality: homespun safe creativity found in the safety of Disney World. Freud's sublimation contained all of the angst involved in the family drama. To borrow Marcuse's criticism of the cinema, Disney's fantasy of a utopian civilization allows for the "emptiness," self-hatred, and personal dreams exiled from, and recuperated into, the Disney psychosis soft-version of creativity.

In his exploration of the "influencing machine" experienced by schizophrenics, Victor Tausk describes something which very closely resembles Disney's virtual reality. His article, "On the Origin of the 'Influencing Machine' in Schizophrenia," written in 1933, represents one of the most important contributions to psychoanalysis (Tausk 519–56).[3] This machine, as described by schizophrenics, "consists of boxes, cranks, levers, wheels, buttons, wires, batteries, and the like" (Tausk and Roazen 186). This detailed technological explanation of the strange influence the schizophrenics report demonstrates how they use science to explain the sense of persecution, which, at first, appears beyond scientific explanation. In describing how the mechanism works, patients describe how the machine produces pictures similar to a "magic lanterns" or from a "cinematograph." These pictures are not hallucinations, but rather two-dimensional single-pane images projected on to walls. This description is remarkable not just for being an apparent invention of a paranoiac, but also, and more importantly, for its suggestion of a Disney ride as an influencing machine. Although the "influencing machine" described does not appear in a socially acceptable way (i.e., the general community does not see these projections), it so closely resembles the Disney ride, that one can not help but wonder if Tausk's analysis was prescient. The machine produces and removes thoughts and feelings by means of "waves or rays" and patients sometimes describe the machine as a "suggestion-machine" if they have less familiarity with technology. EPCOT seeks to "influence" rather than "suggest" as in a simulation of psychosis in a deep hypnosis. We do not follow in a trance the images projected, we interact with them allowing them to influence our movements, thoughts, and feelings.

Although not technically a geodesic dome, because it is a full sphere, the Spaceship Earth pavilion (built in 1982) uses the Buckminster Fuller dome design, and his metaphor of our world as a spaceship. The Fuller design famously uses a framework of self-bracing triangles (in the pavilion's case 954 triangular panels of polyethylene cores sandwiched between two anodized aluminum plates), which creates the strongest and most efficient structure ever designed because no other form of enclosure can cover as much area without internal supports, and the larger these structures, the stronger they become rather than weaker in most rectilinear structures. Spaceship Earth encloses 2,200,000 cubic feet of space inside a globe 165 feet in diameter. It is an icon of efficient and strong systems of organization and composition, an icon for a brand one might call foundations of composition and communication: clear, concise, cogent, and cost-effective—a monument to Disney's world view.

World View, Dream

At the end of seventh grade I found out we were moving to Orlando. I was under the impression that we would live across the street from Walt Disney World. If not across the street, then within walking distance perhaps? I would not visit Walt Disney World for years after moving to Orlando. I did, however, attend a junior high school where the seventh grade classes were at least a year behind Tennessee and chewing tobacco was a major disciplinary problem.

World View, Future

We brought my grandparents to Epcot Center a few years after moving to Orlando. Due to my grandmother's use of a wheelchair, we went to the front of nearly every line. Epcot was not intense enough to be an intense disappointment, but viewed from the perspective of a mid-1980s teen standing in CommuniCore, near Spaceship Earth, the future was already outdated, indicated by interactive kiosks that functioned no better than paper maps and consumer device displays that showed the same shoddy video phones that television constantly told us were coming. Did anyone ever believe in space farms on distant planets shown at the "Listen to the Land" ride? At least we can now make restaurant reservations online. It was only a couple years after this visit that I discovered Commodore 64 Bulletin Board Systems, "anarchy files" and "zero day warez." A future much better than what Epcot was promising opened up.

World View, Trip

We stopped to get the acid and waited outside while our friend driving the car went inside. Once inside she was pushed to do a "depth charge" (a way of shotgunning marijuana). We got to Disney and dropped in the parking lot. Throughout the line to get in our driving friend was passing scrawled notes to everyone. She was already having a bad trip. She wanted to call her mother to come get her. She was the one with the car so we tried to change her mind. We headed to an unoccupied corner of Future World to hopefully help our driving friend calm down. While there, we came to the realization that we were at Disney and while you could, at the time, smoke cigarettes at Disney, you could not buy cigarettes at Disney. This required an immediate inventory of the cigarettes remaining between the four of us. We had less than two and a half packs. Cigarettes had to be rationed. As we became aware of the cigarette crisis, we became aware that Disney wasn't a very good place to be on acid. What is a delightful or at least amusing artifice becomes more sinister. We'd had a similar experience at the Orlando International Airport some weeks earlier. While the massive, patterned carpet and the airplanes were engaging, the music was insidious and we had a long discussion about what airport music was intended to do. Were subliminal messages were contained within the soft-pop ballads? They were telling us something. Disney was worse. Everything was covered in a thin veneer of fun but we were very high and could only see the glue holding down the glitter, and our driving friend was chain-smoking our supply and still talking about calling her mom.

World View, Space Coast

We had been strung out on white crosses (fifteen miligram ephedrine, fifteen dollars for one thousand at Father Nature's store) for most of the school year and decided to celebrate a birthday by renting a motel room at Daytona beach with another couple. The acid was very strong and we took more of it than usual. It was not our spring break, but it was apparently someone's spring break because the parties around us started nearly immediately after we dropped. Speed and acid combined, and paranoia set in, at least for some of us. One of the friends we brought spent some number of hours replaying Robert Johnson's "Malted Milk" over and over again while, from the sound of it, frat boys next door were utterly destroying their motel room. Everything stretched out and no one talked much. Some of us later admitted to near death experiences. Some of us broke down crying on the beach in the early morning. The frat boys never stopped destroying their motel room.

World View, Church & Surveillance

Church Street was shopping simulacrum of the rail station that used to exist in the same spot in downtown Orlando. It was for tourists, drinkers, and drunk tourists, but it was also one of the few places teens could go and avoid (much) harassment (at least white, suburban teens). The main draw was a tobacco shop where clove cigarettes were available, otherwise all activity consisted of walking around aimlessly. At some point security cameras were installed at every intersection of every hallway and watching over every restroom. We amused ourselves one night jumping up and blocking a camera while standing behind it, until a friend missed and smacked the camera loudly, sending it flying into the wall and down the hallway. We scattered and spent an hour regrouping and avoiding security. Another time a college-aged guy asked for a cigarette, revealed he had stashed a pipe bomb near the trash bins and asked for a ride. While we did not believe him, completely, we declined to offer him a ride.

World View, Sinking Psychogeography

In 2013, a massive sinkhole swallowed a man, killing him in his sleep, and suddenly Central Florida was on the front page again for its psychogeographical foreclosure and crises. When the officials were forced to demolish the house, pieces of the family's memories were spit up out of the collapse into public view. Suddenly, the notion of place—a Devil's Millhopper if you will—seemed to be an abreaction of an entire State Apparatus; not the Althusserian notion of the State Apparatus, but an actual State of Florida's—specifically Central Florida—affectivity. As the crews worked, the walls with picture frames slipped down into the hole along with baby toys and clothes on hangers—some avoiding the hellish decent and instead laid out across the ground like make-shift memorials and markers. A woman wept as she held a framed portrait. The cranes demolished the blue, cement brick, one-story house trying to protect family belongings. The work began on a sunny Sunday, and by Monday afternoon, the house was mostly gone. This led to what seemed like a rampant outbreak of sinkholes all over the United States with a banker being temporarily swallowed on a golf course. It was the sad realization of the meaning of Central Florida in the cultural imaginary: foreclosed denial with the eventual bad trip and sinking feeling.

Gregory Ulmer examines the role of "places in electracy," and suggests a heuristic rule for imaging place: "some feature of a site is selected, put into a representation (in any medium), inflected, as a receptacle for a possible feeling felt. From this shift away from topos, story becomes 'a poetic figure' in which "certain details of a situation create atmosphere capable of attracting and holding a thought. This choral 'traitment' (management of traits, attributes, properties of things for non-conceptual effects) opens and maintains a dimension that [. . .] gives access to a register of reality previously only glimpsed by means of art" (Ulmer)[4].

World View, Military Entertainment Complex

Right before the foreclosure crisis and housing bubble crash, we brought our son back to Orlando, to Sea World and to Walt Disney World. Our high school was falling apart. What were two lane roads had become eight-lane highways. Residential and commercial development had increased by several orders of magnitude. Having already been to Disney Land, our son found Disney World to be large, spread out and tiring. Future World had been invaded by Buzz Lightyear and the formerly charming Tiki Room was ruined by an incredibly grating Iago the parrot. We had, for reasons we cannot explain, decided to visit in the summer and the heat was unbearable. We spent two hours with our son sleeping on our laps next to a shooting gallery, where tourists of all sorts where taking up arms against cowboy-themed targets. Watching the steady stream of tourists shooting at targets, it was hard not to think of the wars still going on in Iraq and Afghanistan. We left well before the fireworks.

World View, Reality Ride

"Why is Disney getting into so many things that are apparently unrelated to the entertainment industry? What can Disney possibly contribute? . . . To make today's dreams for EPCOT, tomorrow's reality for everyone."

—Card Walker, President, Walt Disney Productions

When you enter EPCOT, the flow of the crowd leads you into this first pavilion you encounter the world inside a world as a mise-en-abyme. Once inside, you take a ride through the history of communication technologies in a vehicle (a plastic bucket-like train car). It is not surprising that Siemens (and initially AT&T) has sponsored this ride, but it is surprising that the ride seems to introduce and frame the rest of the EPCOT experience, and in Baudrillardian style is an outline of the media-world history and future.

The ride does not explore anything to do with Fuller's notion of spaceship earth as an ecological system delicately balanced and in need of stewardship and guidance. Instead, the entire ride and pavilion explores the history of writing systems and technologies (grammatology) as the essential aspect of our spaceship earth. Like other rides, the vehicle or car moves past a series of posed scenes, pastiche, with animatronics—a neologism Disney coined to mean automatons (but which sounds more like animations mixed with electronics). The ride begins with separate scenes depicting cave paintings, Egyptian hieroglyphs and taxes, and the Phoenician's invention of an alphabetic writing system and increased commerce with the narrator's voice-over explaining the significance. In each case, the advance in technology led to a major advance in systems of organization, thought, and commerce. The next scene of Ancient Greece depicts an animatronic unidentified-Plato talking to a student-like animatronic. The voice-over explains that the Greeks invented school and had great advances in mathematics (as a language system of communication); these advances led to the development of mechanical inventions and innovations. Building on the success of the Ancient Greeks, the Romans built "the first world-wide web" with their roads and aqueducts.

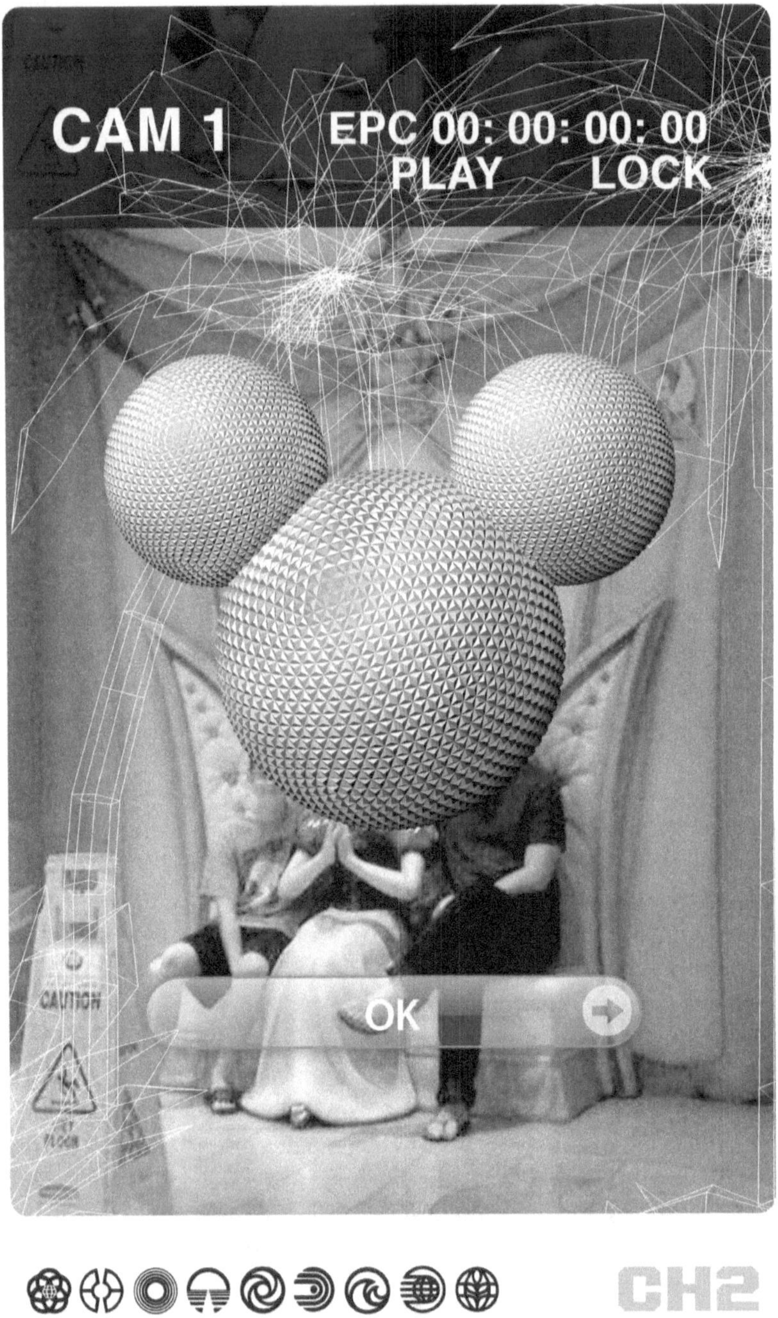

Figure 2. Disney as Grammatology

The ride turns dark, and the air fills with the smell of smoke, one can see simulations of embers smoldering and the wreckage of buildings. The narrator explains that the library in Alexandria burned, and the Rome fell. The next scene takes out of darkness, and we learn from the voice-over that the Jews and Muslims in the middle-east had copies of the books, and preserved the tradition to eventually to be re-discovered in the European Renaissance, where we see Michelangelo on his back above us painting the Sistine Chapel with God's finger reaching out and touching man—and suggesting the AT&T slogan, Reach out and touch someone. Next we learn of Guttenberg's printing press, and the huge advances in communication associated with the mass reproduction of writing.

> We saw this as an opportunity to reach a broad audience and tell them about the Bell system. Disney expects at least ten million people a year, here, and there are opportunities to reach even more people through publicity and advertising and promotion. We want to tell the American public, show them how Bell system is a leader in new technologies and new products and services for the information age. (Bruce Strasser, AT&T Director, EPCOT Project, Chronicle News Update: EPCOT)

The ride ends with a series of scenes and atmospheric sections about the rise of the computer age, but, before it fully articulates the implications of that new system of communication, it dumps you out into a place to send yourself a video postcard from the future in an endless feedback loop of foreclosures. EPCOT promises a dream and a dream-like world-view, or the dream of perfect communication systems. This inflated sphere of influence carries with it an increasing need to inflate the current best of all possible worlds of pure-communicating into a giant geodesic bubble. The Lacanian version of Freud's insight was to see in this type dream-world an uneasy and, often, disjunctive relationship among desire, love, and socially sanctioned, and accepted, innovations and world-views of a perfect future. That system is constantly contradicted and foreclosed by the new set of rules of always, by necessity, new models of communication. This double-bind and foreclosure of real estate, psychogeography, and perfect invisible-media forms of communication is precisely the mechanism that leads to a cultural psychosis and foreclosure called Florida.

Figure 3. Geodisc Sphere 2

Notes

1. See also, Freud, Sigmund. "Leonardo da Vinci and a Memory of His Childhood." Trans. James Strachey. *The Standard Edition of the Complete Psychological Works of Sigmund Freud*. Ed. James Strachey. Vol. 11. London: Hogarth Press, 1957. 59–137.

2. See also, Marcuse, Herbert. *Five Lectures: Psychoanalysis, Politics, and Utopia*. Trans. Jeremy Shapiro and Shierry Weber. Boston: Beacon Press, 1970. Print.

See also Freud, Sigmund. *Group Psychology and the Analysis of the Ego*. Trans. James Strachey. New York: W.W. Norton, 1975. Print.

The relationship between invention and sublimation, and the particular workings of invention cannot be addressed in the space of this article. See also the analysis of the metaphysics of invention in, Derrida, Jacques. "Psyché: Inventions of the Other," in *Reading De Man Reading*, Ed. Lindsay Waters and Wlad Godzich. Minneapolis: U of Minnesota P, 1989, 25–66. Print.

See also, Saper, Craig. "Posthumography: The Boundaries of Literature and the Digital Trace." *Rhizomes: Cultural Studies in Emerging Knowledge* 20 (2010): n.p. . Electronic journal.

3. See also, Saper, Craig. "Sublimation as Media." *Discourse: Journal of Theoretical Studies in Media and Culture* 31.1 and 31.2 (2010): 51–71.

4. See also, Saper's "The Felt Memory On YouTube." *Enculturation: A Journal of Writing, Rhetoric, and Culture* 8 (2010).

Works Cited

Freud, Sigmund. *Civilization and Its Discontents: The Standard Edition*. Trans. James Strachey. Vol. XXI. London: Hogarth Press, 1929. Print.

—. *The Moses of Michelangelo: The Standard Edition*.Vol. XIII. Trans. James Strachey. London: Hogarth Press, 1914. 211–38. Print.

Rickles, Laurence A. *The Case of California*. Baltimore: Johns Hopkins UP, 1991. Print.

Tausk, Victor. "On the Origin of the 'Influencing Machine' in Schizophrenia," *Psychoanalytic Quarterly* 11.3–4 (1933): 519–56. Print.

Tausk, Victor, and Paul Roazen. *Sexuality, War, and Schizophrenia: Collected Psychoanalytic Papers*. Trans. Roazen. New Brunswick, USA: Transaction Publishers, 1991. Print.

Saper, Craig. "Imaging Place: GIS Databases in Digital Humanities." *Rhizomes: Cultural Studies in Emerging Knowledge* 15 (2009): Electronic Journal.

14 Orlando, Florida's Ubiquitous Libidinal Boxes

Lauren Mitchell

> "We don't go to cities. Cities come to us, stream towards us. To occupy a city today is to surf in a dense array of overlapping media streams. The limit of the city is not the limit of some physical terrain but the limit of its packaging. To go to Manhattan is only to go to the hard copy, as it were, of all the images that you know so well, to swim in the source of the flow."
>
> —Mark Wigley, "Resisting the City"

Opening Boxes

Orlando, Florida is made up of packaged experiences. It is a relational web of physical and virtual spaces each with supporting spatial, material, visual, and textual rhetorics. It is a series of destination points—boxes, operating in support of a libidinal economy. Drawing from Mark Wigley's assertion above, to physically visit Orlando is "to swim in the source of the flow," it is to confirm the hardcopy. The institution of

American tourism, embraced so heavily in Orlando, significantly facilitates in constructing a shared sense of what it means to be on vacation.[1]

I am intimately familiar with this flow. Orlando's boxes have always had a pull on me. I grew up forty miles east of Orlando in Titusville, which is situated across the Indian River from Kennedy Space Center. Orlando provided my family access to franchised experiences that the city of Titusville, with all of its coastal beauty, could not. We drove forty-five minutes west to Orlando nearly every weekend for dining and recreation experiences, and for a lot of boxes.

My car is still equipped with an E-pass, offered by Orlando's Expressway Authority for the comfort of smooth transit along the city's uncongested expressways, free from the hassle and interruption of tolls. This drive to Orlando is pleasurable. In contrast to the uncompromising flatness of the terrain, the expansive sky is so frequently breathtaking that it goes unappreciated. The reflective surfaces of the marshy waters, sand, and asphalt merge with the bright sky in a hypnotic haze providing a contemplative mood for much of the duration of travel, unless passing through a storm. I remember anticipatively waiting to resume our transit as my mother stopped to take photographs of herons and egrets wading in retention ponds behind the many franchise restaurants and big-box stores populating this seemingly disorganized urban condition along Orlando's eastern fringes.

The delicate jewelry boxes on the dresser as well as the wilting cardboard boxes in the humid garage allured me. My attraction to boxes, the anticipation of their arrival, along with my fond and foundational memories of Orlando's pull help me to side step disciplinary *stasis* loops surrounding contested architectural and development practices of *big-box culture*.[2] This culture is prevalent within much of this country, yet wildly exaggerated and more observable, more despicable (architecturally), within Orlando. The opening sequence for the first few seasons of the Showtime television series *WEEDS*, featuring and popularizing the 1962 song "Little Boxes" by Malvina Reynolds, captures well the ubiquitous nature of such development practices within this country.

Figure 1–2. Big Box Recreation

In this chapter, I would like to offer an unlikely reading of this city's boxes—its mega-malls, strip-malls, big-box stores, hotel rooms, tollbooths, porta-potties, gas stations, timeshares, hotels, warehouses, tract houses, theme parks, etc. My reading steps outside of typical conversations about sustainable building and urban practices, by focusing instead on how human desire shapes Orlando. I argue that architects are unable to find (or invent) ways to begin designing within these conditions because they have a restricted set of conceptual starting places, known within the field of rhetoric as *topoi,* from which to pull. I invite other disciplines to this discussion, hoping for more actionable reception of this prevalent urban condition within the field of architecture. Placing more awareness on the libidinal complexities at work on us and in us in relation to box culture will open up new strategies for engagement. In the following chapter Ulmer offers the *kunsult* as one such strategy, applying a shifted perception of space, "choragraphy " in order to render disasters into moments for epiphanies. Feeling into libidinal economics requires an Ulmerian perspective. Put very simply, if we were to see/feel Orlando's libidinal forces in action, architecture's capacity for engaging with the community's well-being would radically increase. A fuller understanding of waste would ensue.

Finding ways to look beyond the wastefulness in construction, and lack of architectural sensibility found in the fantastic fictional realities of Walt Disney World's Magic Kingdom, for example, reveals the "utilidor" (short for utilities corridor) infrastructure on which the Magic Kingdom is constructed. The tunnel's careful precision and architectural sophistication—its spatial material rhetoric—facilitates Disney's fantasy. Disney is a libidinal box; it is an experience driven by libidinal economics. Walt Disney provides this fantasy, an escape from our daily lives and economics, and we asked for it, if not directly then indirectly through our persistent participation.

There are roads and pedestrian walkways within utilidor marked clearly with a graphic color-coded system ensuring that characters from Frontierland don't disturb the experience by accidentally emerging through Fantasyland's entrance stair. Even the park's trash is fantastic. Collected within utilidor, an automated trash collection system (AVAC) sucks vast quantities of trash through the tunnels to a centralized collection area. One is aware of trash flying by their body when walking under the parks "stage" level. At the conceptual and physical intersection between Disney's stage and utilidor, we can see the juxtaposition between the spatial material rhetoric of Magic Kingdom and the infrastructure supporting it. This intersection exposes the relational nature of libidinal boxes at work. The utilidor system is as much a part of Disney's packaging as are the brochures at Orlando's official visitors' center on International Drive, the billboard seen on the side of Orlando's Turnpike, and www.disneyworld.disney.go.com. Further understandings of the relationship between these layers of libidinal packaging present opportunities for disciplinary expansion.

Theorist Jean-François Lyotard's text *Libidinal Economy* (*LE*) provides an ideal theoretical lens through which such a reading of Orlando's libidinal boxes can be generated. Within *LE*, Lyotard develops a set of figures as a method of depicting libidinal dispositions as they compete for energies of libidinal events. Through the construction of these figures, Lyotard attempts to portray a complex relationship between the libidinal and *dispositifs*, or apparatuses (controlling mechanisms such as capitalism).[3] The resulting libidinal affects are concrete material entities, which he explains through emphatic phenomenological descriptions. Below I overlay these figures onto aspects of Orlando, expanding Lyotard's visualization of a libidinal economy at work, illustrating further that ubiquitous aspects of our environments proliferate and are repeated in response to desire.

In addition to working with Lyotard, in participation with rhetoric scholars and others in this collection, I wish to open up the following questions: Are there architectural techniques, such as the static "plan," driving the field of urbanism that need to be reconsidered within big-box culture? For example, are such documents incapable of capturing the many layers of urban conditions such as the ones that Jeff Rice's *Digital Detroit* (an exploration into rhetorical invention) points us to? Might we similarly consider appropriating Ulmer's "electracy," a form of literacy based upon the image, as an added layer in order to augment and reconsider the usefulness of traditional architectural *techné*? How, for example, might we invent an "electrate" equivalent to the scaling up and down that occurs within architectural design?[4] Merging architecture and rhetoric, by way of invention, I'm hoping to stretch our understanding of the term urbanism to include areas of big-box culture.[5]

Big-Box Urbanism

I graduated in 2003 from the University of Florida with a bachelor's degree in architectural design. I realized much too late that the highly nuanced design skill set that I had unquestioningly and passionately, even obsessively, devoted my life to for four years had very little relevance around much of my hometown, nor much of my home country. The divide between the culture of architecture and my *habitus* could not be more pronounced. Populated primarily by capitalistically driven developments comprised of big-box franchises and tract homes, or "suburban sprawl," Orlando holds very little value for the kinds of objects and spaces architecture students are taught to create. Bernard Tschumi suggests,

> . . . a pervasive network of binding laws entangles architectural design. These rules, like so many knots that cannot be untied, are generally paralyzing constraints. When manipulated, however, they

have the erotic significance of bondage. To differentiate between rules or ropes is irrelevant . . . what matters is that there is no simple bondage technique: the more numerous and sophisticated the restraints, the greater the pleasure. (536)

The vast majority of Orlando's physical environment is limited by very few tectonic and material restraints beyond value engineering. The fewer corners a building has, generally speaking, will reduce the cost of construction. This is why Orlando has so many boxes. Yet, a realm that is foreign to the field of architecture governs its predominant construction practices. Market segmentation data, I will expand upon below, actually aid in the development of much of our shared public and private space. If we can tap into such data collection and manipulation, through the integration of rhetorical invention and architectural design, these bondage techniques may become pleasurable to designers as well.

Upon graduation from UF in 2003, I felt I would either have to move to one of the few densely populated areas within this country with enough design culture to sustain a living as an "architect," or I would have to find a new profession. Tschumi holds, "Neither space, nor concepts alone are erotic, but the junction between the two is" (537), and I had become addicted to the particular cocktail of concept + space. I was too hooked on the pleasure of architecture to give it up. Ignoring my nagging concerns about the potential uselessness of my profession, I applied to graduate school in Architecture.

An answer to my concerns arrived in the mail as part of the acceptance package to the University of Michigan's Taubman Collage of Architecture and Urban Planning. The school had sent a copy of *Dimensions*, a yearly student publication of the school's work. In it I found images of tract homes, shopping carts, semi trailers, Walmart, and French fries along with the images I expected to see in a publication on graduate architecture student projects. I obsessed over a series of short essays titled, "Contested Urbanism," and was struck in particular by a quote from Jason Young about his recent studio project, a truck stop. In the article, Young notes, "Often referred to as 'suburban,' many of these sites are significant given their frequent repetition and virtual ubiquity within the American lifestyle. Big-box retail, strip center developments, franchise space . . . each is an example of an urbanism which falls outside of the comparative taxonomy of traditional, central, dense cities . . ." (19).[6] Young's agenda attempts to shift the discipline of architecture's focus from the form and space of cities in order to gain, "more penetrating understandings" and more insightful strategies for urban work.

This set of short essays gave me hope that my diametrically opposed worlds might actually be allowed to touch. At Michigan, as a participant in a seven-year initiative to explore this notion of "Contested Urbanism" within the first-year graduate studio sequence, I began to make sense of my addiction, and of my home. Young's pedagogy guided me toward a legitimate place within the field, in the *doxa,* of architecture to consider the "ugly" architecture from which I, just like so many Americans, have come.

Figure 3. Behind the Strip

As a result of my experience within this pedagogy, one which Michigan's school of architecture has sadly let fall away in the last few years, I feel confident arguing for the inclusion of ubiquitous systems of production, and digital publics within urban analyses. I'm hopeful that my investigation into Orlando's libidinal boxes will add further legitimacy and interest in this conversation by offering new *topoi,* or new ways to "begin" working on and in big-box urbanism.

Strip Appeal, http://www.strip-appeal.com, is a design competition that seeks participants who will join them in their efforts to address the "blight" that small-scale strips have become in neighborhoods throughout the United States. Orlando is littered with strip malls fitting this description, long past their prime, yet somehow hanging on. Just west of the Walmart Supercenter on Highway 50, for example, are several strips that have steadily fallen out of favor since 1999 when the Waterford Lakes Town Center, a Simon mall, débuted around the juncture of 408 and 50.

Strip Appeal participant David Karle notes, "The thinness of the strip mall roof is one of hyper efficiency, developer driven economic reasoning, and a maximization of materials, but the roof could still be conceptually and physically thinner . . . Reinterpreting the flat datum strip mall roof . . . repositions the roof as a spatial driver for *new* suburban strip mall typologies."[7] Others and myself would enthusiastically welcome these proposal's to intervene on the roofs of the strips along Highway 50. However, because participants in Strip Appeal such as Karle view the strip-mall as "problematic," advocating for "new" typologies, their proposals would likely become targets in the same cycle of "blight" in generations to come. Projects within big-box culture require an added dimension. This dimension requires invention oriented toward greater awareness and willingness to understand the desires that warrant the proliferation of these ubiquitous boxes.

Ubiquitous Boxes

The Waterford Lakes Town Center, a Simon Mall, is the first major retail shopping experience one reaches when traveling west along Highway 50 toward Orlando.

Figure 4. Waterford Lakes Town Center Entrance

We shopped at this elaborate outdoor mall most regularly after its construction in 1999 because it dramatically shortened our commute. Simon Property Group must have accurately predicted that the eastern fringe of Orange County would become a hub for residential development in Central Florida. The property's success can be seen clearly in satellite imagery of the area. These images expose the sheer quantity and variety of libidinal boxes, the fast and loose architecture that has quickly surrounded the plaza.

Figure 5. Waterford Lakes Seen via Google Map's Satellite Imagery

Nielson, a global information and measurement company, has developed a "segmentation" system called *My Best Segments* that helps to explain how and why such construction proliferates in this country. This product provides one example of libidinal infrastructures made visible. PRIZM, one of three available *My Best Segments* products combines demographic, consumer behavior, and geographic data in order to help marketers identify, understand, and reach prospective customers. The site states that PRIZM defines every US household in terms of sixty-six demographically and behaviorally distinct types, or "segments."

My Best Segments catalogues desire (spending habits) by way of statistical data and analysis that I am not qualified to explain. However, this record is made visible and easily searchable, allowing the information to inform business strategies to repeat, adjust, or morph as needed from place to place depending upon what kind of libidinal intensities might persist there. This operation results in the ubiquitous and sometimes surreal spaces seen in and around the eastern portion of Orange County.

Orlando, Florida's Ubiquitous Libidinal Boxes / 257

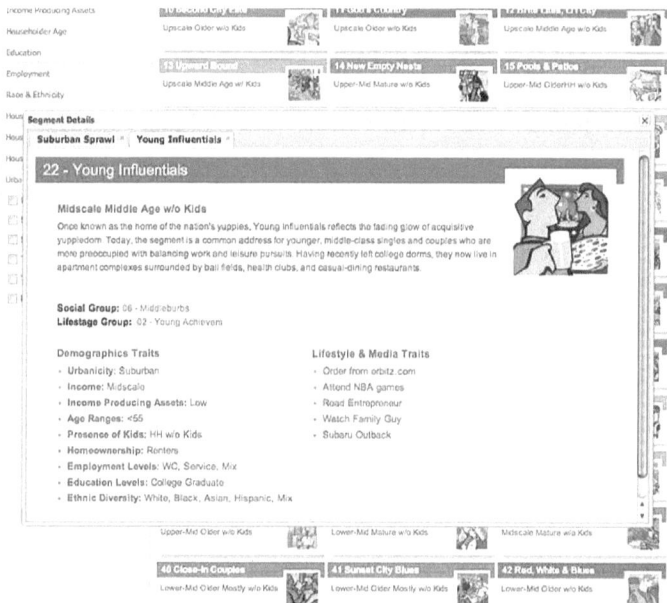

Figure 6. Screen capture of PRIZM online interface to help marketers discern those consumers' likes, dislikes, lifestyles and purchase behaviors. Used by thousands of marketers within Fortune 500 companies, PRIZM provides the "common language" for marketing in an increasingly diverse and complex American marketplace.[8]

Figure 7–8. Behind Waterford Lakes

Entering the zip code 32828 into My Best Segments' zip code search query renders the five most common of the sixty-six PRIZM lifestyle groups found in this section of Orange County. These five groups are, Blue Chip Blues, Home Sweet Home, Kids With Cul-de-sacs, Winner's Circle, and Young Influentials. Each group provides corporations such as Simon Property Group a snapshot of the group's lifestyle and media traits in addition to 2011 demographics data. The Winner's Circle, for example, is described as follows:

> Among the wealthy suburban lifestyles, Winner's Circle is the youngest, a collection of mostly 35 to 54 year-old couples with large families in new-money subdivisions. Surrounding their homes are the signs of upscale living: recreational parks, golf courses and upscale malls. With a median income over $100,000, Winner's Circle residents are big spenders who like to travel, ski, go out to eat, shop at clothing boutiques, and take in a show.[9]

The influential nature of this data collection and visualization on our shared public environment recommends the possibility for intervention within it. What if designers were to use this product as a model for what could be achieved by incorporating a closer look at desire's influence? I don't mean to suggest architects should forget about physical construction, or about Tshumi's pleasurable binding laws of spatial and material design, taking up market segmentation research instead. Areas bound by the hooks of such segmentation data, exemplified by the Waterford Lakes Town Center, escape the common definition of urbanity in architecture. But, these areas are significant to so many in Orlando and much of the United States. Thus, they are viable conditions for serious urban analysis. Such analysis must be willing to consider the perspective of those individuals making up the "Winner's Circle" lifestyle segment, living adjacent to Waterford Lakes Town Center, and loving it.

Lyotard's term *differend*,[10] used to describe a situation that defies resolution, is useful here. In *Libidinal Economy* he explores the *differend* in the chapter, "The Desire Named Marx." Lyotard demands that we consider Karl Marx's humanness—his potential madness—simultaneously while we are considering his writing. Victor Vitanza has suggested that the text actually be conceived *as* Lyotard's madness even more than as a theory.[11] Lyotard portrays "fat bearded Marx" and "little girl Marx" as one conflicting figure, as one hermaphroditic and conflicting body. Captured in this section, Marx's non-rational forces of sensation and conflicting emotions allow Lyotard to express that the world is actually moved in the ways that feelings move people.

Lyotard does so controversially by comparing a prostitute's body of work with the work of "intellectual sirs," academics in their ceaseless efforts to produce "more and more words, more books, more articles." Lyotard is questioning why we, "political intellectuals," tend to commiserate towards the proletariat, suggesting that a proletarian would hate us because we are unwilling to accept the reality "that one can enjoy swallowing the shit of capital . . ." Lyotard posits further:

> You situate yourselves on the most despicable side, the moralistic side where you desire that our capitalized's desire be totally ignored, forbidden, brought to a standstill, you are like priests with sinners, our servile intensities frighten you . . . And of course we suffer, we the capitalized, but this does not mean that we do not enjoy, nor that what you think you can offer us as a remedy . . . does not disgust us, even more.[12]

Vitanza similarly exaggerates and prioritizes the importance of holding contradictory thoughts/ emotions when "making" rhetoric.[13] This is undoubtedly a critical skill for architects and urbanists to develop also. However, very few pedagogical strategies are currently being developed to strengthen such a skill. Both Vitanza and Lyotard allow their writing to fold and zigzag. There is an obvious pain and pleasure involved in the process of both thinkers' writings. This pleasure and pain is marked by shifts away from the intention to inform (although a transaction of information does happen) toward an intention to inspire perpetually new realizations about commonly accepted principles. There is a shift away from a finite, or set amount of information to be conveyed through neutral language, toward an understanding of writing as capable of uncovering the unknown, suppressed, or forgotten—the ubiquitous. This shift can also be conceived as a process of discovery or design.[14] Lyotard would have us all bear witness first, initiate reasons to pause, before seeking solutions through trending theories, technologies, or structural systems.

It is with this intention that I offer the phrase *ubiquitous libidinal boxes*. With it I call attention to externalized (physical and/ or digital) manifestations of human desire-driven energy flows. Though ubiquitous libidinal boxes, such as the Waterford Lake Town Center shopping experience, are prevalent within and around Orlando, representing one is difficult. They are hard to pin down because they are backed by statistical and numeric feedback loops acting upon constructed data and market research. Desire is manipulated by this data. Franchises channel this information toward our discretionary income most easily while within a libidinal economy—when we are on vacation, immersed within a franchised experience, when using our iPhones, or even when driving our car. As a hybrid rhetorician/ designer I have allowed myself to view this reality with fascination—to regard it as an opportune moment from which disciplinary invention and expansion might occur—rather than to resist it. The logics found in big-box culture, while studied in marketing and packaging design, have outlived most of the static and formally oriented strategies and tactics found within most architectural design studios.

Operating virtually, behind the scenes, ubiquitous mechanisms actually aid in forming vast amounts of our shared public and private environments.[15] Such research endeavors literally materialize desires. Bringing further rhetorical scholarship to bear on this situation will offer architects and urbanists an opportunity to design with more awareness about the ubiquitous, what drives it, and why it is there.

Offering designers a way into the intricately woven realms of both market segmentation and the spatial experiences they statistically track, I diverge in my exploration of Orlando's ubiquity from Venturi, Scott Brown and Izenour in their iconic project *Learning from Las Vegas*. Within this project, only the physical aspects of Las Vegas's everyday-ugly ubiquitous nature are considered in relation to architecture and its communication. I argue that we must see beyond the physical appearance of Orlando's libidinal boxes so that we may actually see them. The physicality of these boxes, their transient nature is so ubiquitous that they are nearly invisible. To be in and around Orlando's boxes is to exist in a realm of heightened desire. In this state, we exist in our minds and bodies, acting quickly upon impulses. This invisible force points to the distributed networks that drive urban forms today. Such driving forces require more disciplinary concentration.

My investigation is supported by designers Studio Sputnik who examine what opportunities the study of mass culture can offer architecture by shifting the field's traditional analytical focus away from the physical aspects we see around us in the process of spatial design toward a more relational view of how culture and space construct one another with seemingly unexplainable complexity. Sputnik suggests that architecture "can be approached as 'packaging machine' rather than either Duck or Decorated Shed, demonstrating that objects and the lifestyle surrounding objects become entrenched into a vicious circle where each become symbols for the other, they become a package."[16]

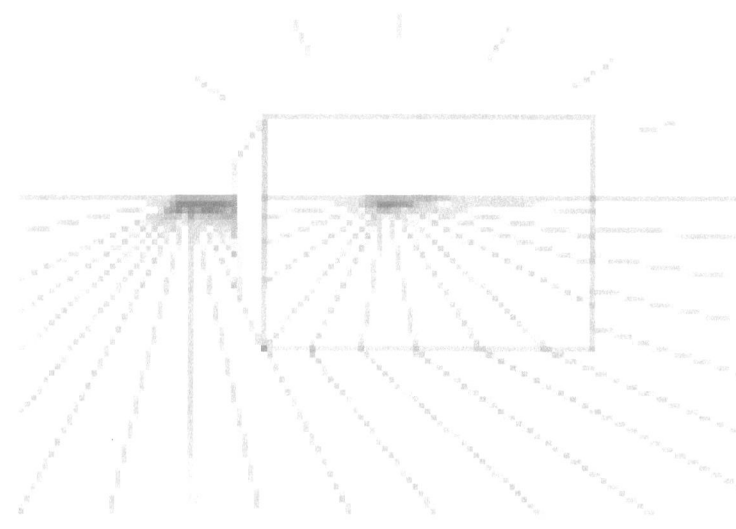

Figure 9. Packaging Machine Diagram, Reproduced with permission of Jaakko Van 't Spijker

Studio Sputnik, like architect and urbanist Rem Koolhaas of OMA, now place a premium on the experience of architecture.[17] Kazys Varnelis explores this disciplinary evolution in *Networked Publics*. Varnelis describes such architecture as similar to the work of Artist Andreas Gursky, Andrea Fraser and Cristoph Buchel, dubbing them, "studies of the real." [18] It is to this emerging fascination/ excitement about urbanism that I wish to offer my interest in Orlando's *ubiquitous libidinal boxes*.

Sputnik's "packaging machine" diagram helps support my claim that the field's relationship to representation is in a state of flux.[19] I'm interested in harnessing the design potential imbedded within human desire, in imagining ways to visualize the impact invisible libidinal intensities have on materiality. The simultaneous ubiquity and fantasy found in Orlando, offer a perfect subject matter. I realize, with Lyotard as my guide, that suggesting a singular, overarching solution would be inappropriate. What I offer here is an example—one approach. I wish to lay the foundation for architectural projects that are more capable of operating—employing aesthetic and critical thinking skill sets—within ubiquitous libidinal infrastructures of urbanism. Resting on the assumption that such spatial practices derive solely out of capitalism results in resistance and criticism, and limits the possibility for a fuller spectrum of inventive design processes from occurring there.

Destabilizing fixed *stasis* loops surrounding the unsustainable nature of these building practices offers more architectural operability. The construction found within these seemingly infinite boxes could perhaps be considered more architecturally if this language game were to become altered. This shift might happen if students of architecture were provided opportunities to develop work with the cultural agency of projects like *Libidinal Economy*, stressing destabilizing, inventive cultural research methods alongside the important inventive design and composition, and empirical research that will always persist. Lyotard refers to this unique process as a "theatrical fiction."[20] It is an additional or alternative—alternative to what we might automatically assume or discern—description of how social structures and reality operate.

The area surrounding the Waterford Lakes Town Center could alternatively be described as an ethereal context of transient dreams where loose mediums and connectors such as paint, asphalt, and thin unarticulated surfaces can easily authorize fast and loose associations. Here a loose impulse can result in overabundance, indulgence, and a lack of restraint, resulting in a radical transformation of over five hundred acres in less than five years. Large modulated contextual elements can be deployed to create an immediate loose connection with what has been communicated to "be," resulting only in the hunt for something new. The immediate trucking of portable modules of context acts in response to these transient dreams that never seem to be fulfilled. The large modulated context might begin to morph with the truckability of the ubiquitous asphalt surface. This aleatory surface might loosen, becoming thin layers, which thicken and fold to house more libidinal boxes, thus continuing to indulgently allow for even more immediate trucking of portable libidinal infrastructure.

Exaggerating the libidinal nature of these architectures might offer more transparent awareness of how desires influence space. Such a shift in architectural agendas, away from problem solving and onto inventive cultural observation, reveals my interest in overlaying rhetorical scholarship onto the field of architecture.

Mobilizing Libidinal Boxes

A libidinal economy can be described simply as a system that attaches value or exchange onto human fantasy or fear. Orlando's tourism industry, as well as its emphatic acceptance of franchised experiences exemplifies libidinal economics. Lyotard uses his figures to demonstrate that the libidinal exceeds representation. Again, Orlando's network of packaged experiences is similarly a moving target.

In Lyotard's theatrical fiction, the *libidinal band* is used to represent the "primary processes" of desire or libidinal intensity. He describes this band with the help of the visual/ formal metaphor of both a Mobius strip and a Klein Jar. The *libidinal band* is continuous, like both of these examples, it has no inside or outside. Libidinal energy circulates along the band in a random fashion with "red-hot intensity," or potentiality. Ian Hamilton Grant suggests in the introduction of *LE,* "As a kind of persuasive fiction, the various descriptions of the band . . . account for the closures and exclusions inherent to re-presentational thinking and suggest a 'pagan' manner of affirming the differences and singularities that run through the libidinal band in an aleatory and indeterminate fashion."[21] Lyotard's vivid treatment of flesh aids in expressing the corporeality inherent in libidinal investments, a shift away from rigid opposition toward a system of continual framing and reframing of the same surface into *this* and *not this.*

I like to think of Orlando's unending roadways in relation to Lyotard's libidinal band. Using Orlando's corporeality, we can expand Lyotard's figures in order to further materialize them. For example, there is a drag strip called Speed World off of Highway 50 along the eastern fringe of the city. The sign for this place is a tricked out school bus claiming to be the fastest in the world.

Figure 10. Speed World Bus

The thrill of drag racing is tied up intricately in working on your vehicle, putting yourself in real danger, and of course the documented speed-time and bragging rights that winning offers. Speed World would not exist without the cultural inheritance of the ubiquitous asphalt band that twists throughout Orlando, its auto dependency, and the junkyards this dependency renders. The obsessive passion for cars, loud ones with elaborate muffler appendages, white powder coated wheels, and other more radical customizations, is born from the ubiquitous flat and expansive highway in and around Orlando. Eliminating the highway system would mean the eventual extinction of this particular manifestation of libidinal intensity, a significant subculture in Orange County.

Lyotard considers the bar and the band to be one and the same.[22] Orlando's unending asphalt band and its libidinal boxes are also one and the same. The ubiquitous highway system is understood as goods transport infrastructure, as a hardcopy of a network, as a way out, and a way back home. The truck stop, the rest stop, the gas station, and the fast food joint all rely on and also support this undervalued life supporting substrate of American urbanism.[23] Orlando natives treat everything as if we are moving on a roadway, having no time for fine grain subtlety. We always have somewhere further to go.

Yet, Orlando's highway and its libidinal boxes are also not the same. Lyotard suggests that in time the red-hot band begins to slow and cool, forming bars. *The Bar* references stable structures that exploit libidinal intensities. Contingent upon one's speed, as with Lyotard's bar, Orlando's boxes become unique experiences that are distinguishable from the relational yet distinct experiences one feels while driving. The billboard signs populating Orlando's 408 can be seen similarly, as yet another manifestation of libidinal intensities slowing and cooling. Paul Virilio poignantly describes this driver as a "voyeur voyager," a non-passive subject position, who unlike the cinema spectator, penetrates the screen, perforates the landscape, and composes moving imagery with the steering wheel, the brake, and the accelerator.[24] With Virilio's voyeur voyager as a new urban subject, we can see how desire manifests Orlando's urbanism rather than the other way around.

Desires are mobilized in capitalism's design along the asphalt band offering a continual flow of consumption. The uncanny correlation between what is consumed and consumable in relation to Nielson's *My Best Segments* predictions for Orange County provides proof of the inability to easily break from the pervasiveness of these building practices. Thus, I feel compelled here to urge designers and scholars to work with rather than against them.

Figure 11. Mobilization of Libidinal Desires

Lyotard's Figures help to expose a suppressed awareness of the agency of objects—how they operate in and on us. Along with the jacked-up, the chopped, and the low-riding vehicles surrounding Speed World, the more universal narrative mythologies of highway space and its frontier narratives such as the Marlboro man, and ad campaigns like "Built Ford tough," and "Chevy: like a rock," operate beyond means-ends capitalist objectives. Conceptual opposition to these apparatuses, Lyotard maintains, can be reconsidered through an exploration of material figures. With this added dimension, architects can conceive of the simultaneous pleasure and pain of *incompossibility*.[25] That is, we can suspend our conceptual opposition to big-box urbanism in order to understand the libidinal as a powerful influence over it, in the process of developing an expanded understanding of urbanism.

Wrapping Up

Libidinal intensities and *affects* are two concepts that Lyotard uses to refer to unpredictable occurrences, or events exceeding in logical/ rational interpretation and/ or representation. The notion that more exists than can be clearly accounted for by a theory or model—an excess or slack—is central to *LE*. We forget how much we abstract and omit in the process of "disciplining," of becoming and sustaining a discipline. This significant thought experiment, explored within this collection, is one I would like architecture to take a larger part in as a strategy to balance its current bend toward architecture as an act of problem solving.[26]

An acute awareness of Virilio's "voyeur voyager," and her libidinal potentiality, her invisible yet material *puissance,* ought to reconfigure the way we teach and learn about space, architecture, and urbanism today. This will require participation from many disciplines, blending the sciences and the humanities even more carefully and thoughtfully. My transdisciplinary call to action should be viewed positively toward disciplinary expansion on urbanism.

It is impossible to clearly state goals and anticipated outcomes of such expanded projects at this time. I can simply suggest that such works consider rhetorical invention as part of the design process, and exaggerate and/or reframe human desire, affirming that "the manmade landscape is a cultural inscription that can be read to better understand who we are, and what we are doing."[27] Such works must never start the invention/design process with the sole premise of solving problems. They must also be willing to look beyond the formal and material aspects of a built work in order to understand more fully its relational context. Scholarly works on urbanism aught not attempt to directly solve world, or even disciplinary problems. Rather, such research, borrowing here from Greg Ulmer, should address what we can't yet understand about these problems (xxxi).

I would like to conclude by discussing Douglas Darden's project "Sex Shop," from the book, *Condemned Building.* This compilation of design projects provides an example of how architecture has integrated poetry and literature successfully in the past as a means to address what we cannot yet understand about the field of architecture and its purpose. Darden asserts, "The ten works of architecture cited in this book were constructed from a particular canon of architecture that has persisted throughout the centuries and the varieties of architectural styles. The buildings are a turning-over, one by one, of those canons. Like the action of the plow, this was done not to lay waste to the canons, but to cultivate their fullest growth" (9).

One of these projects is particularly useful in exposing my claim that disciplinary expansion must continue within urbanism. Peter Schneider notes, "Of the ten projects illustrated in *Condemned Building,* Sex Shop is marked by the dramatic fact of the absence of the project itself. All of the other projects in Darden's corpus are compellingly present" (Darden 9). Examining Orlando's corporeality in relation to Lyotard's figures frames Darden's struggle to represent Sex Shop. The tight urban site chosen for the project is problematic. A sketch of the proposed site configuration can be seen in the unpublished drawings Schneider has uncovered, highlighted here in figure 12.

Orlando, Florida's Ubiquitous Libidinal Boxes / 267

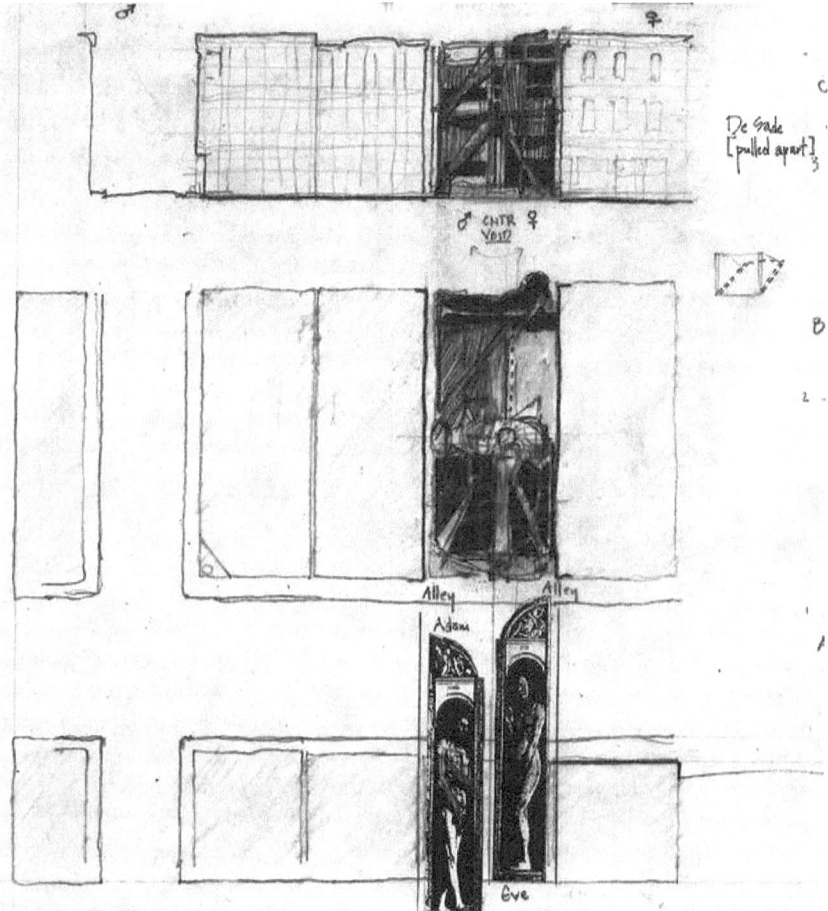

Figure 12: Douglas Darden's sketch of Sex Shop in context, image reproduced with permission of Peter Schneider, estate archivist.

Darden's Sex Shop is better suited for the urban condition of Orlando's ubiquitous libidinal boxes, where infrastructures supporting wild desires thrive. Orlando's boxes exist within a vast, flat expanse affected by minimal formal constraints. Such a condition is needed in order to explore the cultural mythologies that Darden used to map the ground for Sex Shop's rhetorical territory. As I have demonstrated in this chapter, there are other laws governing this territory that are not currently included within studies of urbanism. We do not currently understand, and typically don't even consider the immaterial forces acting upon physical environments. As such, architectural projects are very rarely conceived as "fitting in" among the urban conditions I have chosen to explore here.

Sex Shop is also distinct in the collection because it attempts not only to turn over the canons of architecture, but it also forces us to consider the relationship between architecture and desire. Architectures within a libidinal economy such as Orlando can be described through this relationship. To study the ubiquitous architectural practices of immediacy between desire and the strange and surreal physicality of Orlando's libidinal boxes is to approach the problem currently defined as unsustainable building practices from a radically new direction. My investigation might be described simply as a pause, as an attempting to map a new, yet ubiquitous territory. This is an example of research that aims to describe, to map, that which can't be understood about the problem.

Notes

1. Orlando has the second largest number of hotel rooms, second only to Las Vegas, Nevada and is called the Theme Park Capital of the World. See wikipedia's entry for Orlando, FL, http://en.wikipedia.org/wiki/Orlando,_fl.

2. Big-Box culture is a term developed by Jason Young within the course "SUB-Situation. Urbanism. Big-Box," a graduate course at University of Michigan.

3. Lyotard's definition or treatment of the word *dispositif*, (set up or apparatus), diverges from that of Giorgio Agamben's in his text *What is an Apparatus?*. Lyotard's reading complicates Agamben's careful analysis, such that where Agamben argues that a struggle exists between the organic living being and *dispositifs*, Lyotard would argue that both are fundamental elements of the libidinal economy, mutually constructing one another. Lyotard refers to such *incompossible*, logical violations, as Grant offers in the glossary, as expensive and metamorphic economics. See Agamben 11–14.

4. See Rania Ghosn et al. "The Space of Controversies: An Interview with Bruno Latour," in New Geographies 0, 129. In this interview, Latour mentions his colleague, Albena Yaneva's article, "Scaling up and Down, Extraction Trials in Architectural Design," Social Studies of Science, 35(6) 867–894. Her article articulates, from the perspective of someone outside of Architecture, how scalar shifts are crucial to the design process after observing the firm OMA.

5. Shift from dense urban conditions to include these types of spaces as "urban."

6. Young, "Contested Urbanism," in *Dimensions* 19, 60–62. Dimensions is available online at: http://taubmancollege.umich.edu/architecture/publications/dimensions/.

7. See David Karle, "The ~~Strip~~ Mall Stripped," in the proceedings for the National Conference on the Beginning Design Student, 28. Italicized emphasis mine.

8. Explore Nielson's products at: http://www.claritas.com/MyBestSegments/Default.jsp?ID=20&menuOption=ziplookup&pageName=ZIP%2BCode%2BLookup, (parenthetical insertion mine).

9. http://www.claritas.com/MyBestSegments/Default.jsp?ID=20

10. See Lyotard's *The Differend,* particularly Nos. 21–24, pages 12–13, and *Just Gaming* for more information on this.

11. This comes from seminar notes from course on Lyotard with Victor Vitanza at The European Graduate School in June, 2010.

12. Lyotard, *LE,* 115.

13. See Vitanza's explorations on "what to do with the Sophists," found in *Negation Subjectivity and The History of Rhetoric,* 27–55, and his discussion of "Making" rhetoric, found in *Chaste Rape,* 186–224.

14. The Center for Land use Interpretation (CLUI) has been a very influential inspiration in conceiving of exploring the *differend* in relation to urban intellectual work. The center believes "the manmade landscape is a cultural inscription that can be read to better understand who we are, and what we are doing see http://www.clui.org/.

15. I began research on My Best Segments in 2005 as part of my Masters Thesis in Architecture. I am published on this project titled, "Seeing Practices," in *Journal of Architectural Education,* Blackwell (2008). Another useful, and more recent reference on this topic is the book Karma Queens, *Geek Gods and Innerpreneurs: Meet the 9 Consumer Types Shaping Today's Marketplace,* by Ron Rentel."

16. See Studio Sputnik 22–23.

17. See Ibelings' discussion of this. Ibelings refers to this focus on experience, or affect, as "Supermodernism."

18. See Varnelis,152, bolded emphasis mine.

19. Sputnik's "packaging machine" project, resonates with a number of similar projects such as Kazys Varnelis' *Networked Publics,* Alan Berger's *Drosscape,* Lars Lerup's *After the City,* and Hans Ibelings' *Supermodernism: Architecture in the age of Globalization.* These works suggest that the field's relationship to representation, and cultural analysis more generally, is in a state of radical flux. Each of these projects exposes a need for more expansive modes of thinking about space and identity, thus challenging standard approaches to representation/communication. I believe that seeking influence from outside of architecture will continue to be more important.

20. This phrase also seems to be a suitable term to refer to conceptual architecture, such as those developed by Lebbeus Woods and John Hejduk. See Hejduk's *Bovisa* and *Mask of Medusa: Works 1947–1983,* and Wood's *BorderLine* and *War and Architecture.*

21. Lyotard, *LE,* xii.

22. Lyotard, *LE,* xii.

23. In *America,* Jean Baudrillard uses both the desert and the freeway as models for articulating the American sensibility.

24. See Virilio, 101–150.

25. See Greg Ulmer's pleasure pain transversal diagram by clicking on "Kant" at the folowing link, < http://www.clas.ufl.edu/users/glue/diagrams/diagrams.html>.

26. I argue within my dissertation that you, my readers as well as my co-authors here, might make more of a difference with your work by finding an architectural audience to influence and inspire.

27. See CLUI's site, http://www.clui.org/

Works Cited

Agamben, Giorgio. *What Is an Apparatus?: And Other Essays*. Stanford, CA: Stanford UP, 2009. Print.
Ben-Joseph, Eran. *ReThinking a Lot: The Design and Culture of Parking*. Cambridge: MIT, 2012. Print.
Berger, Alan. *Drosscape: Wasting Land in Urban America*. New York: Princeton Architectural, 2006. Print.
Darden, Douglas. *Condemned Building: An Architect's Pre-text*. New York: Princeton Architectural, 1993. Print.
Debord, Guy. *Society of the Spectacle*. Detroit: Black and Red. 1983. Print.
Haynes, Cynthia. "Writing Offshore: The Disappearing Coastline of Composition Theory." *JAC* 23.4 (2003): 667–724. Print.
Ibelings, Hans. *Supermodernism: Architectre in the Age of Globalization*. Rotterdam: NAi, 2002. Print.
Lyotard, Jean-François, and Jean-Loup Thébaud. *Just Gaming*. Minneapolis: U of Minnesota P, 1985. Print.
Lyotard, Jean-François. *Libidinal Economy*. Bloomington: Indiana UP, 1993. Print.
—. *The Differend: Phrases in Dispute*. Minneapolis: U of Minnesota P, 1988. Print.
Lerup, Lars. *After the City*. Cambridge: MIT P, 2000. Print.
Saper, Craig J. *Artificial Mythologies: a Guide to Cultural Invention*. Minneapolis: U of Minnesota P, 1997. Print.
Schneider, Peter. "Douglas Darden's Sex Shop: An Immodest Proposal." *Journal of Architectural Education* 58.2 (2004): 9–13. Print.
Sputnik, Studio, and Lars Lerup. *Snooze: Immersing Architecture in Mass Culture*. Rotterdam: NAi, 2003. Print.
Tschumi, Bernard. "The Pleasure of Architecture." *Theorizing a New Agenda for Architecture: an Anthology of Architectural Theory: 1965–1995*. Ed. Kate Nesbitt. New York: Princeton Architectural, 1996. 532–40. Print.
Ulmer, Gregory L. Electronic Monuments. Minneapolis: U of Minnesota P, 2005. Print.
Varnelis, Kazys. *Networked Publics*. Cambridge: MIT P, 2008. Print.
—. *The Infrastructural City: Networked Ecologies in Los Angeles*. Barcelona: Actar, 2008. Print.
Venturi, Robert, Brown Denise Scott, and Steven Izenour. *Learning from Las Vegas*. Cambridge: MIT P, 1972. Print.
Vitanza, Victor J. *Negation, Subjectivity, and the History of Rhetoric*. Albany: State U of New York P, 1997. Print.—. *Sexual Violence in Western Thought and Writing: Chaste Rape*. New York: Palgrave Macmillan, 2011. Print.
Virilio, Paul. *Negative Horizon: An Essay in Dromoscopy*. New York: Continuum, 2008. Print.
Wigley, Mark. "Resisting The City." *TransUrbansim*. Rotterdam: Nai Publishers, 2002. 103–122. Print.

15 "Murphy's Well-Being": The Konsult

Gregory L. Ulmer

Best thing to do is to dig one thing or place or man until you yourself know more abt that than is possible to any other man. . . . One saturation job.

—Charles Olson

Introduction

This chapter samples an archive of notes and images produced for the Florida Research Ensemble collaboration, creating an interactive installation experimenting with the genre of *konsult* for the EmerAgency (online virtual egency). The *konsult* addresses the on-going disaster of ground and air pollution associated with a Superfund site—the wood-treatment operation at the Cabot-Koppers site in Gainesville, Florida, in continuous operation from 1911 until its recent closing. Entitled "Murphy's Well-Being," the *konsult* uses Arts & Letters knowledge and methods to educate communities on the relevance of well-being for public policy formation. FRE collaboration: Theory (concept) by Gregory Ulmer; photographs and videos of

Stephen Foster neighborhood and residents by Barbara Jo Revelle; interactive installation by Jack Stenner.

Figure 1. Map

Capability

Well-being is a primary concern of the metaphysics emerging within the apparatus of electracy, to complement the concerns of the previous apparatuses (Orality = Religion, Right/Wrong; Literacy = Science, True/False). EmerAgency consulting introduces Arts & Letters research on well-being (Electracy = Attraction/Repulsion) into the public sphere in the context of democratic policy formation. In the *konsult* our point of departure specifies well-being in the terms formulated by Amartya Sen, winner of the 1998 Nobel Prize in Economics. The goal of the *konsult* is to express Sen's thought-provoking vision in the context of a specific community disaster.

The question for Sen concerns how a free democratic society measures the in/justice of its policies, relative to the well-being of individuals and communities affected. He admits that public reason (deliberative or practical reason) has its limits, but he insists that it is imperative to apply reason to problems to the extent possible. Referring to both the Enlightenment tradition in philosophy, and a tradition of jurisprudence in his native India, Sen identifies two overall approaches to social justice (each identified by the Indian terms):

niti—organizational or institutional propriety and ideals; *nyaya*—the actual lives that people are able to lead. The philosophical division is between contractual approaches (Hobbes, Rousseau) or comparative approaches (Bentham, Marx).

What recommends Sen's vision for electracy is his focus on *capability* or capacity. Well-being and quality of life, are relative to an ability (power) to reason and choose, with freedom to decide according to one's values and preferences, the kind of life (life-style) one lives. Every term in this summary statement is problematic in a positive sense, meaning that this vision helps organize our consultation. Sen clarifies that his approach differs from utilitarian welfare economics, or approaches that center on resources, happiness, or fairness. He claims that examination of the actual lives people live suggests that the best measure of thriving is not outcomes, not accomplishment or achievements, but conditions in which citizens have both the capability and the opportunity to act upon their preferences. One of his most telling points, made while observing the lack of correlation between the wealth of a society and its measurable happiness, is that there is precisely a capacity for happiness. An implication is that it might be useful to revise the United States Declaration of Independence to identify the inalienable right not as the "pursuit of" but "capacity for" happiness.

There are four terms structuring Sen's measure, constituting a dynamic tension: *agency* and *freedom* on one side, *well-being* and *achievement* on the other. As you might expect, Sen in his books qualifies and justifies his position fully, at least relative to the academic discourse within which he is working. Sen acknowledges that Martha Nussbaum noted the relevance of Aristotle's ethics to the capability approach, and this context is the one that we will explore, by adding another pair of terms to Sen's dichotomy: potentiality/actuality. This context references the entire tradition of Western philosophy, from Aristotle to Deleuze, a tradition that has undergone a fundamental change in modernity: not only a change of epoch, but a change of apparatus. (See Amartya Sen, *The Idea of Justice*, 2009).

Region

Retrieving an assumption of theology (that nature is God's book), *konsult* operates as if the disaster (accident) addresses us in a peculiar kind of discourse. *Egents* (EmerAgency consultants) are Technics-Whisperers. *Technics* refers to the autonomous but interdependent ontologies of tools and humans. *Technics* reoccupies in a secularized metaphysics the old position of "God." We need to communicate with our machines, and one of the most direct expressions on the part of *technics* is the accident (the disaster). In our case, we ask: what is the Cabot-Koppers Superfund intimating?

Figure 2.

The vocabulary associated with descriptions of the event (the disaster) is expressive, read as "choral words" (taking terms in all their meanings). Several keywords appeared in accounts of the disaster. The first term that connected with our larger context is "Region." Gainesville is in "Region Four" according to EPA classifications, for example. Although some commentators find this terminology alienating, associated with "District Nine," "Region" has a positive connotation in our context. It is a translation of *Chora*, the term Plato introduced into Western metaphysics to name the dimension of interface between *Being* and *Becoming*.

The vocabulary with interesting possibilities is associated with the process of *solidification*, proposed by engineers as primary remediation, to prevent the creosote pollution from the waste lagoons on the Koppers site reaching the Murphy (Murphree) Wellfield that supplies the drinking water for our area. The procedure involves creating a *corral* for the pollutant. This vocabulary resonates with the lexicon activated in deconstructive architecture, in the collaboration of Jacques Derrida and Peter Eisenman on the Parc de la Villette.

Solidification

Inventional consulting, site whispering, includes reviewing the vocabulary of conventional consulting for egent terms, pivot or switch features in the expository field of documentation (applied to all documentation of the site). The ROD (record of decision) calls for the use of a remediation technology known as solidification, as treatment for the most polluted lagoons on the Koppers grounds—sites of creosote leaching into the acquifer, and moving towards the Murphy Wellfield, northeast of the property. The need for this process is so common that Wikipedia has an entry on it, listing a variety of contaminated places to which it has been applied. *Solidification refers to the physical changes in the contaminated material when a certain binding agent is added. These changes include an increase in compressive strength, a decrease in permeability, and condensing of hazardous materials. Stabilization refers to the chemical changes between the stabilizing agent (binding agent) and the hazardous constituent. These changes should include a less soluble, less toxic constituent with hindered mobility.*

Perhaps the most persuasive recommendation for this procedure is that it is the one God used to bind Satan in Hell, according to Dante's authoritative account known as the *Divine Comedy*, in the part covering the *Inferno*. Dante's eye-for-an-eye ethics suggests a moral remediation procedure that might be part of an overall clean-up policy: let the punishment fit the crime. Here is the *Sparknotes* summary of the relevant Canto.

Virgil and Dante proceed to the Ninth Circle of Hell through the Giants' Well, which leads to a massive drop to Cocytus, a great frozen lake. The giant Antaeus picks Virgil and Dante up and sets them down at the bottom of the well, in the lowest region of Hell. In Caina, the First Ring of the Ninth Circle of Hell, those who betrayed their kin stand frozen up to their necks in the lake's ice. In Antenora, the Second Ring, those who betrayed their country and party stand frozen up to their heads; here Dante meets Count Ugolino, who spends eternity gnawing on the head of the man who imprisoned him in life. In Ptolomea, the Third Ring, those who betrayed their guests spend eternity lying on their backs in the frozen lake, their tears making blocks of ice over their eyes. Dante next follows Virgil into Judecca, the Fourth Ring of the Ninth Circle of Hell and the lowest depth. Here, those who betrayed their benefactors spend eternity in complete icy submersion.

A huge, mist-shrouded form lurks ahead, and Dante approaches it. It is the three-headed giant Lucifer, plunged waist-deep into the ice. His body pierces the center of the Earth, where he fell when God hurled him down from Heaven. Each of Lucifer's mouths chews one of history's three greatest sinners: Judas, the betrayer of Christ, and Cassius and Brutus, the betrayers of Julius Caesar. Virgil leads Dante on a climb down Lucifer's massive form, holding on to his frozen tufts of hair. Eventually, the poets reach the Lethe, the river of forgetfulness, and travel from there out of Hell and back onto Earth. They emerge from Hell on Easter morning, just before sunrise.

Part of the interest of contemplating Dante as a relay for our own project is that many of the characters the protagonist visits during his descent with Virgil are people Dante knew personally from his hometown of Florence, Italy. The heuretic principle is to ask: what is that for us, in Gainesville, Florida, 2012? Cosmology is local. The most striking resonance in Dante's representation is the hierarchy of sins, the vices and their punishments. Treason is the worst offense. We may suspend judgment for the moment, especially since the EmerAgency motto is *Problems B Us*. In this framework, we suspect that civilization is an opportunity to design one's own *Comedy*. There is at the outset, however, at least one traitor to the community who could be identified: the man who deliberately breached the berm that allowed the festering lagoon to spill into and pollute the local creek system (Hogtown Creek).

Figure 3.

Murphy

We depend upon a semantic domain classified as *murphy*. A choral device is to pay attention to any semantic domain associated with the disaster condition. Murphy's Wellfield gives us a generative term for a series (keeping in mind that this name is a slippage from "Murphree"). Most people are familiar with "Murphy's Law" (*if something can go wrong, it will*). Evidence for this law accumulates around disaster. There is a confidence game known as the *Murphy Game*. "To deceive or swindle by means of the murphy game" (to be murphied). There are many confidence (con) games and get-rich-quick schemes recorded in folklore and that have found new marks through the Internet. What is the relevance to disaster in general? Perhaps the industrial revolution is a murphy, that is, what it promised humanity is too good to be true. Another slang meaning of "Murphy" is "potato," used in England as a disparaging reference to an Irishman (the associative slide: "Murphy" a common Irish name; the Irish live on potatoes). Samuel Beckett's novel *Murphy* is worth a look in our context (describing the efforts of an Irishman to overcome Cartesian dualism). "The sun shone, having no alternative, on the nothing new" (the first sentence).

Narrative

Konsult is expressed in an interactive narrative. Narrative takes a point of view, expresses an attitude with respect to the circumstances in the diegesis (representational world). *Care* transforms contingent circumstances into *situation* by adding intentionality, project (in the existential sense). "Experience" here is *Erfahrung* (the event happens circumspectly through telling). It perhaps goes without saying, then, that the FRE is responsible for this *konsult*, which expresses our point of view, our perspective. We are the authors, and our voice is narrator of Murphy.

The dimensions of narrative are story and discourse. "Story" refers to the events (the plot, characters, setting); "discourse" refers to the manner of telling, the style or treatment. The attitude of the narrator/author is expressed primarily indirectly, in the design of story and discourse. Attitude towards what? The primary guiding force working through narrative is some value, a belief or commitment fundamental to the culture within which the narrative is composed. This value is often "transcendental"—freedom, justice, beauty—meaning that it is without properties, and must be made particular through examples. Theorists refer to such terms now as *floating signifiers*, or dialogical words, the site of struggle among different factions of a society, directing the dynamics of rhetoric in the public sphere.

What is the value? *Well-Being*. What calls for *konsult* is that *Well-Being* is in crisis, presenting itself to thought as problem, problematic. *Murphy* does not know what *Well-Being* is or should be, but *that Well-Being* is, may be, and must be (real).

CHORAGRAPHY

Cabot-Koppers Superfund disaster is located for administrative purposes within Region 4. *Konsult* theorizes region in terms of the metaphysical notion of *chora*. Chora (space, region) was introduced in Plato's *Timaeus* as a third dimension interface relating *Being* and *Becoming*. Derrida repurposed *Chora* in his collaboration with Peter Eisenman on a design for the *Parc de la Villette* in Paris. In *Heuretics* Ulmer introduced choragraphy as the rhetoric of electracy, replacing literate "topics" with choral imaging. *Murphy* konsult is choragraphic.

Chora produces coherence in a holistic manner, appropriating modernist imaging, as exemplified by Pound's vortex (Cantos), Benjamin's constellation (Arcades), Situationist hubs (Debord). The sense of *chora* emerges as pattern, through juxtaposition, repetition, intensification, and distortion. The compositional structure borrows from allegory, using the device of miniaturization (mise en abyme, play within a play), through which a manifest partial property is made to evoke the (concealed) whole.

To say that Cabot-Koppers is choral means that the geographical place includes several cultural strata (plateaus). The Stephen Foster neighborhood (and the region served by Murphy Wellfield in general) is shaped by cultural forces, and choral mapping (in the tradition of choragraphy dating back to Ptolemy) is cultural (psycho-) geography (partly mimetic, partly geometric). The implication for *Murphy* is that our map should represent or register in some manner the composite nature of the region. The supplemental places include the ones noted in a preliminary outline of the allegory (the four-place popcycle of discourses).

- Testimony: Gainesville, Stephen Foster neighborhood (narratives of denizens).
- Mythology: Hollywood films, e.g. the California of Erin Brockovich, but also the brand identity of the relevant corporations (Cabot, Koppers, Beazer), sited at their headquarters. Values expressing beliefs about agency.
- History: The history of the corporation, perhaps beginning with the East India Company, and its connection with the spice trade originating in the market for pepper as commodity (the story of colonialism). The larger story of which the invention and production of pine tar and wood treatment is but one part (documentary films).
- Analogy: Philosophy, Arts & Letters disciplinary account of reality.

Figure 4.

Prosopon

The *Murphy konsult* is a *fable* needing a moral; it is didactic, with a lesson to impart. But what lesson, what is the moral of the story? What do we know, what disciplinary knowledge guides our communication with the community? The assumption of this experiment is that we are testing our knowledge against the reality manifested in the disaster. Blanchot's title was "the writing of the disaster," suggesting that what we want to relay to our community is "what the disaster (itself) writes."

The key to this service is to understand who or what speaks or writes in the event. Or rather, it may be that the event is a message without sender, or, a *konsult* is a way to "divine" an event as message (for those who have senses). Theory tells us that the experience of the industrial revolution (the epochal origin of electracy) is *alienation*, *reification*, and *objectification*. These terms name the loss of *agency* in the industrial city, such that our own actions return to us (like the repressed) as if originating elsewhere, from some external power, thus separating us (traumatically) from responsibility.

This effect in the frame of electracy is due to the emergence of a new identity formation, a group subject, whose institutional instantiation is the corporation. *Konsult* in general has the task and opportunity to bring into appearance this event as such, that in the drama of modern disaster we are witnessing the equivalent of Thespis stepping forward out of the Chorus, to speak as an individual actor, on behalf of a new subject (selfhood). The corporation is a collective Thespis.

Just here is the crucial opportunity for intervention. Corporations already walk among us, have donned a mask in order to appear, and this mask is Brand (Logo logos). The history of the corporation foregrounds this event of collective personhood, since that status is precisely what defines the institutional nature of this entity: a company or group of people authorized to act as a single entity (legally a person) whose speech is money and is recognized as such in law. Recent decisions by the US Supreme Court have extended this legal standing of personhood even further, recognizing the first amendment rights of this being. Comedians have enjoyed mocking the implications of this development, proposing that corporations could run for president or date their daughters. From the point of view of electracy, corporations are the institutional order within which the digital apparatus will unfold, just as school and science nurtured literacy.

What is the immediate point of relevance for the design of *Murphy?* We know that corporations communicate with society by means of the commodity sign (this sign is one of the fundamental innovations of electracy). As Marx noted in his revolutionary analysis of commodity fetishism, if commodities could speak, they would be the most ingratiating, lovable, obsequious, pet-like creatures imaginable, for they see every passerby as a potential customer. Theory picked up this insight and developed it extensively, realizing that commodities do speak a kind of pure language, consisting entirely of exchange as such, pure relational circulation. There are positive opportunities offered by this circulation, but the immediate point for konsult is that the commodity operates a con game, specifically the game known as a "Murphy": bait and switch, offering an opportunity too good to be true and fleecing the suckers who bite (one born every minute). It is the lesson of conduction, of electrate flash reason: the secret is hidden in plain sight. Why did the vulgate translate "Murphree's Well-Field" into "Murphy"? As a warning, for those with ears. Buyer beware.

Figure 5.

Konsult Design

Knowledge

The *konsult* intimates (it neither reveals nor conceals) to the community what is known, what may be learned, in a way that is useful, leading perhaps to some action. The theoretical and historical insight (disciplinary knowledge) is that human desire for well-being (the Good), manifests itself as a history of "goods & services," culminating in our time in the commodity form and sign. Capitalism as economy and the corporation as an institution were created (invented) to meet the demand for the Good with goods, with unforeseen consequences. Murphy evokes this historical event within which our disaster is a commonplace. Understanding prepares the community for action.

Interface Metaphor

Installation design calls for a metaphor to guide the interaction or participation of users with the konsult. This metaphor is suggestive only, a figure, whose familiarity lends depth of meaning while allowing intuitive participation with the medium. A provocative metaphor supported by knowledge, including electrate conductive inference, is the Murphy Game. This well-known con game is defined as "any of several confidence tricks in which something worthless is substituted for something of value, often in a sealed envelope." A related definition specifies a certain scenario: *Any of various confidence games often having the services of a prostitute as a lure and brought off by switching an envelope containing the victim's cash with one containing scrap paper.* In our context this bait and switch trick is a supplement more than a substitute, of something not worthless but dangerous or destructive. We previously associated the game with the theoretical meaning of "gift" (in German, both present and poison): *pharmakon* in Derrida's terms. The lure (prostitute) is the commodity sign, the promotional representation of the use value of the product (everything is for sale).

Assessment

The value of the con game figure is that it calls attention to the active participation of the "victim" in the trick. The confidence agent commits fraud by appealing to the "vicious" (as opposed to virtuous) nature of the mark. It is important to include the historical origins of the pine tar commodity, invented to preserve wood, which is ancillary to the larger history of the spice trade. Cabot-Koppers is in the lineage of the first modern corporation (the East India Company), itself produced within the history of the spice trade. The corporations exist to feed the demand of human bodies for goods, and these goods promise to accomplish the Good (well-being). Our bodies are the mark, wanting benefit without cost. The marks are not innocent, even if victimized by a Murphy game. Technics works for the operant subject (human embodiment).

Wisdom

The fundamental wisdom of the konsult, relevant to every one of the nine Superfund Regions, is that we are complicit as marks in a confidence trick. It is a *confidence* game in that there is no honest *enowning* of responsibility. It isn't only corporations that often shirk responsibility, but also citizens, who refuse payment for the sins of the Fathers. The proposal, then, is to design *Murphy* as a fable, with an open moral, whose wisdom implies the lesson of being victimized by one's own desire for good(s). The point is not to blame victims, but to shift the scenario from victim/villain to community well-being in which corporations are macro-persons.

Figure 6.

Murphy's Well-Being

A wood treatment plant owned by the Cabot-Koppers corporations operated in Gainesville, Florida, for a hundred years. Including in its 140 acres some of the most polluted ground in America, it has been listed as a Superfund Site since 1983. This konsult renders perceptible some of the forces at work in the conditions that produced the Koppers slow-motion catastrophe. The consultation does not offer solutions, but provides the terms of understanding that prepare citizens to participate in the decisions affecting their well-being. This concern, the priority of Philosophy since its inception, resonates with one of the threats to the community—the pollution of the Murphy (Murphree) Wellfield that supplies the drinking water for the region. This instance of pollution is just one of several kinds of contamination associated with the site. Murphy's Law states that if something can go wrong, it will, and in our case, it did. The danger is not just to the community's well, but its well-being.

The Koppers' dilemma exists within a larger context: it is one of 52 Superfund sites in Florida; one of forty-three Koppers sites in the United States; Region 4 is one of nine Regions collecting a multitude of environmental disasters (1280 sites) compromising the *well-being* of our society. These statistics are familiar and unpersuasive. What needs to be appreciated is the extent to which our disaster is the norm, business as usual. Or rather, that the cost incurred by our citizens constitutes a sacrifice required to maintain our American way of life. The purpose of "Murphy's Well-Being" is to locate this sacrifice in a discursive matrix, in order that it may become an object of public deliberation and review. Thus the goal of the consultation is to pose the disaster as an opportunity to take stock of our values and options going forward.

The structure organizing the project design is known as a *cognitive map*, or *popcycle*, an updated version of the four-part allegory (based on religion) by which pre-modern society made sense of the world. The Koppers popcycle, based on art, brings into relationship the following discourses:

1. Family: the Family narrative documents stories of Gainesville citizens most affected by Koppers, such as those living in the Stephen Foster neighborhood adjacent to the site. Denizen testimonials.

2. Mythology: Hollywood cinema has developed a genre of disaster films, specifically stories in which individual citizens confront and triumph over corporations or other institutions violating the public trust. *Erin Brockovich* may be the most apt, but the most recent example is Cameron's *Avatar*. Such films illustrate the mythology of individual agency informing American values, but belied by events. Contemporary mythology lives through Entertainment.

3. History: Documentaries such as James Burke's *Connections* remind us that while the production of pine tar for wood treatment in Gainesville started in 1911, the industry is as old as the Colonies themselves, since wood treatment was a necessary technology for the maintenance of ship hulls. The larger historical narrative of our dilemma includes the entire history of European colonial expansion, all the way back to the original spice trade in ancient times. When Columbus bumped into "America" he thought he had arrived in the Indies. Temporality escapes us.

4. Philosophy: Arts and Letters disciplines have developed a set of practices within the framework of modernism for transforming immediate embodied experience of pleasure/pain (attraction/repulsion) into a logic for conducting practical reason necessary for ethics and politics in a democratic society. With these devices, the Koppers site is generalizable as a microcosm for understanding the threat posed by the Superfund phenomenon to the well-being of the macrocosm itself. The chief insight is that these dilemmas are not anomalies, but the result of a habitus, an ethos, a collective

way of life. The question posed is: what is to be done? *Ereignis* (Heidegger) is the relevant philosophical notion: Enowning. Event, Appropriation. Individual lives play out within collective forces and histories, for which we must take ownership.

Figure 7.

Design Concept

I. Konsult

A. EmerAgency Frame

1. Collective pedagogy = consulting. Goal: to provide the community, both citizens and decision-makers, an insight into the policy problem based on knowledge available through our disciplines.

2. Konsult is a genre, with its own constraints and affordances. It is not entertainment, propaganda, activism, advocacy, documentary, or even story, finally.

3. Konsult is "art," in that it shares many features with various schools of modernist and postmodernist practices, but its function is consulting, as a form of institutional education.

B. Knowledge Insight

1. Chora: "Chora" means "region," functioning in metaphysics as interface between necessity (reality, what is, Being) and change (Becoming). It is a holistic or composite place, supporting the intersection or intertextuality of the primary discourses recording and shaping events in any particular location. "Reality" may be comprehended allegorically, through the pattern emergent in the juxtaposition of these discourses (the popcycle): experience, mythology, history, philosophy. Gainesville is a chora. To understand "what happened" requires access to the full popcycle account.

2. Well-Being: Human civilization is organized to seek improvement of the human condition, that condition being our embodied sensory nature. This striving for improvement in quality of life produced ultimately the present order of industrial technology, the corporation and capitalist economy, the commodity form of exchange. Pine tar production at the Superfund site is an industrial commodity.

3. Insight: any commodity is a gift/poison, meaning that it has costs as well as benefits, by-products and side effects. Pine tar is a "gift" in this sense.

C. Cabot-Koppers Superfund Site

1. There are nine Regions in the Superfund project. Florida is in Region four, and is one of 1280 active sites of environmental disaster remediation in the United States.

2. Cabot corporation (for example) is a global enterprise, producing "performance materials to improve products," and as such is typical of the institutional form.

3. Pine tar historically is a detail in one of the central threads of world history, stretching from the spice trade in ancient times, through colonialism, to the present. The original purpose of pine tar was to preserve the hulls of wooden ships used by the East India Company (the first modern corporation) and its equivalents to carry out European trade with Asian. The discovery of America is one of the "accidents" of this history.

D. Deliverable?

1. Our Superfund disaster is normal, a cost of doing business in industrial capitalism. Accidents are calculated in cost/benefit terms. This social model is founded on a fundamental value within a worldview

and as such is not reparable, (or not without changing the value). The consequences of this civiizational decision may be ameliorated to some greater or lesser degree.

2. All citizens benefit from this world order, and hence are complicit with it, and therefore responsible for the risks. Some few citizens are sacrificed as "hostages" of fortune, exposing a position of "anyone."

3. The intended or desired insight of the konsult is an experience of identification with the testimonials collected in the archive, at least to the degree of recognizing responsibility as community for "anyone."

Figure 8.

II. Figure

A. Wellfield = Well-Being

1. The ordinating form of the konsult is a figure, an analogy, informing the primary interface metaphor of the design: the condition of Murphree (Murphy) Wellfield may be understood figuratively as a measure of the well-being of the community. The literal threat to our physical health is also a threat to our ethical stature. As Ben Franklin once said, we either hang together, or hang separately.

2. A Well of Stories: The installation platform, including all the equipment of the installation, the touchscreen map accessing the database of video clips, introduces users to the figure.

3. A trailer is the default video, constituting instructions by simulating not only the well in action but contextualizing it with some commentary, rationale.

B. "Murphy"

1. A principle of conductive logic native to electracy is that "nothing is hidden," or that at least the starting point of a consultation should be the lexicon associated with a disaster. One of the oldest con games is the "Murphy Game," as it was called in the nineteenth century. The scammer uses a lure appealing to the mark's naiveté and/or greed, to switch the bait for something worthless.

2. The commodity structure, transposing use value into exchange value, is inherently a process of substitution, replicating in the economy the fundamental nature of language and rhetoric. One proof that a system is a true language is that it supports lies.

3. The name of Murphy Wellfield suggests that we are in a Murphy Game, and so is anyone who relies on commodities (or language). Any con game may evoke this condition. The analogy is loose, in that the switch leaves its marks not with something useless, but dangerous.

C. Insight

1. The konsult is not an interactive narrative, but an interactive allegory (extended metaphor, figure).

2. A primary intended signification: a) We've been tricked; b) It is our own fault.

III. Narrative

A. Fable

1. The figure of the konsult is expressed through an allegory. The allegory effect is created through repetitions across the tracks of the popcycle, each track including clips from narratives and documentaries. The basic effect is that of micro-cosm rendering legible the order of the macro-cosm.

2. Fable is structured as a particular anecdote suggesting a lesson or moral derived by generalizing the anecdote situation to other kinds of situations (it is a didactic form).

3. Testimonials (Stephen Foster neighbors): the denizen interviews, whatever they might "mean" on their own, are re-motivated to express the insight of the konsult.

B. Cinematography

1. The General Cultural Interface (GCI) today is cinema, such that devices of montage, mise-en-scene and the like are familiar and legible.

2. The 2-screen display supports a montage juxtaposition, correlated with the fable anecdote + moral. It proposes an implicit equation, leaving the final lesson open to interpretation.

3. Popcycle: the second screen or track is supplied by the popcycle discourses, supplying with mythology, history, or philosophy a context whose juxtaposition with the anecdote produces a comment effect.

Figure 9.

IV. Interactivity

A. Participation

    1. Interactivity is a distinct feature of composition, on a par with narrative, with its own constraints and affordances. The assumption of interactivity is that some degree of control over the construction of the narrative and figure is entrusted to the user.

    2. The well interface prompts users to make selections, and the subsequent events of display solicit further investment of the user in the experience. The tradeoff in author control is potential greater user ownership of the meaning.

B. Competence

    1. Interface metaphors guiding participation draw on cultural constructs already familiar to users.

    2. Our design assumes general familiarity with cinematography, con games, fables, and consumer culture.

C. Crowdsourcing

    1. Further engagement with both the spirit of fables and of consulting is encouraged by inviting users to rate the value or insight of the presentation they selected (1 to 5 stars?)

    2. The assumption is that in any case each set of choices is recorded by the database, to allow some analysis later of signification generated through the process.

    3. Is it possible for users to annotate the rating, for example, to enter some text (perhaps tweet length) making explicit the moral of the fable?

V. Implementation

A. Selection and Sequence

    1. In principle, given the reliance on repetition for the creation of meaning effects through patterning and montage, the popcycle archive maximizes testimonial clips, to be paired with a highly selective collection of clips representing the rest of the popcycle. The design idea is that testimonial clips are unlikely to repeat, while lesson clips are more likely to repeat across different testimonials, thus establishing through repetition the point of the konsult.

2. Choice: users first select a testimonial. The clip is short, but they may choose to continue the interview, even up to the exhaustion of clips from that denizen. Then they choose a clip to pair with the anecdotes for the second screen. The choice is restricted to one from each category (mythology, history, philosophy).

3. The reason for restricting popcycle matches to a maximum of one from each track is so as not to mix the metaphor, and thus dilute or confuse the fable. It is the same principle that discourages querents of an oracle to keep trying the system until they get the answer they prefer.

4. Users may run the choice sequence as often as desired.

B. Control

1. There are several options for the design of clips and their combination.

2. Simulation: complete control of clip content and which clips may combine with which is retained by the authors. This control is partially masked, and users' selection is limited to the number of edits that they initiate. This option requires more work from the authors, and returns less feedback about community experience.

3. Randomizing: at the other extreme from simulation is randomized access to a lightly edited archive of clips. This option turns over to crowdsourcing the task of generating possible significance, within the fable framing. The risk is that many of the combinations are "surreal" or meaningless, discouraging participation.

4. A third option is somewhere between simulation and randomizing.

5. Users know when the work is finished when the repetitions accumulate and they recognize the pattern: they get "it" (the figure).

C. Effect?

1. The final determination of design depends upon what effect we want the konsult to have. A related criterion might be effects we want to avoid.

2. Given the brief time many users are likely to spend with the konsult, it is desirable to select the more pithy minutes of the interviews and other videos. As for control of matches, there is a tradeoff between eliminating unwanted ironies or matches that contradict our inten-

tion (on the one hand), and losing the potential for unanticipated insights (on the other).

3. Selection of clips for the lesson screen should have in mind the production of potentially interesting, moving, and or provoking combinations with the anecdotes.

4. Shot lists?

Figure 10.

Murphy's Wellbeing

A Trailer (http://emeragency.electracy.org/projects/murphys-well-being)
1. [MONTAGE of Denizen portraits]

VO: *Murphy's Wellbeing* is a Konsult, a genre for community deliberation on a Superfund emergency. There is a disturbance in the Wellness Field of North Central Florida. There is an appeal, a call from our neighborhoods, and from one neighborhood in particular, named for the songwriter Stephen Foster. It is a test of response-ability. What is that feeling: is it *obligation?* The stickiness of pine tar is an allegory of what bonds us with our neighbors.

2. [MUSIC FADES in: "Old Folks At Home," instrumental version. Clip: *Gone With the Wind*. Music continues under throughout trailer]

VO: How can the Stephen Foster neighborhood serve as a fable about the wellness of America? First, because Stephen Foster is acclaimed as the Father of American music. Composing "Old Folks At Home" for a blackface troupe in 1851, Foster needed a name for the river referred to in the lyrics. Foster never visited the South, but he found the name "Swanee" in a dictionary. A version of the song, bowdlerized to remove reminders of the slavery institutionalized in the antebellum South, is now the State Song of Florida. Stephen Foster imagined our plantation as an image of happiness. If only it was as easy to purify our water as it is to clean up history!

3. [Clip: *Citizen Kane,* Orson Welles, conclusion, the mansion "Xanadu."]

VO: Who else imagined our happiness? Samuel Taylor Coleridge, in "Kubla Khan," one of the greatest poems of the Romantic imagination, invented a composite city called "Xanadu." "In Xanadu did Kubla Khan a stately pleasure dome decree." Coleridge based his description of the pleasure dome mostly on Bartram's *Travels,* published in the late eighteenth century, in which Bartram described the karst topography of North Central Florida. Four sites are composited in Xanadu: Shangdu (Kubla Khan's capital city), the mountains of Kashmir, the caves of Abyssinia, and the sinkholes and underground river of Alachua County. In other words, what happens to us, is happening in Xanadu! Xanadu is polluted, and the old folks at home testify to the disaster.

4. [Clip: Demo of the Well with user using the touch screen, making choices, scenes appearing on the two screens, making more choices . . .]

VO: The Florida Research Ensemble produced *Murphy's Wellbeing,* to help us understand our *fix*. Other consultants inform the community about engineering options, or corporate calculations of cost-benefit outcomes. EmerAgency consultants add the insights of Arts & Letters expertise, concerned with the measure of wellbeing, which we know is "priceless." The testimony of our neighbors is a call not just to duty, but to Xanaduty.

5. [Demo continues, now a simulation . . . A Denizen Interview]

VO: The Well of Stories is a database Xanadu, a potential fable to remind us that the local is global. As Xanaduans, we live in four places simultaneously: Alachua County, India, Hollywood, and Utopia. Four forces shape our destiny, recorded in four subplots, the first of which consists of the testimonies of neighbors, reporting from the disaster zone. The second track is the history of pine tar. It is the story of corporations, going back to the discovery of America by Europeans trying to get to India to trade in pepper and other spices. They treated the hulls of their ships with pine tar. The third subplot is our mythology, dramatized in Hollywood tales of superheroes that express our belief in the capacity of individuals to change the world. The fourth subplot is philosophy, the voice of wisdom, explaining our ideals about well-being, about how the world should be.

6. [Still: Chinese Ideogram "Happiness," FADE to chorus singing, FADE to Demo of the Well in use]

VO: If the story of *Murphy's Wellbeing* is a fable of Xanaduty, its moral remains to be constructed by interacting with the Well. What is our answer to the ancient question *how should we live?* The Well is an archive of narrative tracks, to be explored in basic montage units, a collective fable composed one ideogram at a time. The fable emerges by juxtaposing neighbor testimonies with passages from the other Xanadu places. You consult with the Well by selecting neighbors, and relating them to one or more of the subplots shaping their world—History, Mythology, Philosophy (repeat as often as you like). The inventors of cinema learned from Asian ideograms how to express thought by means of images. An ideogram combines two sensory properties to evoke an immaterial thought. The Chinese character for "Happiness" combines the figure of "Music" (a hand striking a drum) with "Singing" (an open mouth). "Happiness" is a feeling like that expressed in a song, a song such as "Old Folks at Home," way down upon the Murphy Wellness Field. How do these ideograms make *you* feel?

7. [Demo continue]

VO: A clue to the moral of the fable is in the very name of "Murphy's Wellfield," since "the Murphy Game" is a classic confidence trick, a bait and switch scam native to American folk culture. We wanted pepper, and got poison. If you used pepper today, you helped pollute Xanadu. The pine tar commodity produced at the Cabot-Koppers site is a kind of tar baby, like the one created by Br'er Fox and Br'er Bear to catch Br'er Rabbit, in the fables adapted to cinema in Walt Disney's *Song of the South*. But is that really our song, our South? There is a note of optimism in these stories, since the trickster rabbit always extricated himself from the fix. Let us hope that is also our story.

Figure 11.

The EmerAgency: http://emeragency.electracy.org/

Index

agency, 64, 126, 158, 162–163, 170, 262, 265, 273, 278–279, 284
Ali, Muhammad: Clay, Cassius, 36, 42–44, 46, 49, 134
Amelia Island, 222–223, 226, 227
anecdote, 3, 13–14, 37, 289
anti-Semitism, 136
Apollo, 76
Army Corps of Engineers, 84, 157, 161, 167, 169, 171
Arvida Jr. High, 146
assemblage, 11, 87–91, 96, 104
association, 98–99
Augé, Marc, 195, 197, 201, 204, 210

bar mitzvah, 141–143, 145, 147
Barthes, Roland, 6, 14, 39, 46–47, 49
Bayshore Drive, 80, 145
beach, 12, 35, 75, 113, 135, 151, 157, 208–209, 212–220, 222–225, 227–229, 241
Betsch, MaVynee: The Beach Lady, 225–226
Biscayne Boulevard, 135, 138
Bitzer, Lloyd
Blue Palace, 224
bones, 11–12, 19, –23, 25–26, 28–31, 129, 196
boundaries, 56, 89, 91, 153, 158, 196, 200, 219
boxes, 12, 180, 239, 248–255, 259–261, 262, 264, 267–268
Brooklyn, 34–35, 139

Brown, James, 11, 31–32, 40, 44, 49, 108, 117, 260, 270
Burdines, 43
Burroughs, William, 200, 204, 210
Burton, Tim: E*dward Scissorhands*, 28, 32, 196, 211

Calvino, Italo: *Mr. Palomar*, 217, 229
canals, 10, 12, 47, 77, 152–155, 157–160, 162–164, 167–171, 201
capitalism, 197, 252, 262, 264, 286
Caroline Brevard Elementary, 110
Casey, Edward, 18, 32, 87, 106
Cayo Hueso, 20, 21
Celebration City, 9
census, 91, 105, 201
chora, 10, 18, 19, 28, 31, 278, 286
cigar, 21, 31, 78
cinema, 238, 264, 284, 289, 294
commonplace: topos, 9, 10, 38, 40–41, 46, 89–91, 96, 99, 104–105, 197, 281
Coral Gables, 133–134, 145, 148
Cubans, 23, 136, 155
Cutler Ridge, 7
Dade County, 36, 49, 52, 129
Dadeland, 134
Dante, 275, 276
De Certeau, Michel, 49, 89
De Landa, Manuel, 88
Deleuze, Gilles, 88, 106, 196, 198, 200, 208, 210, 273
Derrida, Jacques, 10, 18, 32, 247, 274, 278, 282

design, 12, 53, 56, 63, 174–179, 183, 187, 189, 191, 193, 199, 234, 239, 252–254, 258–259, 260–262, 264, 266, 268, 276–278, 280–282, 284, 287, 290–291
diegesis, 35, 40, 42, 46, 48, 277
differend, 258, 269
discrimination, 10, 12, 36, 111, 127, 229
Disney, Walt, 5, 9, 10, 11, 14, 75, 76–78, 103, 206, 233–234, 236–240, 242–245, 251, 294
Dixie Highway: US 1, 4, 129
drainage, 154–155, 157–158, 161, 167, 192
dwell: dwelling, 11, 69
education, 76, 138, 210, 285

Electracy, 242, 252, 272–273, 278–280, 288, 292, 295
Epcot, 233, 240
Everglades, 83–84, 129, 152, 155, 157–158, 161, 166–167, 169–171, 173

F.C. Martin, 36
Facebook, 6, 7, 8
fantasy, 192, 236, 237, 238, 251, 261, 262
Fantasyland, 78, 251
FEMA, 52
Fisher, Carl, 42, 44
Fiske, John, 212–215, 217
Flagler, Henry, 23, 129, 154, 158, 218
Florida A&M University, 127
Florida Research Ensemble, 271, 293
fragment, 6, 8, 23
Frenchtown, 111–115, 117, 123, 127
Freud, Sigmund, 25, 198, 237–238, 245, 247
Frontierland, 78, 251

Gainesville, 32, 67, 74, 194, 271, 274, 276, 278, 283–284, 286
gaze, 12, 53, 110, 116, 174, 175, 179, 184, 189, 190–192, 228

Giroux, Henry, 9, 14
Gleason, Jackie, 43, 46, 49, 187, 194
golf: PGA, 10, 12, 42–44, 46, 74, 151, 156, 158, 174–178, 182–183, 187, 191–193, 222, 227, 242, 258
grandparents, 4, 9, 34, 73, 101, 151, 153, 156, 240
Greater Jacksonville Open, 187–188
Greek, 29–31, 59–60
grid, 11, 129, 130, 136, 146, 154, 159, 164
Guattari, Felix, 88, 106
Gulf Coast, 89, 93, 99, 208
Gulf of Mexico, 55, 80, 91, 97
Hillsborough River, 80, 82
Hollywood Sportatorium, 4
HUD, 58
Hurricane Andrew, 51–52
Hurricane David, 46, 47, 48, 50
Hurston, Zora Neale, 157, 168

image, 7, 17–19, 21, 26–28, 30, 39, 42, 47, 56, 103, 158, 161, 182, 193, 200, 212, 236, 252, 267, 293
income tax, 74
interface, 257, 274, 278, 286, 287, 290

J. Geils Band, 5, 143
Jacksonville, 73, 170, 175, 179, 187–189, 194, 213, 218–219, 222, 225, 229
Jewish: Jews, 11, 12, 37, 38, 41, 44, 47, 49, 128–132, 134–137, 139–141, 143, 144–148
Jim Crow, 108, 119
Joel, Billy, 35–37, 41, 46, 49
Jolly Roger, 21, 30

Kaplan, Kivie, 37, 50
Kendall, 4, 11, 13, 34–36, 41–42, 47, 49, 129, 137, 141, 146, 147
Kendall Lakes, 4
Kennedy, John F., 10, 40–42, 44, 49, 139, 145, 148, 249
Key West, 11, 12, 17, 18–32, 38, 83, 129, 153, 155

Kissimmee River, 152, 154, 158, 159, 161, 164, 168, 171
Konsult, 12, 271–273, 277–283, 287–291

Lacan, Jacques, 236
Lake Okeechobee, 152, 154–159, 161, 163–165, 167–168, 171–173
Latour, Bruno, 10, 87–91, 105–106, 268
Leewood Elementary, 131
Liberty City, 36
Libidinal, 237, 248, 251, 252, 254, 255, 256, 259, 260, 261, 262, 263, 264, 265, 266, 267, 268
Lyotard, Jean-Francois: grand narrative, 252, 258–259, 261– 266, 268–270

Mailer, Norman, 43, 47, 49
Manhattan Beach, 218–220
Marcuse, Herbert, 238, 247
marijuana, 13, 31, 240
Matheson Hammock, 4, 145
McDuffie, Arthur, 36, 141
McLuhan, Marshall, 6, 14, 177–178, 194
Mellencamp, John, 73
metaphor, 30, 239, 263, 281, 287–288, 291
Miami, 3, 4, 5, 7, 10–12, 34–50, 54, 74, 82, 90, 128–130, 133–136, 138, 139–148, 152, 155–156, 167, 171, 189, 213, 220, 224, 229
Miami Beach, 37–38, 41, 43, 46, 49, 129, 135, 138, 140, 142, 189, 213, 224
Miami Dolphins, 7
Miami Herald, 4, 167, 171
Miami Vice, 44, 49, 82, 146
Miccosukee Indian Village, 129
Moon Lake, 92, 96, 100–104, 106
Morgan Woods Elementary, 199
mounds, 10, 12, 179–183, 191
muck, 11, 158, 164–170, 179, 181, 191

narrative, 4– 9, 11–13, 35, 38–39, 41–42, 44–45, 47, 59–60, 87, 90, 96, 99, 158, 160, 162, 204, 265, 277, 284, 288, 290, 294
Nazis, 143, 238
network, 6–8, 10, 11, 13, 18–19, 30, 88, 90, 105, 123, 153, 155, 158–159, 169, 177, 179, 204, 252, 262, 264
New Port Richey, 11, 86, 87, 89–92, 94, 96, 98–100, 102, 104–107
New York, 3, 14, 31–33, 35–38, 43, 49–50, 63, 69, 84, 106, 136, 142, 148, 171–172, 177, 194, 197, 210, 211, 219, 225, 226, 229, 236, 247, 270
Nicklaus, Jack, 175, 176, 188
North Florida Fair, 114, 118–120, 122–123
North Miami, 74, 137, 139

Ocala, 74, 207
Old Lincoln High School, 116–117, 122
Orlando, 12, 74, 79, 83, 152, 170, 194, 208, 234, 240–242, 248–249, 251–255, 258–264, 266–268
Overtown, 141

palmetto bug, 84, 202
Panama Canal, 36, 154, 155
Panhandle, 73
parade, 79, 82, 87, 93–94, 114–116, 118, 120, 179
Parrot Jungle, 4
Pasco County, 86, 93, 95–97, 99, 100, 102, 106–107
pattern, 10–13, 18, 30, 39, 41, 44, 48, 84, 278, 286, 291
place, 4, 8–13, 17–19, 30, 39, 47, 86–91, 104, 130, 140, 152, 189–190, 196, 198–200, 202, 203–204, 206, 210, 213, 217, 227–228, 233, 245, 254–256, 261, 263, 271–278, 286
Plato, 18, 23, 28, 274, 278
Players Championship, 174–176, 178, 190, 194

Ponte Vedra Beach, 12, 174–175, 187, 189
popcycle, 12, 278, 284, 286, 288–291
Publix, 137
Punta Gorda, 52

Rascal House, 37–38
reef, 20, 21
Rickels, Lawrence, 238
Rickert, Thomas, 18–19, 31–32
riots, 36, 74–75, 141
Rosh Hashanah, 38
Ross, Andrew, 9, 14

Sears, 109
sediment, 163–164, 166
Seven Mile Bridge, 23
Sex Shop, 266–268, 270
Shamrock Heights, 91–94, 96, 99, 102
shells, 22, 68, 198, 202, 206–207, 210, 226
Sloppy Joe's, 25, 27
sludge, 10, 48
South Florida Water Management District, 153, 162, 170–172
Spartan, 11, 51, 53–55, 57, 58–65, 67–69
spectator, 174, 177, 179–183, 186–187, 190–192, 236, 264
St. Augustine, 75, 221, 222, 224, 229
St. Lucie River, 151, 155, 161, 163, 167, 170
story, 8, 11–14, 39, 47–48, 59, 60, 64, 78, 83, 86, 89–90, 96, 163, 169, 198, 226, 242, 277–279, 285, 293–294
suburb, 12, 34, 81, 129, 197, 200, 210
suggestion, 10, 12, 239
Sunshine State, 5, 10, 38, 73, 82, 87, 129, 212

Tallahassee, 11, 12, 109, 111, 117–119, 123, 127, 171, 229
Tampa: Cigar City, 11, 12, 54, 73–74, 76–84, 87, 91–92, 103, 106, 111, 129, 138, 156, 169, 172, 196, 201, 205
tans, 215, 216
Tausk, Victor, 239, 247
Ted, 83
television: ABC, CBS, 25, 78, 119, 174, 176–178, 182–183, 186, 188, 189, 193, 240, 249
Temple Israel, 38, 132, 141–142, 148
topos: commonplace, 9, 10, 18, 19, 242
tourists, 22– 27, 53, 83, 129, 186, 188, 191, 212, 224, 234, 241, 243
Town 'n' Country, 12, 105, 196–197, 199–203, 205–210
trailer, 11, 51–52, 54–56, 58–61, 63–68, 288, 292
Trouse, 54, 67, 68, 69

University of Miami, 133, 135

Vitanza, Victor, 258–259, 269–270
Voisinet, Robert L.P., 164–166, 170–171, 173

Walt Disney World: Magic Kingdom, 223, 233–234, 240, 242, 251
West Palm Beach, 11, 87, 153, 155–156, 165, 166, 171

Xanadu: Kubla Khan, 293, 294

Ybor City, 78–79

Zayre, 7, 8

Contributors

James P. Beasley is Assistant Professor of English at the University of North Florida, Jacksonville, where he teaches courses on rhetorical history, theory, and research. His work has been published in *College Composition and Communication*, *JGE: The Journal of General Education*, and *Rhetoric Review*. His article, "Demetrius, _Deinotes_, and Burkean Identification at the University of Chicago" was the winner of the 2010 Theresa J. Enos award from *Rhetoric Review*.

Cassandra (Sandy) Branham is a PhD student in the University of Central Florida's Texts and Technology Program. Cassandra's research interests include military rhetorics, prison literacy, digital writing studies, and embodiment and identity theory.

Lillie Anne Brown teaches literature and composition courses in the Department of English and Modern Languages at Florida A&M University. Her work has been published in books and journals, including *Southern Quarterly*, *Revista Lingua & Literatura*; *Pakistaniaat*, *Black and White Masculinity in the American South*, the *Journal of the Pennsylvania State Universities*, the *Encyclopedia of the Environment in American Literature*, and online at *Feminist Wire*. Her research interests center on images of the female body politic and the intersection of race, power, gender and identity in southern literature. She has written and lectured extensively on the works of writer Ernest J. Gaines and is at work on a project in celebration of the author's writing career. She has laid the groundwork for *Kaleidoscope: Essays on*

Kinship, Community and Cultural Traditions. She holds a PhD in nineteenth and twentieth century literature from Florida State University.

Channel TWo (CH2), Jessica Parris Westbrook and Adam Trowbridge, is a studio/research construct focused on mixed reality, media, design, development, distribution, authorized formats + unauthorized ideas, and systems of control + radical togetherness. CH2 recent projects involve interactive landscapes/game environments, augmented realities, and computer viruses. CH2 was awarded a Rhizome Commission in 2012, a Turbulence Commission in 2011, and a Terminal Commission in 2009 for projects involving information, systems design, and net art. In addition to exhibitions and commissions, CH2 contributes to panels, platforms, publications, and collaborative scenarios intersecting new media and social practices.

Bradley Dilger is Associate professor of English at Purdue University, studying networked writing and technical communication. His current research focus, a collaboration with Neil Baird, is a longitudinal study of writing transfer which explores the influences of ease, negotiation, and ownership. With Jeff Rice, he edited the collection *From A to <A>: Keywords of Markup*, winner of the 2010 Computers & Composition Book Award. Bradley lives in West Lafayette, Indiana, with his bride Erin Easterling and two daughters, Madelyn and Amelia.

Sidney I. Dobrin is Professor of English and Director/Editor of the TRACE Innovation Initiative at the University of Florida. He is author and editor of many books and articles, including *Gone. Fishing. Recreational Saltwater Sportfishing and the Future of the World's Oceans* (forthcoming, Texas A&M University Press).

David M. Grant is Associate Professor of English and Writing Program Coordinator at the University of Northern Iowa where he teaches courses in rhetoric, professional writing, and literature. His research focuses on place, memory, and craft. He has recently started a project on the Lakota *chanupa* as a rhetorical object. His work has appeared in *Pre/Text, JAC, Kairos* and in the edited collection, *Rhetorics, Literacies, and Narratives of Sustainability*. His two children continually inspire him to recognize wonder and to use it well.

Charlie Hailey teaches design, history, theory, and design/build at the University of Florida, where he received his doctorate. A licensed architect, he also studied at Princeton University and UT-Austin and has worked with the designer/builders Jersey Devil. His books examine camping as placemaking (*Campsite*, LSU Press), camps as contemporary spaces (*Camps*, MIT

Press), and most recently, islands as manufactured cultural landscapes (*Spoil Island,* Rowman and Littlefield). He has lectured nationally and internationally, most recently at Harvard University, UCLA, NYU, UC–Irvine, and SUT in Macedonia, where he was a Fulbright Scholar in 2011.

Megan McIntyre is a PhD candidate in Rhetoric and Composition at the University of South Florida. Her dissertation focuses on social media responses to the 2013 Boston Marathon bombings. Her research interests include rhetoric and technology and social media

Sean Morey is Assistant Professor of Rhetoric and Professional Communication at Clemson University where he teaches writing and digital media in the Department of English. His research focuses on developing theories of writing at the intersections of rhetoric, new media, and technology, primarily through the lens of electracy. He is the author of *The New Media Writer* (Fountainhead Press, 2014), and has co-edited the collections *Augmented Reality: Innovative Perspectives Across Art, Industry, and Academia* (Parlor Press, 2015) and *Ecosee: Image, Rhetoric, Nature* (SUNY Press, 2009).

Steve Newman is Associate Professor of English at Temple University. His first book was *Ballad Collection, Lyric, and the Canon* (U Penn) and his current project is *Time for the Humanities: Competing Narratives of Value from the Scottish Enlightenment to the 21st Century Academy.*

Jeff Rice is Martha B. Reynolds Professor of Writing, Rhetoric, and Digital Studies at the University of Kentucky. He is the author of *The Rhetoric of Cool: Composition Studies and New Media* (SIU Press, 2007) and *Digital Detroit: Rhetoric and Space in the Age of the Network* (SIU Press, 2012).

Craig Saper is Professor and Director of the Language, Literacy, and Culture Doctoral Program at UMBC in Baltimore, and from 2012–2015 the Bearman Family Foundation Chair of Entrepreneurship. He is the author of *Intimate Bureaucracies* (2012), *Networked Art* (2001), *Artificial Mythologies* (1997) and has edited or co-edited volumes on *Posthumography* (2010), *Imaging Place* (2009), and *Drifts* (2007) and edited editions of Bob Brown's *Words* (2010) and *Readies* (2010). He has published widely on Fluxus and visual poetry and serves as the Reviews Editor and "Blog Report" columnist for *Rhizomes*. His curatorial projects include exhibits on "Assemblings" (1997), "Noigandres: Concrete Poetry in Brazil" (1988) and "TypeBound" (2008), and folkvine.org (2003–2006). In addition, he has published two artists books, *On Being Read* (1985) and *Raw Material* (2008). Saper is currently completing a biography of the poet-publisher-impresario-writer in every imaginable genre, Bob Brown.

Todd Taylor is the Norman and Dorothy Eliason Professor of English at the University of North Carolina at Chapel Hill. He attended Thomas Jefferson High School and the University of South Florida in Tampa. His most prominent publications include *The Columbia Guide to Online Style* (with Janice Walker), *Literacy Theory in the Age of the Internet* (with Irene Ward) and *Take 20*. He previously served as Director of the Writing Program at UNC, and he last rode vert on his fortieth birthday.

Gregory L. Ulmer is Professor of English and Media Studies at the University of Florida, and Joseph Beuys Chair at the European Graduate School. His work with the Florida Research Ensemble is coordinated through the EmerAgency consultancy *http://emeragency.electracy.org/*, and includes a book-length study, *Miami Virtue, http://smallcities.tru.ca/index.php/cura/issue/view/5*, as well as an interactive *konsult*, "Murphy's Well-Being." His most recent book is *Avatar Emergency* (Parlor Press, 2012). Ulmer's current project is a collaboration with the Florida Research Ensemble on an introductory pedagogy to facilitate electrate approaches to online education (Electracy 101).

www.ingramcontent.com/pod-product-compliance
Lightning Source LLC
Chambersburg PA
CBHW030524230426
43665CB00010B/757